Everybody Knows

The publication of this book was assisted by a bequest from Josiah H. Chase to honor his parents, Ellen Rankin Chase and Josiah Hook Chase, Minnesota territorial pioneers.

Everybody Knows

Cynicism
in
America

WILLIAM
CHALOUPKA

University of Minnesota Press
Minneapolis / London

Published by the University of Minnesota Press
111 Third Avenue South, Suite 290
Minneapolis, MN 55401-2520
http://www.upress.umn.edu

Library of Congress Cataloging-in-Publication data

Chaloupka, William, 1948–
    Everybody knows: cynicism in America / William Chaloupka.
      p.   cm.
    Includes bibliographical references.
    ISBN 0-8166-3310-X (hc.).–ISBN 0-8166-3311-8 (pb.)
    1. Public opinion—United States.   2. Cynicism—United States.   I. Title.
HN90.P8C545   1999
303.'8'0973—dc21   99-21025

Printed in the United States of America on acid-free paper

The University of Minnesota is an equal-opportunity educator and employer.

11 10 09 08 07 06 05 04 03 02 01 00 99   10 9 8 7 6 5 4 3 2 1

for Annie, a kynic

Contents

Acknowledgments

This project accumulated a large roster of friends, critics, and editors. Jane Bennett, Gregg Cawley, Bill Connolly, Bill Corlett, Jodi Dean, Fred Dolan, Tom Dumm, Kathy Ferguson, Tom Kuehls, Andrew Light, Tim Luke, Mike Shapiro, Chip Stearns, Paul Taggart, Michel Valentin, Rob Walker, Julia Watson, and several anonymous reviewers commented on presentations and essays that formed an early basis for various chapters. Dennis Judd and Mark Reinhardt read the entire manuscript and offered excellent comments and much-appreciated encouragement.

A sabbatical leave sponsored by the University of Montana in Missoula provided the chance to begin the project, and my colleagues and students there are a continuing inspiration. Amherst College, Goucher College, the University of Hawaii at Manoa, and the University of Wyoming provided me the opportunity to present parts of this work while it was in a formative stage.

I wish to thank Carrie Mullen, my editor at the University of Minnesota Press, for her support. Wendy Jacobs offered careful and wise copyediting. I also thank Robin Moir, Mike Stoffel, and Laura Westlund at the Press for their work on the project.

Eric Johnson, the much-missed former editor of the Missoula *Independent*, edited a weekly column I wrote for six years, and in the process taught me many lessons in the art of the political essay. Any number of friends in Missoula, a writers' town, encouraged this project. My partners in the Missoula New Party continue to teach me about political activism.

More than anyone, Dan Baum and Margaret Knox pushed, encouraged, criticized, and cared about this book. Over an endless string of dinner-table discussions and debates, they convinced me that I had something to say and helped me find ways to say it. I am deeply grateful.

Introduction

Everybody knows that the dice are loaded.
Everybody rolls with their fingers crossed.
Everybody knows the war is over.
Everybody knows the good guys lost. . . .

Everybody knows that the boat is leaking.
Everybody knows the captain lied.
Everybody got this broken feeling
like their father or their dog just died. . . .

Everybody knows the deal is rotten:
Old Black Joe's still picking cotton
for your ribbons and bows.
Everybody knows.

     Leonard Cohen and Sharon Robinson,
       "Everybody Knows"

Americans use names to mark events. The name "Monica Lewin-sky" will forever refer to more than one young woman and more than a sequence of revelations about President Bill Clinton. As sure as "Watergate" now calls forth a cultural memory of abused power, "Monica Lewinsky" seems sure to mark a high-water moment for American cynicism.

To be sure, the diagnosis of cynicism had been well established before we ever met Monica. Since the end of the Cold War, Americans have become acutely aware of a cynical thread running through their country's social fabric. Americans are cynics. That diagnosis of America's social ills, seldom heard before the tumultuous 1960s and 1970s, has become obvious. Cynicism pops up constantly as description and explanation. The appeal of the singer Madonna is cynical. The Gulf War was a cynical ploy to benefit oil companies. Voters are cynical about Congress. A syndicated columnist praised the success of the film *Titanic* because it refuted the prevailing cynicism.[1] Many of his readers no doubt muttered cynically about the movie's quarter of a billion dollar budget and associated hype.

Well before Monica Lewinsky became a celebrity, Americans had been practicing the cynical argument, often in relation to Bill Clinton. In the 1996 presidential campaign, Republicans hammered away at incumbent Clinton's "character" but achieved a result they hadn't expected. Pollsters found that Americans agreed that their president was none too trustworthy. But while such judgments usually erode a candidate's support, they didn't work that way in 1996. Bob Dole, generally judged more kindly on the character issue, was unable to translate this advantage into votes. When the votes were in and exit polls tabulated, it was clear that some voters had turned cynical on the character issue. A fifth of voters for Clinton told pollsters that they did not consider their candidate honest and trustworthy.

But this did not fully prepare us for Monica. As a variety of scandals accumulated around President Clinton in the winter and spring of 1998, a dramatic disconnect persisted between citizen support for his job performance and television audience interest in Monicagate. His performance ratings hit all-time highs at precisely the moment scandal revelations reached a peak. And as the scandal flourished, so too did the high ratings. The president's Republican opponents hardly knew what to do. For months, television's talking heads pondered the paradox. Americans expect to trust their president. If they don't, the president's authority erodes. But while Americans seemed convinced that Bill Clinton had engaged in some kind of disreputable behavior, they continued to support him. Everybody understood the implication. Americans are a cynical people.

Struggling to explain the disconnection evident in the poll numbers, the *Washington Post* columnist David Broder at first suggested that "perhaps American voters were adopting 'the French solution,'" playing down the sexual morality of a leader who otherwise performed his job.[2] Broder subsequently acknowledged that other columnists, and most of his mail, rejected this hypothesis. But increasingly precise polling questions seemed to support it. A *Wall Street Journal* poll, for example, reported that only 30 percent of respondents agreed that "Americans have become more cynical and have low expectations about the moral standards" of their leaders.[3] Sixty-five percent thought "Americans have become more realistic," judging leaders on "their performance in office rather than on their personal life." Neither Broder nor the *Journal* noted that both answers offer satisfactory evidence of cynicism. A supposedly realistic willingness to put up with the foibles of leaders during good economic times would strike many as cynical, especially when TV ratings suggested intense public interest in the continuing Lewinsky coverage. Add the two responses together and you get 95 percent. Unanimous.

Our cynicism extends far beyond Americans' attitudes toward Bill Clinton. We say we are shocked — shocked! — to see TV talking heads, politicians, celebrities, or experts promoting projects that coincide with their private self-interest. But nobody really believes a public figure might sincerely pursue the public good. Call this "the season of our national contempt." Our condition may be paradoxical and confused, but cynicism is no longer a sideshow. Although our overt anger may ebb and flow, we Americans persistently deride and flee from public life, mired in a cynicism we don't understand, a cynicism that envelops our political leaders, our media pundits, our cultural heroes, ourselves.

Like good paint, the cynical label can be applied everywhere. The stuffy and pompous politician is called cynical. Regular Joes watching the nightly news and scoffing at the flickering spectacle are cynics. The politicians the Regular Joes accuse of cynicism even use the term to describe themselves. Early in her husband's first term, Hillary Rodham Clinton told an assembled crowd of teachers: "We have to fight against our own cynicism."[4] It is a theme both Clintons have repeated throughout their White House years.

Defined concisely, cynicism is the condition of lost belief. Many American institutions and public practices have simply forfeited their constituents' faith. Leading public intellectuals diagnose this malady but offer remedies that only reassure and then fall short. They urge us to endeavor more resolutely to *believe*—to rebuild values whose failure propelled cynicism in the first place. The current crop of civic preachers has added a behavioral argument: if Americans would become more civil with one another, this would both show that their cynicism had subsided and lead to yet more civility. These "civilitarians" translate every problem into the language of values and manners. They say that public debates, fed by cynicism, have somehow become too strident.

By the mid-1990s, the foundation world had locked onto civility as a buzzword and a bludgeon against cynicism. Late in 1996, the Boston-based Institute for Civil Society dedicated part of a $35 million anonymous gift (among the year's largest single private contributions) to the sole purpose of promoting civility. The institute hired retired congresswoman Pat Schroeder, a well-known liberal, as spokesperson. But the civility strategy is broadly bipartisan. Former drug czar William Bennett teamed up with former senator Sam Nunn to create the Forum on Civility. Former Republican presidential candidate Lamar Alexander signed on to chair the new National Commission on Philanthropy and Civic Renewal. Bill Clinton didn't exactly use the "C" word in his inaugural address, but he did quote Chicago's Cardinal Bernardin: "It is wrong to waste the precious gift of time on acrimony and division."[5] His speech was widely interpreted as a call for civility. Soon after, the new Congress held a retreat designed to teach the methods of civil debate.

But despite its apparent attractiveness, the civility strategy is ineffective. In the first place, much of the public has already dismissed the leadership of public intellectuals as pompously naïve or apologetic or simply irrelevant. Voting rates haven't risen, to cite an obvious measure. After the civility workshop, the attendees proceeded to conduct the 103rd Congress (1993–1994), one of the most acrimonious legislative sessions of the century. On all sides and at all levels, the disbelief and acrimony are more durable than the civilitarians presume. What is more, in a cunning and circular twist, opportunistic politicians and preachers take advantage of civility talk.

Cynicism is a durable cultural strain. It grows vigorously, even feeding on its proposed remedies. Cynics, by definition, have learned how to live with moral contradiction. Telling a cynic to stop being cynical is like telling rain to stop falling. One secret to cynicism's remarkable stability is simply this: not every cynic is an evil villain or a pompous bore. Some cynics are undeniably attractive. The irreverent balloon-busting rogue, a beloved character in both high and pop culture, is a cynic. So too the gutsy "can-do" pragmatist worshipped in American culture.

In a society deeply suspicious of the discrepancies between public pronouncement and the hidden workings of power, there is something genuinely attractive about the way a cynic expresses a truth. Every social movement, from the left or the right, has its jesters, wordsmiths, and lead singers—its engaging cynics. It is not at all obvious that we would be better off without them. Call it a "good cynicism," a successor to "good cholesterol" in the American cultural vocabulary.

Responding to a diagnosis of dangerous cynicism requires sophistication that is, ironically, the reverse of what the civilitarian believers prescribe. The lively, contentious, but ultimately resilient process of democratic practice requires a persistence and a verve not unrelated to cynicism. In short, cynicism is not uniformly an affliction or injury. Indeed, it is more than one thing, and as an ensemble, cynicism does its work at the core of Americans' relationship to political life. But the ensemble effect is important. The cynicism of leaders does not simply produce or reflect the cynicism of citizens. Confronted with cynical institutions, cynical media commentary, and intractable public predicaments, Americans are an angry lot. Nonetheless, even citizen cynicism splits into varieties that differ significantly from one another. Still, despite these complications, Americans keep talking about cynicism, with good reason. We have chosen to call our anger and its causes by a single name that will make good sense once we tease it apart. Americans are cynics. Everybody knows.

This book is neither a call to belief nor an apology for the social, cultural, and political arrangements that have produced a cynical response in American cultural and political life. Cynicism is a subtle and elusive cultural mood, misunderstood by those who issue broad pleas for civility. Cynicism is hard even to measure: committed to several varieties of deception, cynics are poor subjects for the pollsters. As a topic of study, cynicism requires a thoroughly interdisciplinary approach. My aim is not to cover all the bases but to treat the subject with the breadth it requires. Some chapters in this book emphasize cultural interpretation. Others translate works of political and social theory into broader terms than those sometimes used by academic specialists. Still other chapters take on the logic and practice of American politics from an angle closer to history or political science.

No single explanatory device—whether based on human nature, capitalism, liberalism, technology, modernism, or any of the other available alternatives—satisfactorily summarizes American life. To approach the discomforts, injuries, and dangers of contemporary society in terms of a broad reconstruction of one of the available universal "isms" simply won't do. I will mostly leave it to others to argue, point by point, with the legion of communitarian and civilitarian theorists. Instead, I will open another front, focusing attention on the complex, intriguing, and little-appreciated condition—cynicism—that introduces all their works but then leaves the scene too quickly and much too cleanly.

Part I introduces a way of thinking about cynicism that differs from the common analyses. Chapter 1 introduces cynicism's oddly stable role in society by examining its roots in classical Greece and exploring the paradoxical components that a contemporary cynic has learned to manage. Cynicism is a way of life, not an abstract issue or personality quirk. Chapter 2 reviews the civic belief that is called for as an antidote but that interferes with our ability to deal with the most mischievous effects of contemporary cynicism.

Chapter 3 introduces the cynicism of those who rule, as displayed by the kind of maneuver that draws charges of cynical manipulation. The cynicism of the powerful is related to mass cynicism, but the inevitable disproportion between leaders and masses makes a difference. Chapter 4 examines the rampant disbelief of citizen outsiders—a variant I call wig cynicism in recognition of the wiggy conspiracies, mysticisms, and other odd notions of social causation that drive this brand of cynicism. The conspiracy theorist or antipolitics enthusiast is not the same as the cynical insider, but the interaction between these types is crucial.

Part II examines the culture of cynicism, using interdisciplinary approaches to explain both the roots and contemporary effects of cynicism. Chapter 5 charts a brief history of cynicism's emergence in this century, especially since World War II. Chapter 6 argues that long-established structures of American politics inhibit civic belief and encourage cynicism. The American political system, as hallowed as it may be, has set us up for this contemporary cultural crisis. Chapter 7 brings my analysis into the current period, in dialogue with E. J. Dionne's influential book *Why Americans Hate Politics*. For reasons that become clearer as one better understands cynicism, Dionne's favored remedies, among them an insistence on policy solutions and rebuilding a viable commitment to a public good, are not as responsive to rampant cynicism as he imagines.

Chapters 8 and 9 investigate television and journalism in general. The cynical journalist has been one of our best-known social types, but television has been changing both itself and its audience at a rapid pace. The way television interacts with audiences is a key to the development and persistence of cynicism. Chapters 10 and 11 examine political strategies that promote and benefit from contemporary cynicism. Chapter 10 explores backlash, a political technique that is increasingly and systematically deployed, compounding cynical opportunities while also militating against a reconstruction of civic belief. Chapter 11 covers the intensified resentment that both allows backlash to work and is its most radical consequence. Militias and other elements on the far right give resentment its most extreme expression.

Part III examines responses to cynicism. Chapter 12 puts the popular communitarian response into a cultural context, attaching its social costs to its promises and logic. Chapter 13 introduces a different kind of cynical character, present throughout history but absent from the "crisis of values" responses we hear so often. The "kynic," rooted in the role played by Diogenes, the first philosopher of cynicism, is necessary to democratic culture in ways not recognized by most condemnations of cynicism in general. Chapter 14 elaborates the notion of a positive cynicism through a reinterpretation of that odd political form, the street demonstration. Americans have a cultural sense of the moves that might adequately respond to cynicism even if they have not yet understood the political significance of these moves. Chapter 15 takes my analysis into the crucial terrain of political campaigns — an inextricable part of democratic government that is also at tension with the process of producing remedies for cynicism. Chapter 16 makes several explicit recommendations that might assist in a better response to cynical America.

Part I

Cynicism

Chapter 1

Socrates — Gone Mad

Diogenes and the Cynical Tradition

What did Oscar Wilde mean by his blasé statement: "I am not at all cynical, I am only experienced — that's pretty much the same thing"? Or Anton Chekov, who gloomily remarked: "No cynicism can outdo life"?
Peter Sloterdijk, *Critique of Cynical Reason*

Most of us remember the tale of Diogenes, the original cynic, holding a lit lantern aloft as he walked the sunlit streets of Athens, telling curious onlookers that he was searching for an honest man. Diogenes complained that the philosophers did not — and could not — live the life they preached. He complained that their nostrums were a cover for political privilege and comfortable circumstance. He was a classic gadfly.

The historical Diogenes, a contemporary of Plato, is hard to establish. He quickly became a favorite literary character from antiquity, a colorful provocateur put to uses beyond those he himself imagined. The mythic Diogenes stands as a model of cynicism, a force propelling the cynical doctrine through ancient Greece and beyond. The obscurity of the real Diogenes has always troubled historians. But that's the point. Here's a character who so resonated with his audience that they kept adding lines, creating stories, and reinventing him. From the start, Diogenes was a star.

We do know that Diogenes was a familiar figure in Athens, well known for criticizing conventions, debunking hypocrisy, and refusing to respect undeserved reputations. The civic belief — the claims made on behalf of existing arrangements — couldn't hold, Diogenes argued. The philosophers' advice about how to live offended nature and truth. Having been exiled to Athens, Diogenes was unencumbered by the limits of family and reputation, and he played his outsider role to the hilt. Rather than arguing by careful and precise dialectic, which is the true Socratic method, Diogenes intervened with outrageous and challenging criticism, favoring lived example and counterexample. He drew attention to the absurdities of the philosophers' edicts about rationality and social truth.

His most cogent criticisms targeted philosophers and those in power. The contemporary scholar who best interprets Diogenes' legacy, Peter Sloterdijk, notes that Diogenes initiated "resistance against the rigged game" of philosophy: "Since philosophy can only hypocritically live out what it says, it takes cheek to say what is lived." The stories of Diogenes' pranks against the philosophers of antiquity are many and legendary. The absurd conclusions that their abstract philosophy sometimes produced was his favorite target. For example, Sloterdijk tells us that "when Plato put forward the definition of the human as a featherless biped and was applauded for it, [Diogenes] tore the feathers from a rooster and brought it into Plato's school saying, 'That is Plato's human.'" Little wonder that Plato had harsh words for his rival. After all, Plato's greatest contribution to the development of philosophy had been to add a measure of positive abstraction to the rough-and-tumble Socratic method that insisted on endless and often irreverent questions and challenges. At least Socrates had insisted on a standard of logic and the careful definition of terms. One oft-told story has Plato saying of Diogenes, in reference to the rooster episode, "That man is Socrates — gone mad."[1]

In perhaps the best-known philosophical anecdote from Greek antiquity, a young Alexander of Macedonia (not yet "the Great") sought out the famous Diogenes and found him sunbathing. To prove his generosity, Alexander granted the sunbathing celebrity a wish. Diogenes is said to have responded, "Stop blocking my sun!" His impertinence, replicated in today's comics pages by *Doonesbury*'s irreverent habitual sunbather, Zonker, shows disrespect clearly enough. It also makes the point that the king, whatever his delusions of extraordinary power, has a body, too, and is competing for a sun Diogenes has already claimed at that spot, much as a monarch claims his sovereign territory.

Diogenes lived in the streets, in some sort of abandoned tub. He lived poor, but unlike later Christian ascetics, he was not pious about his intentional poverty. Instead, Diogenes remained outrageously funny and shameless. Because of his public performance of various bodily functions, good citizens called Diogenes a dog, and his living standards did approximate that of a stray canine. So he turned their criticism around, adopting that name for his brand of philosophy. *Kyon,* meaning "dog" in Greek, became *kynic,* from which we get "cynic."

Cynicism is Diogenes' direct legacy. As Sloterdijk puts it, Diogenes, "the first in the tradition of satirical resistance, [creates] an uncivil enlightenment."[2] Diogenes modeled a naughty, durable disbelief in pompous pronouncement. He was a rascal, and the tales of his boldness offer a challenge to those who insist that cynicism is simply and solely corrosive, debilitating, and weak. It may be hard to recognize the cynicism attributed to Bill Clinton and Newt Gingrich in this portrait of the original cynic. Diogenes, especially as portrayed by Sloterdijk, asks us to hold the question of cynicism's value open for further investigation. Subsequent chapters in this book, by outlining several types of cynicism, argue the point that cynicism is diverse. But it is good to avoid rushing to domesticate the tensions and contradictions Diogenes represents. The legend of Diogenes gave a name to a whole set of cultural conditions, moods, and attitudes. His legacy persisted throughout the development of European society. Eventually, Diogenes' model made its way to the New World.

Suddenly, it seems, American society is awash in cynicism. That diagnosis, unlikely just a few years ago, seems so obvious that it borders on the banal. Over and over, cynicism pops up as a description of our society's problems. To be sure, the term *cynicism* is often used where simpler words would do. Some uses of the word are simply non sequiturs — people call something "cynical" when they mean that it was mistaken, ill-tempered, tone-deaf, boring, or disagreeable. Such misuse proliferates when pundits, politicians, and even talk-show hosts continually invoke the cynicism diagnosis. It would be a futile enterprise to try to get people to use the word *cynicism* properly. But it is worth the trouble to examine the concept with precision and at length. Despite its overuse, the word turns out to be an apt diagnosis as well as an intriguing one.

Perhaps more than any other political condition, cynicism is both a paradoxical and durable condition. Cynicism undermines the social conditions and moral commitments it addresses. But having contradicted each commitment seemingly required for a productive life, cynics then somehow manage to live on anyway, frequently with style and verve. Functioning cynics are sometimes funny, lively, critical, and compassionate. Their attitudes call into question the morality they have left behind. Cynicism absorbs the refutation it is most likely to confront.

There is another way to phrase the paradox that is central to my argument. Cynicism invites a response it is always already prepared to fend off. Every good citizen scolds the cynics, telling them that they should believe — should acknowledge the traditions, the necessities, and *the reasons for* various values and moral commitments. The cynic is prepared in advance to laugh off this advice. It is stunning that we arrive at this crisis of cynicism so ill equipped to confront actual cynics. Cynicism carries its defenses with it, containing in advance ways to defuse calls to belief, values, and responsibility that cynicism's critics predictably will issue.

By presenting models for such sustained liveliness, cynicism offers the promise of culture and sociability, even if this promise is, perversely, not based on the values of community and civic belief. This social sense might help distinguish cynicism from irony, which, along with skepticism, is something like cynicism's close cousin.[3] Irony makes more sense as a description of an individual statement. "Oh, I get it, you were being ironic," we say when we have misunderstood a joke. To say that an entire culture tends toward the ironic would not quite capture the right sense of shared and persistent disbelief. The phrase "cynical culture" makes sense in a way not quite captured by irony. Skepticism, which in the twentieth century is often associated with scientific approaches, likewise does not quite capture a sense of social condition. A community or a culture can share cynicism because cynicism is rooted in a reaction to shared moral commitments. What a culture rejects can end up informing that culture's most basic self-understandings, if in ways neither simple nor direct.

This paradoxical stability of cynicism, its canny intelligence, poses a dilemma. Cynicism weaves itself into the basic elements of political and social life — the structures, patterns, and habits that frame life in the contemporary world. A culture builds up around cynicism. Any attempt to respond to such a situation is fraught with dangers, among them the tendency to generalize. The cynic is especially good at fending off professors and their theories. A successful treatment of cynicism has to start closer to the ground, perhaps by listening carefully to how we talk about it.

When politics is put under pressure, as it has been in a recent series of crucial elections, cynicism can become more visible as charges and countercharges fly. During the 1992 presidential campaign, Representative Newt Gingrich of suburban Atlanta, not yet Speaker of the House and unknown to most of the public but already a national leader of his party's right wing, upped the ante on the rhetoric of political complaint. In a bare-knuckled approach, Gingrich complained that Bill Clinton, who had been charged with having an extramarital affair, was the moral equivalent of Woody Allen, whose lurid affair with a stepdaughter was then much in the news. Speaking at a rally in Georgia before introducing George Bush, Gingrich said the Allen case "fits the Democratic platform perfectly."[4] The national press, traveling with Bush, picked up the reference.

George Will, a prominent conservative pundit, responded that Gingrich's comments about Bill Clinton's "Woody Allen" campaign "would cost Gingrich his reputation for seriousness if he still had one."[5] Will further remarked that Gingrich's comment revealed an opportunistic streak characteristic of the Bush crowd and "illustrates how cynicism at the top of the Republican ticket pervades the entire party. Gingrich did not, in any meaningful sense, mean what he said." There is more to Will's charge than simple dishonesty. If elementary lying had been the issue, he would have called it that. Dishonesty is a symptom of cynicism, but cynicism is more general. A critic underscores the importance of manipulation and ethical abuses as symptoms of cynicism, which is the encompassing moral and social condition that fosters such abuse, and also makes it a viable political issue.

When Will complained that Gingrich was "just emitting the sort of noise that characterizes what Bush calls his campaign about 'trust,'" he was explicitly charging that the campaign had exhibited a pattern of inconsistency, excuse, and cynicism. What was at stake was not exactly the pattern of simplifications, obscurities, and simple lies that dominate both political speech and its media coverage: "Bush operatives constantly whine about the media, but Bush is benefiting from the mock sophistication of journalists who, striking a world-weary stance, say of his campaign dishonesty, 'It was ever thus in American politics.'"

Will thus identified Gingrich as a specific cultural type, a cynic. Will's comments evoke that culture's mood — its "mock sophistication," its urbanity, its resemblance to the "world-weary" stance of journalists and political insiders. An accomplished and professional scold, Will then slid immediately into a discussion of values, after he had just shown that values can be manipulated. In a preachy, paternalistic style, Will employed cynicism as a way to raise issues of belief and disbelief. Even if it were true that it was ever thus in American politics, "it would be no excuse, and it isn't true. This is extraordinary. . . . Bush calls his campaign 'a crusade to bring back values.' His campaign is powerful evidence of the need for such a crusade."

But cynicism, like the dandelion, is much easier to denounce than to eradicate. Will later endorsed Bush, if reticently. That endorsement probably struck some of his readers as a replay of just the sort of cynicism Will had identified in Gingrich. This is how it is with cynicism. Once started, charges of cynicism spiral and multiply. Cynicism recruits, captures, and encloses. It is remarkably agile and hard to escape.

Will's column also serves as a reminder of how integral journalism is to this issue. The reporter is America's archetypal cynic, dedicated by professional standards of conduct to persistent doubt and disbelief. The news media have become so important to the political world that the two share, and darken, each other's stains. Everyone — politico, reporter, and audience — knows that words and images rule. They also know that those who generate words and images can and do misuse them.

For every such sophisticated deployment of the cynical as Will's, there are dozens of others that are cruder and even hilarious. The diagnosis of cynicism crops up at the oddest times. During the first Clinton inauguration, when a little unself-conscious celebrating might have been allowed the Democrats, who, some thought, would never pocket the White House keys again, the talk turned to cynicism. Harry Thomason, one of President Clinton's Hollywood intimates, staged a spectacular show for inaugural week. Fireworks burst overhead in a benign replay of the Gulf War pyrotechnics that had so eerily turned night into day not so long before. A concert worthy of Woodstock held forth from the base of Lincoln's statue. At that event, Aretha Franklin, resplendent in a huge fur coat, sang "Respect" and knelt at the edge of the stage to shake hands with the Clintons and the Gores. But even this outbreak of showbiz-style entertainment required an odd justification. Thomason said he hoped the $25 million inaugural ceremony, festival, and parade — complete with a lawn-chair drill team — would help "alleviate the country's cynicism."[6] It is, one can fairly say, a solution only a TV producer would imagine.

The cynicism so easily diagnosed in political talk resists spectacles, sermons, and editorials. Its resilience raises an interesting possibility. The cynic may be cynical for good reason: the objects of a cynic's contempt might richly deserve such a response. American political structures long have been set up for the current cynical outbreak. From the beginnings of modern Western democracy, intricate institutional arrangements of representation have relied on strategies for managing the citizenry's trust and activism. Cynicism is a matter of lost belief, and American politics has worked long and hard to rebuild belief.

Consider Bill Clinton's first inaugural address, which launched a rhetoric of reconstruction in its surprisingly strong first paragraph: "My fellow citizens: Today we celebrate the mystery of American renewal. The ceremony is held in the depth of winter. But, by the words we speak and the faces we show the world, we force the spring."[7] It was a surprisingly lyrical speech and also unexpectedly short, filled with critical references to the regime he was displacing: "the depth of winter," "an economy...weakened by...deep divisions among our people," "an era of deadlock and drift." But these complaints gave way to a call for renewal, as political critique so often does in American life. The debacle of Jimmy Carter's "malaise speech," which had scolded too much and uplifted too little, taught a lesson to aspirants for power, including this bright young star that biographer David Maraniss would dub "first in his political class."

President Clinton's speech invoked the word "change" nine times. Toward its conclusion, he tied the rhetorical knot: "Yes, you, my fellow Americans, have forced the spring. Now, we must do the work the season demands." The new president's appeal was well received by the enormous crowd. No cynical back-chorus here.

That would come soon enough, of course. It is the dirty little secret of American politics that every call for reconstruction — for community, for belief, for meaning — can immediately be turned on its head. This inversion is the simplest of rhetorical tricks and perhaps the one that Americans have learned best. A call for values either manipulates or is received as manipulation, no matter its intent. Modern citizens have long since learned how to handle overt partisanship, an impulse much distrusted in a culture caught between democratic values and resistance to politics. Masked, repressed, then desired as a guilty pleasure, out-and-out politics tries not to present itself too boldly. Calls for unity and belief often denote the opposite. And cynics of every variety understand the code.

Cynicism is more than an intellectual topic or a passing malady. It lies at such a central place in our politics that it could be used as an organizing concept, a way to structure an inquiry into politics. Cynicism, it turns out, is something like a worldview. The cynical citizen perceives institutions as cynical, suspecting that manipulators inside those institutions have abused faith and caused cynicism. Those who have power in those institutions exhibit their own cynicism, which comes with strong traditions and reasons for its necessity. The circularity is powerful. Cynicism covers our political and social arrangements like a blanket or, as Ken Kesey called it, a "fog."

Too savvy to be painted into a corner by charges that they have succumbed to evil or anomie, cynics initiate a project. They organize the world as a series of seemingly realistic observations. They organize friends and lovers into communities, marking their sophistication by their ability to function even after they become permanently pessimistic about every larger question. The cynic has found a way to persist in the face of pandering and lying. This arrangement is strong and stable; it can sustain life. Arguments the cynic does not believe still persuade, still help make their proponents legitimate and powerful. Knowing about the gap between what is said and how it is received, cynics are empowered to decide for themselves, to get on with whatever activist project they have chosen. Cynics are seldom apathetic, although they also know how useful it can be to feign apathy.

Belief no longer matters to a cynic, except when its image offers some opportunity. The cynic knows that words and images can be used manipulatively. Cynics know how to fend off criticism or turn it against itself. The cynic may even recall a youthful time when belief of one stripe or another had been personally important. But that memory serves as a confirmation of a mature and cynical vision. Cynics vindicate that vision by recruiting others to adopt it. They are good at arguments but even better at being realists. They justify themselves with appeals to "how the world really is," telling stories of its harshness and necessity and urgency. It is hard to refute a cynical realist.

Belief is a broad and generalized effect, which in turn leads to very specific social practices. Cathedrals are built. Nations, too. And economic systems. Belief's effects survive as institutions. Likewise, the signs and rituals of such powerful belief persist. But once put into doubt, the institutions and rituals alike are susceptible to reinterpretation. Show me a believer and I will find a cynic close by who will read negatively the believer's faith. Catching a hint of cynicism, believers may respond with frenzied efforts to return the cynic to the fold. But having escaped belief, the cynic possesses enormous resources for resisting such a conversion. Abused belief is hard to reconstitute.

Cynics derive a perverse energy from their resistance. Understanding that familiar statements of belief do not carry enough awareness or perhaps carry too much pretension, the cynic acquires an inverse knowledge. Cynics know what words mean, but they also know that these meanings can be manipulated. For believers, faith sustains hope. But it is not necessarily the case that cynicism inevitably produces melancholia. After all, the contemporary cynic lives on quite well after belief is exhausted, after it no longer sustains career and citizenship. This vitality may mystify the believer, but that does not worry the cynic.

Cynicism clashes with familiar and powerful ways of characterizing social life. It resists and subverts the important social themes, such as faith, rationality, utopia, or reform. It undermines how we think about important concepts: freedom, authority, society, self, change, and stability. As cynicism spreads, discontent takes on different qualities. In an era of belief, social discontent might signal a challenge to orthodoxy or systemic change. In a cynical era, social discontent transforms itself into widespread if also often diffuse cynicism. We can no longer assume that adversaries and partners are playing by the same underlying rules. Cynicism is not isolated or singular. Given an opening, it takes over relentlessly. It becomes a condition we share — with each other, through history, written into institutions, cultural patterns, habits, and most everything else.

Cynicism is pervasive, but it is also elusive. Cynics mock belief's role as the glue that holds society together, but the cynical stance itself holds the promise of another way to proceed. At the same time, *cynicism* may imply a simplicity that could not apply in a diverse and complex society. Cynics compose themselves differently in different roles. There is a mass cynicism that establishes itself broadly as a culture. There are outsider cynics capable of cranky and even violent disruption. But cynics rule, too. In our times, the phrase "cynical politicians" is so apt that the two words seem to become one. We can identify cynicism in the vigorous glow of the pragmatic, realistic, energetic mover and shaker. Other cynics are critics, and good ones, too. Abused belief, after all, has long been a prime topic of pop culture, journalism, and even education. Understanding cynicism requires a balancing act. There is a cynical culture to understand, with broadly applicable dynamics and indicators. But there are also specific characteristics and implications for cynicism in its various particular roles.

Cynicism extends beyond politics, of course. But power and manipulation form an important pair, and politics thus makes for a reasonable place to begin studying cynicism. Likewise, cynicism is obviously not only an American affair, although my focus is the United States. In some ways, American cynicism might be singular, if not exceptional. Our political culture has trained itself to avoid too serious a belief in its own public institutions and media. More precisely, it has trained itself in a studied ambivalence toward each of these things, an ambivalence that bends toward belief at some points, perhaps during a war, only to veer away at others, whenever anyone suggests new taxes, for example. The institutional and cultural setting makes a difference for the study of cynicism. Given this country's powerful influence throughout the world, via media culture, economic trade, and political leadership, it makes sense to study American cynicism.

Many journalists, authors, and public figures have proclaimed the age of cynicism. Many others have struggled to come to terms with the mixture of sophistication and lost belief that combine to set the scene for cynical America. In *Great Plains,* a romantic paean to American simplicity and heart, Ian Frazier describes a moment of clarity, a revelation:

> Suddenly I felt a joy so strong it almost knocked me down. It came up my spine and settled on my head like a warm cap and filled my eyes with tears, while I stood there packed in with everybody, watching Mrs. Robinson's lovely daughters dance.
>
> And I thought, *It could have worked!* This democracy, this land of freedom and equality and the pursuit of happiness— it could have worked! There was something to it, after all! It didn't have to turn into a greedy free-for-all! We didn't have to make a mess of it and the continent and ourselves! It could have worked! It wasn't just a joke, just a blind for the machinations of money! The Robinson sisters danced; Prince sang about doves crying; beauty and courage and curiosity and gentleness seemed not to be rare aberrations in the world.[8]

You cannot even be a romantic these days without being a cynic first. Which means, of course, that you will not long be a romantic. The exclamation "*It could have worked!*" is an admission that it didn't work. Frazier probably knows this, too. Searching out some of America's most believing places, letting them carry him away in sublime visions, Frazier still phrases his epiphany carefully. He plays the role of the sophisticated *New Yorker* author, testing his cosmopolitanism out in the plains.

It wasn't just a joke! It could have worked! This is the cosmopolitan at his most aware. The sour taste of the moment—the bitterness of life in a society wracked with so many ugly spasms—was not genetic; it was environmental. The best we can do, Frazier implies, is to acknowledge that some set of historical forces prompted this odd, paradoxical condition, that it was not predestined, that there once was hope. But nostalgia is also a trap. There are manipulations to fend off, and buoyant nostalgia, or worse, apology, will help no more than dogma. The cosmopolitan strives to manage all this contradiction.

Cynicism is large. It includes the cosmopolitan, the politico, the journalist, and many others. At the extremes, cynicism debilitates some of its practitioners, leaving them bitter, manipulative, and uncivil. But cynicism is a way of life; more precisely, it is a way of life against belief or after its exhaustion. At the same time, cynicism is also diverse. The cynicism of the powerful is distinct from, though related to, that of the powerless. Paying attention to the gradations of American cynicism and placing them in political contexts, we can begin to understand what is happening to our culture.

So I propose to analyze American politics as if cynicism mattered. As if cynicism were not simply attitude or fashion, or a way to introduce another tedious argument about belief and reconstruction. As if cynicism were condition and culture, not effect and consequence and symptom. As if it had something to teach us.

Chapter 2

The Values Remedy

Community, Civility, and Belief

Values leap up before our acts like partridges.
John Gardner, *The Wreckage of Agathon*

Every diagnosis of cynicism renews a call to believe, and Americans at least talk believer talk. One moralist after another, whether politician, televangelist, professor, or commentator, announces that we must reestablish belief and reconstruct community values that have fallen into disrepair. These moral complaints are always coupled with recommendations on how authority should present itself, how the media or other institutions should be reformed. Ethical rules must be revived. Victims must rehabilitate themselves. The "values remedy" is always presented as cynicism's antidote. If the problem is cynicism, the solution must be belief—in leadership, education, obedience, and the responsible application of moral criticism.

In a public television special, the journalist Bill Moyers interviewed Michael Franti of the rap group The Disposable Heroes of Hiphoprisy. Moyers repeatedly asked Franti, in effect, why rap culture refuses to conform to an ideal of communitarian language, that is, generalist, sober, gentle, solution-oriented, and values-laden. It is hard to imagine that Moyers, who cares about a lot of things, cares much about rap. This was instead a minor police action, his checking to see whether outlaws of the culture business could be brought into the communitarian mainstream.

Franti did not respond all that well, mostly lapsing into black populist judgments of precisely the sort Moyers wanted. Certainly, Franti said nothing as engagingly ambivalent and political as his group's title cut from their recording *Hypocrisy Is the Greatest Luxury*.[1] But his garb did the trick. He wore a hat—unusual in itself for a serious TV show. More precisely, he wore two hats: a bowler stacked on top of a backward baseball cap. Metaphorically, he was also wearing two hats—that of the populist spokesman-in-training and the rap character. His headgear said, in effect, "I can be multiple. There is more than one way to send a political signal." Moyers never asked him about his hats.

The formation of community requires something other than the solemn remedy talk of communitarians like Moyers. The coherent, calm, rational talk of official community leaders does not match the language of the streets, of the young, of the rebels whose energy the community requires. Believers imply that the crisis of values is not only a matter of social mood or individual psychology. But histories, social structures, and deeply ingrained cultural habits are in play, and these contexts often do not conspire with the believer.

While Americans speak the words of belief, this culture has also diligently trained itself to avoid too serious a belief in its own institutions. We pride ourselves on our pragmatism, in local or private solutions. At its best, this ambivalence clears space for flexibility, a useful thing for a powerful country as it meets shifting circumstances and challenges. But as the culture has swayed between the poles of belief and cynicism during the past decades, a paradox has accumulated around the very possibility of belief. Belief has become less possible, exhausted by conflict, by the enormity of demands placed on a system that seemed more elastic and resourceful than it was, and by increasing opportunities for the successful political and journalistic use of cynicism. Between waves of patriotism and troughs of skepticism about government, civic belief somehow vanished as an overarching way of life. It ceased to be the only practical master strategy for life in democratic society.

Some citizens, deeply bound to communities of faith and drawn to the religious realm, have reacted to this pressure with radical fervor. One of cynicism's many paradoxes is that it flourishes at the same time that religiosity has also become more visibly active. Fundamentalists of various denominations insist that the political realm must serve the edicts of belief. This view works well enough in a single-issue context. In making strong claims about abortion or school prayer, fundamentalists are reassured by their strong personal response to the crisis of belief they perceive in contemporary society. They can build successful organizations, which can indeed generate discussion on their issues. Thus emboldened, they can even elect candidates and take over political institutions, such as local or state party organizations.

But the fundamentalists are blocked from turning our entire society on their proposed axis. Their political strategy can succeed only locally or regionally, or on a small range of linked single issues. A broader success would require durable coalitions and a more inclusive legislative agenda. A diverse culture, thoroughly secular and mostly urban, stymies the fundamentalist project's grandest goals. Opportunities for scandalous behavior emerge as the fundamentalists build financial war chests and institutional structures large enough to have significant national impact. Skepticism on the part of nonbelievers turns scandals into major media stories. The successes of Christian fundamentalists like Jerry Falwell and Pat Robertson are matched by the downfall of their colleagues Jim and Tammy Faye Bakker and Jimmy Swaggart. If anything, the presence of a massive fundamentalist movement drives general cynicism by giving belief an extreme form that can be investigated, criticized, and ridiculed. But the fundamentalists are not the only proponents of the efficacy of belief.

Of course, not everyone who poses spirituality as a response to cynicism is a fundamentalist or a radical.[2] More popular among public intellectuals is a middle position, sometimes referred to as civic belief, or communitarianism.[3] This approach argues for a basic faith in institutions and practices as the context within which interests are advocated and specific issues resolved. Communitarians trace the roots of their belief to antiquity, especially various Roman tracts on citizenship. In this country, Christian belief, with its certainty about universal values and its convictions about the efficacy of moralistic advocacy, provided the basis for political belief. But communitarian belief underwent serious transformation when mass communications and thorough urbanization came to shape American culture. Faith in community acquired a nationalistic and patriotic quality. These are surprisingly recent grafts onto the older traditions of community. As the historian Garry Wills convincingly argued, the nationalist faith emerged, suddenly and with almost instant success, from Abraham Lincoln's Gettysburg Address.[4]

Almost as suddenly, however, belief has been depleted. It no longer provides a credible way to organize political life. In an era of difficult policy problems, the only way to generate remedies is through the messy and inevitably compromised construction of political coalitions. Coalitions must be assembled and thus must accommodate political practicalities. To grow large and successful, coalitions require deals and bargaining. Believers hope that an overlay of values and community talk can survive such pragmatic assembly projects, if decisions are made openly and deals are cut only with the rhetoric of responsibility. They argue that political dealing can have a heart of gold; the dealer can yet be an honest broker. The believer answer is sometimes compelling. Values and community start to sound real in the accomplished sermons of our best intellectuals.

Nonetheless, the believer solution conceals fatal flaws. The focus of remedy politics, the legislative process, is ill suited for a reconstruction of values. For citizens to have faith in "the system," they must believe that legislators do their coalition building on behalf of what President James Madison called the permanent and aggregate community interest. But Madison's approach no longer works, if it ever did. Citizens recognize the endless gridlock between Congress and the president as a succession of cynical games, not as examples of the grand Madisonian scheme. Legislators, as a class, are held in absurdly low esteem, routinely ranked on a level with used-car dealers in opinion polls that try to measure the trust citizens have in various professions. Doubting their legislators' sincerity, Americans turn cynical about Congress. If voters keep returning their district's representative back to the fray, they do so while communicating contempt, bitterness, and jaded sophistication.

It gets worse when one pays closer attention to the legislative process. There are too many deals, too few solutions, too many reasons to lose faith, too little incentive to learn how a bill becomes a law. At the Gerald Ford Presidential Library in Grand Rapids, Michigan, a wall-sized chart diagrams the harrowing process, with dozens of index-card labels connecting circles and arrows in what can only be called the flowchart of hell. One imagines droves of puzzled schoolchildren touring the library, getting their first experience of what is required to make this legislative system work.

There are legions of dissatisfied citizens, in every American locale. Many are well educated and interested in political outcomes. They watch every Moyers series on public television. But for the most part, these citizens are not enlisted in campaigns for legislative or administrative redress. Their activism mostly involves responding to junk mail or telemarketing calls for contributions. They might explain their reluctance to participate in terms of the demands on their time. They might even cite cases when fanatical believers have caused real damage, such as unseating a good legislator with a third-party candidate or blocking a solution to a problem with extreme demands.

But the reluctance of citizens to participate is so resolute and so odd, given their obvious dissatisfaction, that it deserves closer attention. There is something wrong with the somber communitarian arguments and suffering sensitivities, which debilitate the moral intentions these arguments profess. Talk of community turns back on itself. Citizens lose track of even the most basic political divisions and mechanisms. Many discontented Americans seriously believe that the terrible social injuries they perceive are the perverse legacy of government's efforts to right wrongs.

No matter how strong their faith, the believer's morality faces serious and continuous challenge in this cynical era. Some believers will persistently claim that the crisis of cynicism is merely a test of faith. This is, after all, part of belief's stability in the Christian tradition. But the pervasiveness of crisis terminology (the "crisis" of community, of values, and so forth) inadvertently attests to the depth of the believer's worry. And there is good cause for contemporary believers to worry.

Moralism, whether religious or civic, faces predictable challenges in a cynical era. The powerful, manipulative cynic is always measuring the distance from a moral stance to what the cynic regards, secretly or openly, as its false promises and indefensible restrictions. Since Machiavelli, rulers have consciously and deliberately taken advantage of their constituents' belief. The persistent difficulty for belief is that it can be manipulated. Belief can be feigned or tricked.

When we talk of a crisis of cynicism, we are openly worrying that a skeptical, angry citizenry is onto the Machiavellian game and will be more difficult to trick. Most of the responses a believer can formulate in the face of mounting cynicism only make matters worse.

Intellectuals, who in Western cultures have long articulated the need for belief in its several varieties, worry about the social glue. This is what it means to be a public intellectual. Such intellectuals complain that we will be in an awful mess unless we can figure out and implement coherent and successful responses to our ethical and spiritual woes.[5] The remedies vary in form, from better leadership to more studious citizenship to more somber journalism. But the traditional diagnosis always tends toward unanimity and attunement, the attributes of universal faith. This kind of moralistic intellectual practice comes with a persistent problem, however.

The moralist's hope for communal belief undermines itself. In some cases, authoritarian forces seek to impose belief and, in doing so, generate distrust and doubt. In other cases, the pressure of consistency becomes unmanageable, and critics resist, citing episodes of hypocrisy or corruption. In still other circumstances, citizens grow suspicious about the moralist's intention and begin contesting the supposed need for unanimity. As pressure mounts, problems grow. The unanimity the moralists prescribe fosters the fragmentation it was intended to fix. Belief is blocked from creating the outcomes it desires.

One need not search far to find examples of this pattern. American attention to hypocrisy and false sanctimony marks our anxiety about moralism. The spectacle of fallen preachers and politicians captures interest because it matches our predisposed concerns. The political theorist William E. Connolly summarized our fears about morality, especially morality under pressure, as an "overweening drive to assert: 'What I am (believe, demand, pray, do) is what morality (God, nature, reason, science) itself requires.... [A]nything (person, creed, nation, movement) deviating from these exclusive imperatives is ... to be converted or conquered or both.'"[6] In American society, which doubts the efficacy of social or political limits on rampant moralism, the best line of defense is also the last—a resolute and individualist cynicism.

Believers are at pains to describe cynicism in negative terms. The persistence of resentment and backlash has not diminished the confidence of many intellectuals and most media commentators that a solution to our social ills must be based on a renewal of belief. But no matter how often they insist on the importance of civic faith, the everyday patterns of politics and government undermine the commitment to morality they wish to preserve. Sometimes this happens because the stakes are high, and then political adversaries charge their opponents with hypocrisy, personal immorality, or thievery. Sometimes, the charges are accurate.

But this is not entirely a question of the character of leaders and celebrities. In a regular, everyday way, democratic strategies can undermine belief in community values. All of this is exacerbated in a mass society with mass media and mass urbanization. The contemporary language of politics, to cite an important example, continually falls into a cynical dialect. The political scientist Jeffrey C. Goldfarb described this effect with a neat example from the 1984 presidential election: "Everyone knew Reagan was to the right, so he made leftist statements. Everyone knew Mondale was to the left, so he made rightist statements. Add this to the thirty-second political commercials packaged by those who make cola ads, and the cultural problems of mass politics come into view."[7] In a mundane way, the trivial habits of political speech accumulate into a cynical culture.

Voters expect political campaigns to use codes. Most of us know that Democratic speeches about trickle-down economics encode complaints about Republican elitism. Most of us know that tax-and-spend criticisms similarly encode Republican accusations that Democrats are undisciplined and excessively concerned with social justice and pluralist deal. The codes themselves are relatively trivial. Political folk choose their side, accept most of its codes, and go to work trying to get the votes out. On occasion, a code is too flagrant and itself becomes an issue. But no matter how much we reform campaign practices, a variety of codes will remain. This matter of making politics "honest" is not as simple as it might seem. We would agree on extreme cases like bribery. But how about the myriad lesser cases? At that end of the scale, the insistence that political campaigns be honest essentially asks that politicians give up politics.

Repeatedly, the measures we have taken to shore up democracy in an age of mass society have had unanticipated consequences that undermined the project they were intended to implement. Democratizing reforms, such as the party system and an expanded franchise, transformed elitist, exclusive institutions. But such reforms did allow government to function in a large and complicated society. Madison had feared that democratization would also introduce opportunities for manipulation. As literacy spread, so too did the Enlightenment tenet that people can know what is in their best interest and can act on that awareness. But opportunities for manipulation spread along with that positive development.[8] Television, for example, makes political information easily accessible and pervasive at the same time as it encourages the mass marketing of candidates, in a process that debases the democratic project.

The quality of political talk is eroded by a development we support for egalitarian reasons, namely, democracy, and by another development we hardly have much control to stop or reverse — mediated politics. This is not to say that democratic reforms should not have been sought. Indeed, this tension between excellence and the contrary tug of populism is a mainstay issue of democratic theory. My point is that moralism in the political world is never as simple as it promises to be. Solutions routinely undermine themselves, as we work out a political and cultural future that is always more vigorous and unpredictable than we can know. In a setting where cynicism puts pressure on civic faith, believer reforms continually ask for changes that would undermine democratic liveliness by asphyxiating the very values reformers seek to salvage.

At the extreme, believer complaints about the roughhouse democratic mob turn cranky and self-destructive. Consider the ill-tempered sermonizing of Allan Bloom, whose wildly successful book, *The Closing of the American Mind,* spawned many imitators.[9] Bloom captured the topic of "quality" with an appeal to classical European culture and thought. He also had an obviously conservative agenda with which conservative neoclassicists could rally their troops and sell books. But their reform attempts were blocked from the start. Their adversaries know how to fend off these efforts. In a cynical culture, most everyone knows how to ferret out elite interests and celebrity inconsistency.

Cynicism begets more cynicism, but it also gains advantages from other social developments. As ours becomes ever more completely a commercial culture, we develop the habit of thinking of values in terms of market value. As social relations are ever more thoroughly commercialized, so are values. The continuing hegemony of Reagan conservatism accelerates this development, constantly reiterating the claim that traditional, values-oriented conservatism is compatible with free-market libertarian opposition to regulation. The market mediates every relationship. As a result, it becomes standard-issue social knowledge that every relationship can be translated into the terms of commerce. Cynics understand that everything has its price.

Believers insist that a smothering layer of values talk will help reconcile democracy's necessary noise, its many codes and strident voices, with the ongoing need for clear national focus and policies. The problem is that values talk provides an opening for resentful and cynical backlashes that corrupt institutions, including those institutions the believer endorses, such as education and journalism. Democracy has been composed of elements that contribute various cynical pressures that undermine the believer argument. This problem is made all the worse now, when cynicism looms so large. The patterns, institutions, logic, and styles that demand a believing citizenry have become too problematic for anyone to assume that more belief is the remedy for our problems.

Community talk may serve well enough as rhetoric for governors, but it is not a principle for democratic society. The enforcement of "community talk" rules lets believers convene an endless stream of conferences that praise traditions and civility without helping at all to accomplish the necessary political work that could produce better policy. Lunch is usually good; privilege is what is actually served.

The believer plea is issued by both left and right. In chapter 7, I discuss E. J. Dionne, Jr.'s version of a saving civic faith. For now, consider the argument posed by the authors of *Habits of the Heart*, a book that drew attention in the 1980s as a model for a community-attentive social science.[10] The success of *Habits* provides a model of what left-believers take as important and necessary in political analysis. From that angle, the favorites it plays and the political elements it excludes tell us something about the community argument. Most dramatically, *Habits* shows how easily believers forget that some kind of movement has to be generated and supported if politics can ever hope to alter institutions. Underlying causes tend to slip away from the grasp of *Habits'* authors. One does not find out how we fell into our current circumstance by reading it. There is an American character that *Habits* wants to repair, but there do not seem to be general conditions or institutions that created that character.

The authors of *Habits* abhor conflict and love interview subjects who use the language of community and self-help. Their book dismisses interviewees who talk of struggle and challenge, preferring instead those who speak in generalities and promote certain values, while ignoring the dissension and inconsistency of the social world. As the political scientist Michael J. Shapiro has noted, the authors of *Habits* persistently locate "an inadequacy in their subject's discoveries, which they attribute to an impoverished political discourse. But they fail to assess their own discourse, the univocal, moralistic view of communitarianism, which they impose and then treat as a discovery."[11] Believer analysis always risks turning into nagging scold, but it also risks missing the reasons we end up in our current condition. Both tendencies miss the point.

Not all of today's moralists are hypocrites or ineffectual. Some believer critics find ways to insist that powerful institutions be held to high standards of behavior without falling into the traps of ignoring politics or insisting on an improbable spiritual transformation of society. The best believer critics identify abuses that debilitate democratic responses and undermine the confidence citizens have in their institutions. The author and journalist William Greider, activist Ralph Nader, and scholar Noam Chomsky sometimes accomplish this kind of critique. But even the best moralist critics constantly risk misrepresenting politics as a test of the soul rather than an arena to which groups and individuals need to be mobilized, or coalitions assembled and messages communicated to many citizens less concerned with universal moral dictum. Their critiques always risk providing an incomplete basis for political movement, especially in a society that is dissuaded from political activism. The moral high ground is consistently perilous terrain.

This has been a particular problem for the left. As the political theorist Alan Keenan has explained, leftist criticism now depends excessively on a politics driven by guilt.[12] The left complains that this or that condition fails the test of justice, moral purity, or democratic fairness. But in the political world, conditions must be altered through a process rife with negotiation and strategic consideration. Responses to the system's injustices are necessarily formulated and proposed within that same system. The motivation for action is guilt over unjust results, but the remedies all involve more intense interaction with the system that generated guilt in the first place.

Still, the believer is an activist. After all, the system has been set up in the name of belief—in institutional solutions, in formal protections of rights, in the justness of a given economic order. Believers know the system works, for it has worked very well for them. They can be more than a little baffled by the cynicism that surrounds them. Civic believers think and talk and write about recruitment, but unlike their fundamentalist counterparts, they are seldom good at it, certainly not on a massive scale. And why should they be? A believer can make a compelling case that it has been a believer's world for centuries, that all sorts of considerations, including theology, science, and tradition, stipulate that belief is necessary, not optional or negotiable. The elitism underlying calls to civic belief is a durable problem. While partisan Republicans have worked out basic moves to maintain a mass audience, the more proper communitarians are blocked from using their manipulations. Civic belief is constantly in danger of appearing not to have a community, only a faith.

The believer diagnosis has foundered lately on one hard fact. It is always easier to "talk the talk" than to "walk the walk." The best preachers in this cynical age sometimes turn out to be cynics. Former secretary of education William Bennett's ascent to power began at Ronald Reagan's National Endowment for the Humanities, where Bennett honed the pernicious complaint that any critic or victim must be held responsible for having produced the problems that bedevil them. Dialog, struggle, and debate, in Bennett's view, were suspect responses to public problems. When Bennett became drug czar during President Reagan's second term, he insisted that drug abuse is a moral failing unrelated to poverty, racism, and other disadvantage, or that it is a matter of virtue and the lack thereof. This approach failed dismally in the effort to control the drug trade. It succeeded mightily at providing Republicans with a wedge that could leverage middle-class white resentment into electoral victory. And it did wonders for Bennett's career.

Bennett flitted from one prominent position to another during the Reagan and Bush administrations, eventually resigning from leadership of the Republican Party in 1990 when he learned that the post would prevent him from accepting a large advance for his next book.[13] The tome, a light retelling of moralistic fables with the grandiose title *The Book of Virtues,* went immediately to the bestseller list and stayed there for a very long time. Bennett had made himself the preeminent spokesperson of the values crusade, the teller of our virtue stories. Confronted with any catastrophe, Bennett directs attention toward values and away from power, toward citizens and away from institutions and leaders. The disempowered are blamed, and privilege is protected.

Bennett was able to make a classic American tension work for him. The habit of reaffirming and reconstructing belief pulls us one way. The pragmatic, deal-wise business of capitalism, or of government, pulls us in the other direction. Bennett, and eventually others in the Reagan-Bush mold, circumvented the problem by demonizing government even while they governed. Bennett also overcame the incremental inertia of policy making by "freelancing," a term he applies with pride.[14] On his own, without White House sanction, he offered showy policy initiatives, such as his proposal to use the military for drug interdiction. Never mind that he would condemn such freelancing by his adversaries as a grave and unprincipled abuse of power. *The Book of Virtues* sells just fine without a chapter on consistency.

Chapter 3

Cynics-in-Power

Manipulations, Lies, and Empty Gestures

No matter how cynical you get, it's never enough to keep up.

Lily Tomlin

Most of the time we cannot know in any direct way whether a leader is cynical or sincere, and hence are left to the kind of interpretive exercise chapter 1 conducted on George Will, who in turn had been interpreting Newt Gingrich. Was the divorced Gingrich truly horrified at President Clinton's alleged philandering? Did Will sincerely change his mind over the course of three months, from condemning former president Bush in the strongest of terms to endorsing his election? As audience to the political spectacle, we have little direct access to leaders and little trust in the mediated access we do have. This is a problem for any analyst of cynicism. How can we invest such importance in a largely unverifiable diagnosis? But the interpretive character of such questions also reminds us of a political opportunity. Contemporary citizens are free to ascribe cynicism wherever they wish, with little danger that their criticism will be repudiated definitively.

The characteristic opacity attending cynicism does not debilitate our attempts to understand and ascribe cynicism. There are solid, structural incentives for cynical action by those in power. Social, political, and institutional forces could even be said to produce cynicism. Under the guise of strategy, raison d'état, and old-fashioned hardball politics, cynicism has blossomed among contemporary political and governmental leaders. It is much more than a feature of an individual's personality. Part of the reason we are a cynical society is that we have good reason.

Once he became Speaker of the House after the 1994 elections, Gingrich had less to fear from George Will and others who earlier charged him with cynicism and hypocrisy. Voters quickly turned cynical toward his Contract for America, which in the popular lexicon became the "Contract on America." President Clinton's health insurance reform had already failed. Neither Democrats nor Republicans could propose solutions ambitious enough to salve the public's many and varied injuries. Those hurts didn't heal; they worsened, as part of explicit strategies deployed in the struggle for power. Every leader's every gesture is understood, sooner or later, *as a gesture,* a cynical attempt to gain power without regard for the consequences.

The Reagan-Bush years provided endless examples of one of cynicism's key modes — the cynicism of those who rule. Opponents regularly decried the gap between what these two presidents said and what their constituents or their aides or even they could possibly believe. When Bush selected Dan Quayle, David Souter, and Clarence Thomas for his most important nominations, he announced that each was the most qualified person available. Ample evidence indicated that the trio was as ill qualified as any such crucial appointments ever offered by a president. Quayle and Thomas vindicated the harsher judgments when they got their chance. If Bush actually believed what he said, then he was remarkably dense, shallower than any president should be. If he did not mean what he said, he was overtly cynical — saying things for not much better reason than that nobody could stop him, girding his power while reminding us of our inability to hold him accountable.

The word *cynicism* almost automatically conjures the phrase "cynical manipulation." Rulers purposefully misapply principles of justice and democracy, muddling values and ignoring the conscience that would keep them in line. Thus did Bush defend the feudal monarchy in Kuwait in the name of democracy and freedom. Congress created a massive food stamp program, pushed by farm-state legislators like Bob Dole with no prior discernible interest in alleviating poverty or hunger. But there are too many examples of cynicism by those in power even to begin a list. It is all too easy to translate any governmental or political claim into a cynical ploy.

American cynics assume that those in power have been transformed by their climb up the rungs of American life, that they have learned to manipulate. And since citizens seldom have a way to directly measure the sincerity of public figures they do not know and may never meet, there is no limit to the cynicism these citizens can perceive. Often, the citizen cynic has it right. Public officials know that when push comes to shove, as the saying goes, the values and promises can be swept aside if the need is great enough. Having become cynical, those in positions of power project their cynicism outward. When a situation warrants it, they can masquerade as idealists or as pragmatists who know how to balance belief and necessity. Peter Sloterdijk described how any cynic can set the ruses aside and bring down the hammer: "The cynical master lifts the mask, smiles at his weak adversary, and suppresses him. *C'est la vie. Noblesse oblige.* Order must prevail." At its best, the smile is convincing, like a wave from the jaunty World War II pilot image Bush evoked for himself. Audacity marks the cynical leader. "Master cynicism," Sloterdijk summarizes, "is a cheekiness that has changed sides."[1]

Since Machiavelli, powerful cynics have functioned almost as a secret society, a self-conscious band of operators who pervaded the most public professions. These cynics can speak of values well since they are so little restrained by them. They know the system works, and they know how to work it, with manipulations, deals, and muscle. They write and read endlessly euphemistic press releases, knowing they can say anything they want to say. They also know they can punish, or at least exclude, troublemakers who dispute their well-chosen words. These cynics experience power as fun and enlivening, its trappings as scores of their success. Seen from afar, they are often the beautiful people: witty, hip, at the center of things. Only the bitterest partisan could have ignored the attractiveness of the Kennedy clan. And only the narrowest apologist could doubt that they were cynics.

The cynic, whether in power or not, has accomplished several of the psychic goals our culture approves. Cynicism, Sloterdijk notes, is the "widespread way in which enlightened people see to it that they are not taken for suckers." Cynics carry themselves with a healthy and robust bearing because they have resolved the problems of self-preservation that confuse and intimidate so many of us. Cynicism is the stance adopted by "people who realize that the times of naïveté are gone," Sloterdijk notes.[2] This is an attractive posture, so the cynical stance comes to be adopted by cynical citizens who model themselves on powerful cynics. Cynical culture is the barometer of cosmopolitanism, the mood of modernity, the "bright lights" that prompt young folk to flee to the cities. No matter how much we grouse about cynicism, there is no way around the obvious. Cynics know how to live.

Still, the powerful cynic's vitality, audacity, and survival skills are not sufficient to justify their abuses. Too many people have suffered too unjustly at the hands of cynical power. Yet we would not want to discard our interest in the liveliness a democratic culture must exhibit. We need to get more sophisticated about cynicism, to understand how it coheres as a culture at the same time that its several modes are distinct in form and effect. The cynicism of the powerful is related to other kinds of cynicism — all exhibit an energy and activism in the face of belief's demise. But the cynicism of rulers is also singular. Although the cynicism of those who rule traces a history back to Machiavelli, I will argue in later chapters that it acquired a palpably new presence and tone in contemporary American politics.

No logic or evidence can be summoned to guarantee that the cynic-in-power will be defeated. Cynics have advantages, protected both by organized force and the cultural self-discipline they encourage citizens to retain. Cynical false consciousness serves power's interests, even after the citizenry has "seen through" the game. Every cynic has an answer to the complaint that modern power is transparently cynical. Of course it is cynical! Standards, rules, values, and other presumed certainties are not the solid basis for living we say they are. Cynics live in spite of these proclaimed values, not in search of them.

Sometimes powerful cynics beguile us, fending off criticisms with a close attention to self-preservation and an appealing swagger. As much as they are criticized, some cynical performances, even by those in position to manipulate us, hold a sort of fascination. When then budget director David Stockman told William Greider (for an *Atlantic Monthly* article) about the slapdash and coarsely partisan strategies behind the 1981 Reagan budget proposal, many readers — both critics and supporters — found something likable in Stockman's disclosures. The 1981 budget had been Reagan's first, and it had been the boldest proposal in decades. Income-tax rates were slashed, a few social spending programs were "zeroed out," and defense spending exploded. There was good reason to be skeptical about this turn to "supply-side" economics, but the cool, competent Stockman had reassured the plan's supporters. Then, a year later, he told the world that the process had been out of control.

Stockman was a former divinity school student who understood the importance of values. That made his confident realism all the more convincing as he applied those values, with an unevenness that was sometimes relatively open, to the difficult and time-bound world of congressional action. Some critics and supporters alike were pleased to learn that Stockman did not really believe the mishmash of simplistic verities that supposedly drove this novel approach, "Reaganomics." There was something appealing, on the order of a guilty pleasure, in learning that Stockman's competent façade was often precisely a façade, especially when he tossed statistics whose origin he did not remember at a benumbed Congress and public.

Some of Stockman's lines were overtly cynical. He revealed that he had designed the general tax cut as a Trojan horse to generate public support for the huge cuts on taxes paid by the wealthy. But Stockman's admissions to Greider, a *Washington Post* reporter no less, did not destroy the credibility of either the Reagan administration or its irresponsible budget theories. Americans expect powerful leaders to signal ideological belief. But ideology itself is insufficient, even at such a moment as the apex of the Reagan conservative movement. Few Americans expect that politics will really be driven by ideology. Stockman's cynicism was a sign of realism. It reassured the citizenry that someone serious and sophisticated was running the show. Stockman stayed for years as Reagan's budget director. He did, however, stop giving on-the-record interviews to the *Post*.

As quickly as their antagonists could expose Reagan-Bush cynicism, powerful cynics deflected attention. Republicans, themselves susceptible to charges of special-interest influence, loudly condemned the cynicism of special-interest labor unions, whose money kept Democrats strong in Congress. Cynics always charge that their adversaries are cynical. The Reagan-Bush cynics, at their most brazen, became experts at deploying resentment. Media spokesmen for both administrations invented a new meaning for the verb "to spin." If an event had to be explained in such a way as to hide its obvious implications, that event was to be "spun." In a masterfully cynical move, they told journalists that this is what they called the process, and the ploy worked. The spinners convinced voters that the statements of union leaders and congressional old-timers were as cynical as anything Reagan spinmaster Michael Deaver scripted. Their adversaries' political tricks had been exposed by even more powerful cynics, who were then admired for their boldness and innovation.

Cynicism has existed for a very long time. But the character of power changes over time. The blooming of nation-states helped generate opportunities for cynical manipulation as well as for economic and cultural development. More powerful and more distant from citizens, national leaders found opportunity and reason to lie, cheat, and steal. They learned to invoke "necessity" when dirty work had to be done. They learned to appeal to progress and solutions.

More recently, a culture of cynicism among the powerful emerged with contemporary intensity. Franklin Roosevelt set the New Deal in motion as a proto-cynical exercise. The New Deal was all pluralist process, built on the hope that social needs could be met by passing programs, sometimes massive ones, even if more central problems of power and inequality remained unaddressed. Perfectly named, the New Deal was typified by *the deal*—the interest-group negotiation, the wheeling and dealing of elite insiders and economist technocrats whose explanations concealed the familiar congressional pork barrel and logrolling with talk of realism, expertise, and novelty. It was "proto" because so many of the participants, observers, and subjects still retained confidence in the process, when the relations between governor and governed were altered rapidly. The connection and community required for such faith had already begun to dissolve when FDR began his fireside chats on the radio. The real fire of politics to come burned in those early electronic tubes.

Subsequently, the Cold War was the ultimate cynicism, threatening violence in the service of peace. That global cynicism was soon replicated closer to home, in the sort of cloning operation the modern media foster. We had the obviously antidemocratic red hunts of Nixon and associates, in the name of protecting democracy. Aggressive, proselytizing Christianity advanced under the presumably apolitical cover of protected religious practice, with the insertion of the phrase "under God" into the Pledge of Allegiance during Eisenhower's administration. John Kennedy, when campaigning for the presidency against Nixon, expressed his dissatisfaction with Nixon's bellicosity by trumpeting a false "missile gap" and advocating yet more military spending. In these instances power manipulated, but it did so in the name of belief, values, and traditions.

Over time, the mismatch of gesture and consequence started to look cynical. Interest-group liberals as well as conservatives and many others began to take on the flinty glow of the cynic in power. This is what a "crisis of meaning" looks like on the nightly news. It is no coincidence that television and cynical power advanced together. I will return to television elsewhere in this book; suffice it to say here that our leaders are inaccessible except via television, and they learned to use television to represent their sincerity. We are skeptical about the false immediacy offered by the tube. We scoff at leaders and flip channels. But the gap between leader and citizen always makes it possible that we are being fooled.

The cynic-in-power is adept at protesting sincerity. George Bush protested mightily when critics complained about the overt cynicism of his most important appointments. He deployed all the power of his office to impose a tone of seriousness on his string of bizarre choices. He protested that he had researched his appointments exhaustively, a protest not inconsistent with the possibility that they were offered cynically. The seriousness of politics is useful to powerful cynics. It discourages observers from laughing at the baroque oddities that parade under signs of grave importance. Even the most cynical reporters hesitate to scoff at Supreme Court nominees, if only because they need to protect their access to sources.

In an institutional and social setting where structural incentives routinely debilitate prospects for change, those who nonetheless wish to promote change inevitably become strategists. When politicians and governmental officials ponder strategic considerations, manipulate appearances, and appeal to rhetorical verities as a cover for less lofty intentions, they are implementing the cynicism of the powerful. One could interpret their cynicism as personality disorder or moral weakness. But the systemic arrangements these cynics perceive can also be seen as inducing their cynicism. Given the access to media powerful cynics have, they can be convincing in representing their choices as necessary and inevitable responses to "the way the world is." Thus cynicism becomes realism, and the reverse.

The familiar "politics" story changes when we become attuned to the operations of strategy. Public opinions — something Americans truly love and insist on as both democratic right and process — are not necessarily independent readings of reality. More often, opinions respond to political cues formulated and publicized well before the individual gave the matter much thought. No political science teacher can long abide the phrase "in my opinion," which so often functions as an excuse for laziness or an introduction to thoughtlessness. So many unoriginal pronouncements are protected under the "Opinion" sign, which functions something like a diplomatic license plate on a double-parked car in D.C., with the message "don't even think about contesting me"!

Sophisticated citizens have learned how to rephrase their "opinions" in the form of democratic dialog. Such talk seems designed to reach agreement or consensus. But this political practice often misfires. Arguments polarize, at least as often as they "resolve." When solutions do result from political debate, they often emerge before issues are clarified. Powerful cynics use publicity to frame a problem and present choices, then reach solutions that enhance their authority to deal with the problem they've framed.

Child kidnapping is a problem, for example. The image evoked by the phrase is so awful that it seems callous to analyze it. But the powerful cynics, having framed child kidnapping as a problem, get busy. They work, it would seem, to terrorize children, by fingerprinting them, by putting reminders on milk boxes of other children who have disappeared. Never mind that such events are extraordinarily rare. In Montana, where this concern briefly captured headlines a few years ago, not a single such kidnapping by a stranger had been reported in more than a decade. Even in more populous areas, such disappearances are usually a side effect of divorce proceedings, not random acts of violence. But to have identified the problem is to have stifled such counterevidence.

The relationship between problem and solution is susceptible to all kinds of cynical meddling. Real solutions may not be all that useful. Some activities that are commonly called solutions positively contribute to the perseverance of the problem they seem designed to alleviate. Sometimes the solution comes first, then the problem. As the saying goes, if you got a hammer, many things begin to look like a nail. Popular solutions can create problems of their own. In *Alice's Adventures in Wonderland*, Lewis Carroll satirized those who govern, exposing an abiding paradox of politics. Solutions arise, then the problem is found:

> "Let the jury consider their verdict," the King said, for about the twentieth time that day.
>
> "No, no!" said the Queen. "Sentence first — verdict afterwards."
>
> "Stuff and nonsense!" said Alice loudly. "The idea of having the sentence first."
>
> "Hold your tongue!" said the Queen, turning purple.
>
> "I won't!" said Alice.
>
> "Off with her head!" the Queen shouted at the top of her voice.
>
> Nobody moved.[3]

Just so. First we describe something, using sentences. Something is a subject, something else is a verb, and so on. Having fitted an event into a sentence, the verdict is almost automatic. The judgment is foretold in how the event has been framed, how its story has been composed. And if the monarch cannot, at the moment, enforce her edicts, the judgment will live on anyway. As will Alice.

Those who govern discover any number of ways to ease their difficult task. They learn that modern power has its advantages. The French philosopher Michel Foucault's enduring contribution to political analysis was to illuminate this aspect of contemporary power. Most of us continue to think about governmental power as command-and-obey, talking about it in metaphors of parenthood, or sports or military training. Government commands, and citizens obey. But contemporary power has become much more adroit than that, finding ways to generate cooperation but without the messy resistance command often produces as its inevitable side effect. Power does not require that citizens consciously "sell out," nor does it depend on an evil manager who hides behind the scenes, plotting our oppression.

Power formulates problems, applies solutions, and limits possibilities, and it does so regardless of the sincerity, cynicism, or intentions of the various professionals who wield influence over our lives. Power somehow positively constructs us, constituting us in particular roles and identities, at the same time as it also produces other features of our social and political map. If we suddenly came into a situation in which power had much less effect on us (if we won the lottery, say), we would still be constrained in some very important ways, regardless of our good intentions or the weight of the oppressions that have been lifted.

Although we love to play the parlor game, guessing which television personality is sincere and which is cynical, this is the wrong game. Political stakes are so high, the incentive to win is so overwhelming, that the pressure to cynical action—whether conscious or not—overwhelms every better impulse. The lesson? Give up the game of trying to identify a sincere public figure. Focus instead on their strategies and constraints. Cynics-in-power have been captured by a very tough game and we would do well to be more clearly aware of it. Hoping that an "honest" leader will somehow miraculously emerge from the ooze is a sucker's game. The structures and constraints of power bend hard toward cynicism. Even the most attractive of American public figures cannot, these days, long swim against the cynical currents.

Even Colin Powell, as winning a public figure as can be found on the American scene, fell into the role of cynic-in-power. He was Chairman of the Joint Chiefs of Staff under Bush, a black man running the Pentagon. Before we even get to know him, Powell symbolizes the triumph of integration, which had been implemented in the armed services only a generation before Powell's career began. Powell demonstrated integrity and independence. He moderated the hawkish impulses of others in the Bush administration on several occasions. In 1992, when many Democrats assumed that Bush would concoct some military adventure to ensure his reelection, Powell quietly but publicly told the president no.

It may be hard to imagine Powell as a cynic. He represents what so many of us imagine as the best chance we have. But Powell had learned how to get along. Bob Woodward's *The Commanders* showed Powell swallowing his doubts about the Gulf War as planning for it accelerated. As Woodward reported it, Powell even imagined he could express his concern about the war plans with stiff body language in an Oval Office briefing. His predecessor as Chairman of the Joint Chiefs, Admiral William J. Crowe, had told Powell, "To be a great president you have to have a war. All the great presidents have had their wars." Powell laughed and acknowledged the statement's truth.[4]

Though we always suspect our leaders of the worst, it was a jolt to glimpse a cynical Powell. Later, when Powell had retired from his Pentagon position and speculation was rampant that he might venture a run for the presidency, he published a best-selling autobiography that left no doubt about his deep disagreement with Bush's Republican Party on a subject of intimate interest   race and affirmative action. Nonetheless, he affirmed his membership in Bush's party and declined President Clinton's offer of a top-level appointment. Powell had disagreed with the Republicans about domestic and foreign policies of the greatest personal importance. But he stayed with them.

I have no idea what Powell is like, as a private human being. I have never met him or seen him, except on television. In truth, I have no way to decide how sincere or cynical this attractive public figure "really is." But the cynicism of the powerful is a mighty force. Powell gratified a vain president; he went along. Watching him from a distance, we hoped it wasn't true. But we are always prepared to suspect the worst.

Because it is built into the power game, cynicism is not the sole province of one or another pack of partisans. It is shared across the political spectrum, always available as critique and always discounted among friends. Republicans have been willing to accept many of the obvious foibles of the Reagan-Bush era, sometimes, as in the case of Powell, finding it an attractive combination of sensitive soul-searching and dashing realism. The New Democrats have been just as willing to accept Hillary Rodham Clinton's mix of overtly liberal sentimentality and feminism with her pragmatic, lawyerly, and sometimes dubious deal making. Her advocates overlook a grim spot here and there as the inevitable partisan tariff. When the stakes are high in partisan struggle, the incentives to apply our ethical judgments selectively grow. And so the gulf widens, each side convinced of the other side's insincerity — and each side willing to accept some warts on leaders they like.

In one of her first appearances in a First Lady role, receiving an award in New York for service to children, Mrs. Clinton announced: "We have to fight against our own cynicism and skepticism. We have to fight against our own feelings of hopelessness in the face of such big problems. I know that the president is convinced — and I know that I'm convinced . . . that each of us, every day, can make a difference in the life of some child if we are willing to take the risk to reach out."[5] Throughout the Clinton administration, both the First Lady and her husband continued to voice their concern about the country's cynicism. Mrs. Clinton's concern for children correlated with the much-vaunted Republican concern for family values. Democrats complained that Reagan frequently skipped Sunday services even as he berated Democrats for not believing. The same Democrats meekly acquiesced when President Clinton violated his wife's commitment to children by signing a vicious welfare bill during the stretch run to the 1996 election.

The First Lady's bestseller about her side's codes, *It Takes a Village,* set land-speed records for conversion to trade paperback in time for the fall election. It even provided campaign material. Searching for a hold on a race that was slipping away, Republican nominee Bob Dole mused during his nomination acceptance speech that it takes a family, rather than a village, to raise a child. Cheering Republicans took this silliness as Dole no doubt intended it to be taken, as a coded reminder that the defeated Pat Buchanan's bulldog style had not entirely fallen out of favor. Democrats, for their part, slung village metaphors back.

Republican partisans had no qualms about painting Mrs. Clinton as a manipulator. She is a lawyer, a successful one, and what other profession so invites charges of cynicism? The lawyer vests wisdom and justice in an adversary system, insisting on every side's right to able counsel. To appropriate the journalist Michael Kinsley's brightly cynical phrase, every good lawyer knows how to argue it flat or argue it round. As vernacular, that pretty much defines cynicism.

Her critics saw a hired-gun lawyer whose commitment to children looked like fashionable dressing on a crude bottom line of shady real-estate deals and tax maneuvers, insider commodity investments, legalistic cover-ups, and perpetual fund raising. Why did this high-powered, big-city lawyer settle for a life in Little Rock and marriage to a philanderer? Because she saw his political potential and loved the power game as much as he did. And why did her every clarification sound like a lawyer's clever, hairsplitting evasion? Because that's what it was.

The president's cynicism became a commonplace centerpiece of how he was understood by both left and right. The right screamed about hypocrisy and harassment. When Clinton hired and then fired Republican political consultant Dick Morris, the notion of strategic "triangulation" offered by Morris was hard to hear with face straight. The idea that Clinton should triangulate himself between Republicans and Democrats was nothing but cynical positioning. Nobody thought Clinton's acceptance of the Gingrich welfare bill served his constituency. Just as few took seriously Clinton's denials of sexual or financial scandal.

Convinced that they represent the people, Democrats have long practiced a careful tunnel vision, blinding themselves to the manifest cynicism of congressional bosses like Dan "Rosty" Rostenkowski or Jim Wright in their rush to condemn John Tower or Newt Gingrich. Republicans respond by needling Hollywood liberals like Candice "Murphy Brown" Bergen and various "friends of Bill and Hill," while happily taking advantage of Sonny Bono and Charlton Heston. Republicans probably do cynicism better, practiced as they are at convincing working Americans to support political positions that benefit the very wealthy. Is it any surprise that Americans are sickened by all this cynicism and call in absent on election day?

Cynical leaders generate citizens who are cynical about politicians, who then respond with yet more cynical ploys. This is a circular and deeply reinforced relationship. The cynical mire is deep.

No participant who plays by the current rules of the game can find a way out of the muck—not Clinton, not Newt, not anybody else. Given the durability of America's largest institutions, it seems likely that we will enter an ever more cynical, irrelevant, spectacular, and angry future.

Chapter 4

Wig Cynics

American Antipolitics and Its Uses

> The man of resentment is neither upright nor naïve
> nor honest and straightforward with himself. His soul
> squints; his spirit loves hiding places, secret paths and
> back doors, everything covert entices him as his world,
> his security, his refreshment; he understands how to
> keep silent, how not to forget, how to wait, how to be
> provisionally self-deprecating and humble.
>
> Friedrich Nietzsche, *On the Genealogy of Morals*

The salient figure of the intense election season of 1992 was Ross
Perot. The fervor of his followers' cynicism influenced every element of the crucial campaigns that year. Their discontent was palpably new and universal, if still somehow diffuse and opaque. The
potential Perot vote was massive, at least in June, before the Clinton campaign found its track and while the Bush campaign was
honing the disharmony and lack of purpose it would later perfect.
Cynicism was universal, but it was also diffuse. Surely, the deficit—
Perot's horse to ride—was not the occasion for the discontent as
much as it was a symbol around which to organize. Perot used the
deficit effectively against both "tax and spend" Democrats and the
oblivious Bush.

As savvy as Perot was, he had blind spots, too. The candidate
who repeated as a mantra that existing policy structures did not

listen, in turn was an awful listener, as the constant turnover in his campaign staff attested. Perot spent millions on commercials that were not much more than introductory lectures in macroeconomics — "infomercials," he tried to get the media to call them — but filled them with bad facts and leaps of logic. He persistently posted wrong numbers on his famous charts and never even began to discuss the basic complexities of the deficit issue.

Perot was uneasy with the victims of the corporate and governmental arrangements that helped make him so wealthy. And he had vast bond holdings, investments that stood to further enrich him if he could succeed in getting government to lower deficits. Perot argued that policy was driven by money and that because he had so much money — well, he should drive policy. Vowing to run "on the issues," Perot nonetheless spent his way to credibility. His campaign was perfectly cynical, believing in nothing but his own magical qualities to "get under the hood and fix it," in one of his favorite odd metaphors.

It is as if Perot wanted to invent a politics of contradiction and paradox, against the promise and declaration so favored in American political rhetoric. Each time the media tried to get him back into the mainstream, he found some new way to reject their invitation, exploding angrily, for example, when his paranoid fantasy of black and Vietnamese hit squads aimed against him in the 1970s was raised in a press conference. This was discontent in the act of finding its perfect form — pervasive, diffuse, resentful, cynical, and about as inured to critique as the average UFO sighting. Yet Perot's screed somehow was widely perceived as an effective assault on corrupt systems. This, evidently, is the kind of "alternative" we can expect from American politics.

Ed Rollins, the ex–campaign chief for Reagan who briefly worked for Perot, told his employer that the old politics hadn't died completely and convinced him to run traditional television advertisements. Rollins hired the best media guy he could, the one who did Reagan's 1984 "Morning in America" ads under Rollins's tutelage. The ads were terrific, showing crowds of Perot supporters, suggesting how deep a chord he was striking, and reminding us how much Perot's emergence had disrupted the swamp that is contemporary politics.

After reviewing the ads, Perot immediately pulled them out of circulation. He evidently thought he could do the campaign one to one, in the same way he'd always struck business deals, the same way he'd motivated his employees to make him a lot of money. This outsider was, oddly enough, an insider, too. He seemed to think he could skip even the spectacle of the crowd. He seemed to think he could run for president on CNN's *Larry King Live* show. In that one-on-one setting, Perot reenacted the campaign as a leveraged corporate buyout negotiation. It gradually became clear that Perot could not distinguish his interests and opinions from the concerns of the nation. He didn't understand that his presidential campaign required a legion of supporters with whom he ordinarily wouldn't spend a minute in conversation.

America witnessed Perot's panicked withdrawal from the race as a sideshow to the Democrats' 1992 New York convention. Bill Clinton's campaign had just started to show the tough competence that would carry him to a win in November. Perot's sudden announcement that he was no longer running, and his hint that he might find Clinton acceptable, boosted a Democratic campaign that had seemed to flounder only weeks before. After Perot's subsequent reentry into the campaign's late stages, most of the residual goodwill Perot had won from the media for his earlier performances had vanished. Increasingly, the press emphasized his odd unwillingness to adopt the familiar codes of competence, reasonableness, and caution. In a page-one story illustrated with a photo, the *New York Times* blatantly played Perot as a loony eccentric:

> At times, the man known for his zany campaign stunts even outperformed himself. First, he asked rhetorically: "Perot, why are you doing this? Why are you back into this after all the headaches?" Then he answered his own question by holding up a tape player and switching on the Patsy Cline hit "Crazy," a song he played during the campaign after aides to President Bush suggested he had lost his mental balance. Several times at today's news conference, Mr. Perot played portions of the song as background music while he answered reporters' questions.[1]

The article went on to document Perot's inconsistencies: "Even as he vowed not to attack the President-elect, Mr. Perot's digs at

Mr. Clinton were hardly disguised. He held up several newspaper articles that questioned whether the incoming President had been forthright about handling the deficit, and other articles that suggested that he would not rid the Administration of powerful lobbyists." The article's concern with contradiction extended to an unusual extrapolation of Perot's psychology: "Mr. Perot's motives seemed as confounding and as contradictory as they were in the campaign: he advised people to give the incoming Administration a break, but in the next breath he would attack Mr. Clinton."

Even standard codes of reluctance, codes that journalists routinely ignore in their ambivalence about politics' cynical feel, became part of the story. Perot "insisted that he was heading the organization out of duty to his supporters and that he would rather not be in the spotlight. 'Believe me,' he said, 'I would prefer not to have to do this personally.' His protestations aside, Mr. Perot clearly loved the attention. He reluctantly ended the news conference only after reporters ran out of questions." Near the end of the campaign, ABC's Ted Koppel told the *Washington Post* that "some of the things Ross Perot has said and done over these past few months are, to put it bluntly, weird."[2] Early in Clinton's first term, when Perot's NAFTA debate with Vice President Gore went badly, the national media simply stopped calling and Perot disappeared from the scene, in what everyone suspected would be a temporary sabbatical.

Perot had declared open season on every populist target. He'd made the two political parties vulnerable, if only briefly. The coded resentment of the Reagan era — we're government too, but at least we despise the project in which we're implicated — had been stated more bluntly than ever. Resentment loves simplicity. But more than simplicity was at stake. Every leftist who had pined for an opening of the two-party structure watched in horror as Perot became the one to force the opening. Having set up the demise of the Democrats with reform proposals and utopian dreams of better political architectures, the left saw its complaints usurped. No viable left-populist or Green Party had emerged. The left had misunderstood cynicism and had failed to foresee how it would alter politics.

But if the left was abused in Perot's emergence, political science did not fare much better. Traditional denunciations of third-party politics did not contain Ross, his charts, or his pointer. Something was happening here, something beyond third parties as usually envisioned by historians and political scientists. As long as there are only two positions — two parties, two candidates, two sides of an issue — we can still imagine that the winner represents "the people." In a contest of two, the idea of a center is automatically shored up. This fiction has been under fire, of course, especially with voting rates in perpetual decline. The traditional centrist electoral strategy is mapped on a bell curve, as political scientists have explained to generations of students. The center coincides with "the people" or at least their "norm," in this story of American politics. The struggle is for control of the center, a sort of "capture the flag" game. Perot, always a fan of military maneuvers, understood that there was another option. He could change the game, set his own terms of engagement, and conduct a flanking action like Stormin' Norman Schwarzkopf did in Iraq.

Contemporary cynical culture confounds our expectations. The cynical citizen now is a mass figure, not an eccentric outsider. Citizen-cynics are as easily found in rural Montana as in cosmopolitan New York. The rural westerner, modest of means but immodestly bent toward acrid criticism, supports almost anything that will express his anger, from the candidacy of Ross Perot to tax protest movements to the legislative agenda of the National Rifle Association and perhaps even to cranky conspiracy theories and paranoid survivalism. His cynicism differs from the cynicism-in-power displayed by George Bush or Bill Clinton. Throughout their careers, Bush and Clinton have spoken of themselves as called to public service — calls that cynical westerners presume to be hoaxes. But despite the differences among various American cynics, they share in cynical culture. They have learned how to live with their disbelief.

In the 1990s, the outsider cynics ventured out, finding new and strange outlets for their abused belief, for their sense of loss. They tuned to talk radio, where loudmouth, wise-guy superiority hit just the right key. They found the side channels of the broad Internet bandwidth. Eventually, they discovered they could get on the nightly news. Contemporary society is ever richer in the means of making odd and charismatic individuals extremely visible. In the United States, especially, there are few aristocratic, totalitarian, or com-

munitarian means to keep renegades under control if they are insistent and avoid the obvious illegalities. This is not always a bad
thing, since it creates chances for alternative voices to emerge. But
as the culture of cynicism hit its stride, a more damaged and resentful voice hit the airwaves. Even convicted Watergate conspirator G. Gordon Liddy became a radio star.

Our political culture brims over with the dislocated, bent performance. This is now so visible a trend that it deserves a name.
Call it "wig cynicism" to carry a reminder of the wiggy explanation
that is the wig's primary form of political judgment. The talk-show
hosts Geraldo, Donahue, Sally Jesse, Oprah, and Jerry Springer and
the *National Enquirer* and New York tabloids — all of these inten-
sify a wig outbreak that has long been building on assassination
conspiracy theories, nightmares of Trilateral Commission hegemony, and worries over water fluoridation. The radio talk-show
host, now a salient category of public citizen, sifts through one
wig outburst after another, finding it gratifying for both the republic and the ratings book that so many people have opinions.

All this anguished and ecstatic bleeping forms a category of its
own, wig cynicism, that jumbled, postrationalist, unreal aesthetic
of weird causation and bent social dynamics. Living after belief,
living in the society of the spectacle, a surprisingly large number
of Americans go for the tabloid sensibility, the "why not?" factor.
Each issue favored by the wigs is cynical in that it dispenses with
evidence, reasoned argument, and the authority of all but the cer-
tified wig experts. A significant part of society, dismissive of the
explanations offered by cynics-in-power, prefers science fiction
and joins the odd trek into a Klingon-infested landscape of morality plays and improbable physics. It feels good, so the wigs do it.

Not comfortable with conventional civic belief, not willing to
let their cynical impulses be corralled into boring reform proposals, but not yet attuned to power, the wigs act out. Wigs are inherently manipulable by powerful cynics. Resentment combines with
a willingness to entertain the strangest explanation of cause and
effect, the looniest connection of agency and perceived injury. Wigs
often take their cues from powerful cynics who, when it suits them,
demonize scapegoats and launch resentful attacks on powerless
victims. At the margins, wig cynics also have found ways to threaten
the society they resent so deeply. Sometimes the threats are merely

brave talk, but sometimes the talk packs real explosives. Wigs have found the desperate edge of lost belief and persistent cynicism.

Part of cynicism's genius is that, like liberalism or democracy, it includes both a way of life for the powerful and a way for citizens to live, understand the world, and express themselves. If cynicism were only an attribute of a malignant leadership class, it would be easier to criticize. But cynicism infuses the lives of ordinary citizens. Even after we acknowledge the boom in cynicism, and the eccentric strains pervading American culture, it remains hard to talk about the cynicism of ordinary citizens. The tools of social science were not designed with this investigation in mind. Given the rural and pious roots of American political culture, we are not prepared to see the cynicism of daily life as distinctive and socially important. Few of us publicly label ourselves cynics, nor are journalists equipped to ferret out any but the most glaring cynicism. There is no Cynicism Party. The cranky outsiders I am calling wig cynics seldom have power, except at the state and local level, and then only in some regions, primarily the West and the South.

But the wigs' emergence and their frequent alliance with more powerful cynics make the wig outsiders an increasingly important feature of the current political scene, with its odd array of marginal characters and nasty rhetoric. In the same moment that believers sense distress and begin the search for solutions, plans, and policies, their wig neighbors begin a resentful hunt for enemies, villains, and scapegoats. The wigs became visible with Ross Perot and the big talk-show hosts — Rush Limbaugh, Gordon Liddy, and New York City's Bob Grant, to name a few. Through these wig stars and their big-time ratings, we began to see the wig constituency. At the margins, talk-radio posturing gave way to delusional militias, dressed in camouflage, armed to the teeth, and consumed by their study of odd religion and political paranoia.

The hope for a clear view, for coherence, can go ecstatic. Cynical belief, for a wig, can mutate into conspiracy theory. This move ingeniously solves every problem. It bypasses every aspect of traditional politics, since "they're all in on it," as the conspiracy thumper likes to say. Conspiracy explanations have perfect coherence. They can explain everything. If Bush wins, it is because of secret machinations by conservative business interests. If he loses, it is because those interests became disenchanted with him and pulled the secret levers to dump him. No conspiracy theory worthy of the name is phrased in terms that could be disproved. And conspiracy theorists seldom call anyone to action. To do so would be to underestimate the conspiracy's natural strength and risk putting an end to the fun.

Conspiracy theory is central to wig ideology. In some ways it parallels old leftist ideology, now carried on by a dwindling few cranks, leftist wigs who prefer grandiose certainties of judgment over the tougher work of addressing events in a way that puts politics into motion. There are also leftist wigs who hawk ecoconspiracies or tout a millennial New Age revolution by meditation, acute self-consciousness, and harmonic convergences as mystical as they are improbable. Confounded by the debilitating negativity and guilt that have often characterized the left, or by the impossibility of class-consciousness that Marxism presumed, these elements of the left have gone wig. At its worst, the broader left has displayed an authoritarian streak and a tendency toward exclusion that are tragically wiggish. Wherever winning matters less than venting, wiggism flourishes.

The political abstractions of left talk survive as habits long after their utility has been refuted. The upheavals of Soviet collapse did not much challenge the intellectual left, because a democratic, anti-Soviet leftist argument had long before been developed. But in a response few anticipated, the Soviet collapse became a useful symbol of left weakness in general. Gleefully applied by a robust new conservatism, complaints about left abstractions stuck, and no wonder. Somewhere along the line, leftist abstractions had wigged out. "Property is theft," a position that at least had Marx's formidable philosophical argument as backing, had turned into "marriage is rape" or, worse, "save the planet — kill yourself." Given these opportunities, the rightist backlash stomped the American left. But the right's policing of left excess did not raise the overall level of political rationality. As if by pneumatic mechanism, wig momentum pumped rightward.

Wiggism has a substantial history in American culture, dating back to historic tales of conspiracy and mystical causation. What is new in this century is the extent to which wig explanation expresses general discontent more than fascination with cabal and intrigue.

As some expressions of hatred and bigotry became somewhat less welcome in public discourse, the wigs took a weirder path.

Mike Davis's *City of Quartz,* a chronicle of Wig Central, a.k.a. southern California, presents vivid portraits of emerging wiggism in the first half of the century. One journalist described a speech by Robert A. Millikan, president of Cal Tech in the 1920s: "When he got through with science and religion, they were so wrapped up in each other that a Philadelphia lawyer could never untangle them.... The whole thing was a conglomeration of metaphysical aphorisms and theological sophistry, suffused in a weird and ghostly atmosphere of obscurantism, with occasional and literal references to Santa Claus."[3] In the 1930s, John Parsons, a Cal Tech rocketry pioneer and later a founder of the Jet Propulsion Laboratory, sponsored a Pasadena outpost for the notorious sorcerer Aleister Crowley, who performed "blasphemous rituals (with, for example, naked pregnant women leaping through fire circles) in his secret ... 'temple.'" The young naval officer L. Ron Hubbard was among the temple's attendees some years before he founded Scientology.

It is a mark of wig expansion when wigs offer the most astonishingly offensive actions and opinions, which do them no long-lasting damage. Jackie Robinson's first fight in the major leagues, for example, contested bigoted remarks made by Joe Garagiola, who went on to a long and lucrative broadcasting career. In a 1960 TV debate with Martin Luther King, Jr., James J. Kilpatrick, then editor of the Richmond *News Leader,* asserted that civil rights sit-ins were sexual in character. He warned of miscegenation — of "any intimate race mixing by which these principles [of Western civilization] inevitably must be destroyed."[4] Kilpatrick later became a mainstream commentator and enjoyed a long and lucrative career without ever being discredited for his wig paranoia.

Wig cynicism is by definition an outsider phenomenon. Conspiracy theory or other wig explanation wouldn't be of much use once a politician enters the Washington sausage factory. What wigward tendencies remain are usually well hidden. But cynics-in-power can manipulate the outlander wigs and can find ways to make alliances with them. A crucial figure in the merger and acquisition of wigs and powerful cynics was Richard Nixon.

Look at any of this country's recent historical ventures into the politics of resentment and you'll find wigs galore. Every American red scare is a pageant of wig hegemony. Nixon used a fear of reds to get elected senator from California and, soon thereafter, Eisenhower's vice president. After being temporarily held off from the presidency by John Kennedy (who courted the wig vote by running to Nixon's right on the fear of world communism), Nixon eventually came back with the coded law-and-order campaign of 1968. Never mind that the combined red-and-black scare Nixon invoked that year was truly an astonishing way for a president to get elected during a controversial foreign war. Who could ever have thought that Alger Hiss, the alleged communist that Nixon turned into a symbol for every public fear, was that big a threat to American society? Along the way, Nixon transformed American politics, constructing the bridge to the cynical era. We now routinely make presidents in wig rituals barely disguised as elections.

The 1990s belonged to the right-wing wigs. Especially in the western United States, they acquired enormous potential for damage. At the same time that various preachers of community — some, no doubt, more cynical than others — push for higher standards of reason and morality in community debate, the wigs already have rejected even the minimal requirements of community. The wig right explains a complex world's messy contingency by imagining secret meetings, unaccountable forces, and the unsubtle if also untraceable scam or fix. A difficult world comes back into focus.

The success of Rush Limbaugh provides a workable measure of the wig constituency. Limbaugh blames victims with, as the saying goes, a vengeance. He attributes cynicism everywhere, except, of course, on his side. Loudly proclaiming his role as defender of "truth," Limbaugh rushes to embrace any rumor, no matter how absurd, if it confirms his suspicions. There are millions of faithful wig cynics who still think Vince Foster was murdered in a suburban safe house owned by Hillary Clinton, whose henchpersons surreptitiously moved the body to the park where it was found. Contrary evidence is seldom a problem for a good conspiracy theory. It only attests to the skills of the supposed conspirators. Nobody was shocked when, years after Foster's suicide, it was finally reported in the mainstream press that Pittsburgh newspaper owner Richard Scaife, heir to a Mellon fortune, had funded several of the efforts to promote the Foster story. Wig culture has been so vibrant of late that it even recruits a few wealthy and well-connected insiders.

When *Nightline*'s Ted Koppel pressed Limbaugh on his role in spreading rumors about the Clintons, Limbaugh, perhaps wanting to ingratiate himself on a "real" TV show, told the truth.[5] In a remarkable admission of wig displacement, Limbaugh told Koppel that the real issue was health care. But since it was so hard an issue to debate—all those numbers, complexities, institutions—he was forced to attack the president's character rather than his policies. Limbaugh is fully able to comprehend and discuss the health-care issue, but he cynically knows he doesn't have to enter that debate. He can simply shift the issue to ground where his innuendo and resentment find better footing. His weird admission may have cost him invites to *Nightline,* but it did little damage to his wig mission.

Wigs display an extraordinary propensity for replacing or shifting legitimate issues and questions. The serious feminist claim that "the personal is political" mutated into Monicagate. Identity issues of race and gender twisted until we got O. J. Simpson and Clarence Thomas. Communists, themselves a wig fascination, morphed into aliens, which the top-rated *X-Files* TV show took mainstream. Education, one of our most serious and expensive public policy commitments, became entangled with another great issue, violence, and holds our attention in the form of schoolyard shootings in Arkansas, Oregon, and beyond. The debate over the social effects of technology gave way to claims that nobody ever landed on the moon. Our simultaneous suspicion of and attraction to celebrity served up a strange public blood feud between rival figure skaters. Abortion mutated into a fascination with fertility, and the mother of septuplets became a media star and spectacular charity case. And for some unfathomable reason, Elvis Lives. This is giddy community life, distracted from cause, fascinated by revenge and conspiracy, intrigued with the oddest of public displays. The great wig contribution has been to show how completely our politics has been transformed as centrist arguments are replaced by a politics that eludes standards of reasoned debate and conversation.

Consider how the National Rifle Association (NRA), for example, redefined gun control to preclude any systematic discussion of crime, poverty, and violence. Why participate in old-fashioned politics, such as voting, working for a candidate, or trying to figure issues out? Better to sit back and toss an empty beer can or two at the television set in a mock explosion of anger. It feels good. If you're roused to get up off the couch, you can subscribe to the glossy NRA magazine and maybe send in one of those preprinted NRA alert postcards to your congressional representative. Passive aggression is at the core of the NRA's appeal. Once the left began to build mass organizations through bulk mailings and telemarketing, it generated some single-issue campaigns almost as wiggy as those of the NRA.

When wig momentum gets going, wig cynics can do remarkable damage. Those of us who live in the rural West know how pervasive the hate-radio mentality was, even before fringe spin-offs took hate radio's rhetoric literally, eventually leading to the 1995 Oklahoma City bombing. But Rush Limbaugh is correct when he claims, ever so loudly, that he is distinct from the most extreme of his listeners. Limbaugh's project is to drum up support for a partisan, Republican cause. He represents the Republican wager, riding since Nixon, that resentment and cynicism can be harnessed to defeat Democrats and move politics to the right. In the rubble of Oklahoma City, we saw clearly the downside of that wager.

Why do the odd eruptions of the wigs so seldom disqualify them from public life? Sometimes they do. Limbaugh is much less powerful now, having been ridiculed and refuted for years. But the wig parade has found its own momentum, staying visible thanks to such private funding as Scaife or Perot contributes or such persistent ratings as Jerry Springer gets. The wig outbreak forces us to make some unusual judgments. Conspiracy theorists and resentmentmongers don't lose arguments on the points of policy analysis. Evidence, reason, and the normal standards of political talk don't apply. Confounded by their arguments, we might prefer to laugh and change the subject. Telling them to behave responsibly is usually futile. Because cynicism is durable, wigs persist. Believer talk does not pull them back to the fold.

In our cynical age, the terms of social life become oddly reversible. Conservatism denotes either freedom or order, depending on which rhetoric is required in a particular circumstance. Liberalism evokes self-interest or compassion, depending on whether the "libs" are to be scorned as pathetic or dismissed as pompous. Any public figure's statement, about anything, can imply honesty and integrity or cynicism and resentment. When Perot quit his presidential bid, he dropped his insistent cries that people should "never give in . . . never, never, never." He didn't notice the irony. He had already succeeded at so many smaller reversals.

Cynics have dispensed with solemn civic belief and are free to turn any position inside out. Wig cynics take the lead, and powerful cynics take advantage. Nothing disciplines a cynic, which is why it is so hard to "reconstruct" a civic belief, to use the currently popular vernacular. Nonetheless, such a reconstruction has been precisely what most scholars of cynicism have emphasized. The pundits, scholars, and grant-givers have decided that Americans and their leaders are too cynical, and these opinion leaders have suggested that Americans should reinvigorate civic morality. The wig cynic serves as reminder of how difficult the reconstruction process will be. At the social margin, the most aggravated wig cynics have developed ways to stay in orbit forever. Some are dangerous. Others are pathetic or merely entertaining, at least from a theatrical distance.

But each of their performances tells a story of social breakdown. Whom to believe? What is true? What are the rules of evidence? Can you top this? In a society that has so thoroughly given up the habits and comforts of belief, some cynics will play the wig role, beyond any kind of reasonable governance. It seems odd that this wacky way of life could have been generated by such a reserved, hardworking culture. The usual suspects so beloved by our current pop psychology — TV, family discipline, or the crisis of values — seem inadequate as explanation. The wig cynic's outburst is too striking, durable, and resilient. The cynical age has been a long time coming. It was set in motion long ago.

Part II

Cultural Crisis

Chapter 5

A Brief History of
American Cynicism

Ethical man: a Christian holding four aces.
Mark Twain

There may have been a time when Americans believed. But the
cultural memory plays tricks. We convert history into the Good
Old Days, selecting only the best tomatoes from a motley harvest.
The believer wants to reassure us that we all once believed and
that this condition could be recovered. The cynic might agree that
someone once believed but resolutely assumes that this can no
longer be the case.

H. L. Mencken, a prominent Baltimore journalist in the early days
of national media, was a harbinger of cynical America. Mencken
is a vivid symbol of the sophisticated, urbane culture that he helped
define. The old virtues, and those who promoted them, often to
their own advantage, could be openly mocked by the 1920s, during his heyday. Mencken is remembered for his caustic wit, and as
biographer Fred Hobson notes, his wit had specific targets. From
his earliest *Baltimore Sun* columns, "Mencken was given permis-
sion to fire away at anybody he chose except Baltimore ministers,
and when he lured the preachers into attacking him, they became
fair game too. From the beginning his primary targets were Baltimore politicians, boosters, prohibitionists, anti vice crusaders, and
moralists and reformers of all stripes."[1]

As Americans "wised up," they turned as cynical as Mencken about the reformers and preachers. Mencken's effects were diverse. We misjudge his legacy if we remember only the discredited crank and borderline or outright bigot. His cynicism may have discouraged some of his readers from public action, but it mobilized others. In 1927, a nineteen-year-old Richard Wright used a borrowed library card and a forged note ("Will you please let this nigger boy have some books by H. L. Mencken?") to borrow two Mencken books from the Memphis public library. He read through the night: "I pictured the man as a raging demon, slashing with his pen... denouncing everything American... laughing at the weaknesses of people, mocking God, authority.... He was using words as a weapon, using them as one would use a club." Wright called this night his birth as a writer.[2]

But if a few receptive readers got the message all at once, from Mencken or other critics of the day, these were the early adopters, the first voices in a choir that would take decades to assemble. It took a while for American cynicism to emerge, and starting points are always risky to identify. But this century has seen America turn cynical, sometimes distressingly so, yet at other times with an exuberance we have yet to understand.

We can find convincing believers in American history, even after Mencken. Dwight Eisenhower may have been our last genuine centrist believer. Installed in the presidency by a process closer to shapeshifting than electoral politics, Eisenhower retained the war leader's ability to summon patriotism. He left to others the day-to-day rigors of producing remedies and shrugged off jokes about improving his golf game while in office. His aloofness did not debilitate him or encourage the cranky right—consequences that would bedevil the next two-term president, Ronald Reagan. Indeed, Ike's reputation only improved when he tried to fire Vice President Richard Nixon or when he warned about the military-industrial complex. Ike survived scandal without resorting to bitterness or counterattack.

Eisenhower's administration was surprisingly active. Commitments were made to build the interstate highways and to develop the national parks as tourist destinations and emblems of national pride. Dams for electricity and agricultural irrigation sprouted everywhere. In keeping with this country's then new preeminence, foreign policy was transformed as we worked out the implications of nuclear technology for diplomacy. Ike kept a distance from the opportunists who had started to congregate in the conservative ranks. When the Soviets launched Sputnik, the first satellite, Ike took the occasion not to demonize the evil empire but to apply federal remedies to education. If we now look back on the fifties as a time of repressed conflict and building tension, it was not a thought that occurred to many at the time.

Or rather it was not a thought that occurred to many white Americans at the time. For on the other end of the narrow political spectrum, another of our last great believers was beginning his brief, spectacular run. Martin Luther King, Jr., raised outsider complaints in the language of centrist belief in a way that eventually triumphed. His was the last effective believer protest movement. Calling the country back to principles both Christian and constitutional, King raised the issue Eisenhower ignored. Even though *Brown* v. *Board of Education* was decided early in Eisenhower's first term, he would have preferred not to think about race. King forced the issue. He was the last great civic preacher, always addressing audiences in a loud voice, even when amplified, as a sort of omnipresent reminder of his belief's source—the unamplified and relatively unmediated southern black church.

We can measure the extent to which King's belief was effective by the character of the response he provoked. King's was the last protest movement, opposed primarily because "it moved too fast" rather than because it was a cynical grab for power. The struggle was debated in terms of how much stress it put on the system. Could the system advance diverse black and white interests while simultaneously managing the unifying symbols of nationhood and justice? After King, each protest movement was best opposed by claims that it was cynically opportunist. Women, environmentalists, and gays struggled to find ways to respond to this attack. They insisted ever more vehemently and, hence, less credibly that their preference formed a belief, a credo. But the cynics had already prepared their refutation of that defense, calling reasoned response shrill and applying repressive force when the opportunity presented itself. King's believer assault on entrenched power worked in a way almost unimaginable to later believers who still wished to connect morality with public-policy remedy.

It is a tricky game, trying to locate the cusp of a change as intricate and slippery as the turn toward cynicism. Believer options were up in the mid-century political markets. After Franklin Roosevelt saved capitalism from its own excesses, a pattern of interest-group pluralism emerged. We were into the Eisenhower years before political analysts like Robert Dahl and David Truman presented a new, compelling pluralist explanation of democracy, and into the King years before that explanation began to inform public opinion. Within the huge centrist New Deal coalition first assembled by FDR, remaining disagreements narrowed. Conflict generally turned more polite and easier to manage. Adherents to this broad coalition, which held for decades, played by the rules of the game. Nobody asked for too much, and nearly all understood why they should wait their turn. Their reward came, as a sequential pattern of major legislation and social spending broke through the long-standing American reticence about government.

Indeed, interest-group pluralism seemed like a healing salve for American suspicions, especially regarding politics. Generations of political scientists greased the wheel, explaining how the sequential payoffs and national standards inherent in pluralism would serve as a way to understand the democratic rule of a complex society. Nobody could grasp all of society's ills and inefficiencies in this antimarxist age, but if we politely queued up to air our grievances, those complaints sufficiently meritorious would result in salving legislation. The cynicism of this arrangement only appeared if one focused on the borders of the broad coalition. Blacks and women were notably absent, and there were important regional exclusions, too. But the coalition held for a long time. When it began to break down, the resulting disruptions of the sixties seemed an affront to society itself.

Still, the tensions were there and are easy to see in retrospect. Nuclear technology put a crushing strain on a society that had drawn great satisfaction from its technological and intellectual developments, even while it still largely saw itself as an agrarian small town. Suddenly, Main Street had to deal with nuclear annihilation, deterrence, and counterforce theory. We reassured ourselves that it made perfect sense to prepare to destroy the world precisely to prove that we could do it, so we wouldn't have to engage in the age-old pattern of war and peace. We rushed to domesticate the nuke, both with a rakish nickname and a domestic power-generation industry. Above all, we made the Soviet Union into an Evil Empire, a dark star that justified unprecedented peacetime militarism. We tried hard to make sense of the Bomb, but in retrospect, a turn toward cynicism was inevitable.

Communism was an opportunity as well as the justification for military preparedness. J. Edgar Hoover grasped the opportunity with flair and persistence. From the earliest years of his employment at the FBI, Hoover made his mark by finding conspiracies, sometimes with unmistakable cynicism. After terrorists tried to assassinate Attorney General A. Mitchell Palmer in 1919, Hoover was assigned the task of writing legal briefs on the new communist parties in the United States. Hoover studied the works of Marx, Lenin, Trotsky, and others, according to Don Whitehead's authorized history of the FBI. Hoover discovered "a conspiracy so vast, so daring, that few people at first could even grasp the sweep of the Communist vision." He decided that communism was "the most evil, monstrous conspiracy against man since time began."[3]

American nativism, a bigotry against anything outside the parameters of whiteness and Protestantism, was nothing new. Conspiracy-hunting wigginess also has a long history in America, perhaps dating back to the original witch-hunts. But Hoover commanded a new stage. At the center of American policing for a half century, he spread his venom primarily through prosecutions, often political in character. Hoover's first important target was Emma Goldman. He struggled mightily to place this charismatic leftist in conspiracy with Leon Czolgosz, the Polish-American factory worker who assassinated President William McKinley.[4] A grand jury had already decided there was no connection, but this did not deter Hoover from submitting doctored records of Czolgosz's testimony at Goldman's deportation hearing. Time and again, Hoover cynically employed methods every conspiracy theorist pursues. In a twist, Hoover used these tools, buttressed by his unquestionable authority, to create useful images of conspiracy.

After World War II, opportunities for Hoover to pursue wig conspiracies multiplied. He orchestrated the Hiss and Rosenberg cases that set the Red Scare model for decades to come. Without his help, the 1950s congressional hearings that blacklisted Hollywood writers and celebrities might have been impossible.[5] When Wisconsin senator Joseph R. McCarthy, who liked to use the phrase "a conspiracy of infamy" in congressional speeches, needed to back up his purported list of 205 (or, in a subsequent speech, 57) State Department communists, he called Hoover, who suggested that McCarthy stop using numbers.[6] When contemporary analysts attribute the conspiracy boom to the loss of the communist menace, they forget that Hoover's incessant, self-serving promotion of conspiracy grew in symbiosis with the communist target.

Hoover provides the link between anticommunist wig hysteria and the persistent conspiracy interpretation of John F. Kennedy's assassination. In this instance, Hoover uncharacteristically took the anticonspiracy side of the argument, insisting that Oswald acted alone. After Oswald was killed, the Bureau destroyed the files on him, setting off one branch of the conspiracy theorizing that ensued. Hoover lied about the destroyed files, and his agency conspired to support the allegation that Oswald acted alone. Firmly committed to the idea that an individual could transform history, Hoover did so. His real conspiracy to suppress Kennedy assassination evidence helped fuel a plethora of theories about the event and an ongoing era of conspiracy theory.

The paranoid theorists who began to emerge soon after the November 1963 assassination of President Kennedy marked the first full bloom of wig cynicism. By February 11, 1964, a University of Illinois professor suggested in the *New York Times* that Kennedy had been shot because the communist conspiracy to capture the country had fallen behind schedule.[7] A congressional hearing on a gun-control bill that aimed to stop mail-order gun sales heard testimony from three men who had driven from Bagdad, Arizona, one of whom called the bill "a further attempt by a subversive power to make us part of one world socialistic government."[8] The FBI, too, became the target of the kind of conspiracy theorizing it had pioneered. But Hoover and the Bureau soon found new ways to promote — and benefit from — conspiracy.

With wild, often illegal, actions aimed against both right and left, and eventually even the Mafia, Hoover gave reason for almost everyone out of the mainstream to suspect having been the target of hidden government action. Hoover kept power, but his longevity had effects. In particular, Hoover's success at convincing both Johnson and Nixon that secret forces, not popular conviction, shaped the movements of the 1960s and 1970s likely harmed those presidents' ability to deal with phenomena that were in fact social and political. Johnson had the misfortune to inherit an increasingly paranoid and cynical Hoover. But Johnson also loved the gossip Hoover offered, with its illusion of secret levers that could punish enemies, manipulate history, and solve the vexing problem of how to govern a nation in crisis.

A mixture of modes had intensified through the middle third of the century, as emerging cynicism — visible in Hoover's wigginess, the nuclear establishment's insider manipulations, as well as in accelerating suburbanization of the populace and corporatization of the workforce — displaced the civic belief that had previously prevailed. The tensions of the era finally flipped into an era of accumulating cynicism, and it is hard to find a cusp that better symbolizes the turn than that formed by Lyndon Johnson's presidency. Historians, media analysts, and biographers love to explain that Johnson was much more persuasive in person than in public. This should not come as a surprise. The work of a legislator is inconsistent with the role of leader. The separation of powers principle that informed much of the U.S. Constitution prophesied the problem. Congress, a democratic institution, was assigned to do work no public would ever want or need to see. The age of visibility opened by television put stress on Congress in ways the great legislative leaders never anticipated nor resolved to anyone's satisfaction.

Johnson's legislative triumphs on race and poverty were generally popular, with the prominent exception of the South, which would eventually form a wig bastion. Americans knew that his successes were achieved crudely, that some of his bullying even took place in the executive washroom. Most of us hoped that his skillful management of a recalcitrant Congress would ameliorate the civil-rights crisis. But LBJ soon turned his ability to broker private deals into warmaking. Taken in by the fashionable anticommunism of his Establishment advisers, Johnson lent his vulgar legislative skills to the brutal demands of foreign war. The combination was disastrous: television footage of jungle routs made other images of our coarse and awkward president less sufferable by the month. As Tom Engelhardt explained in a recent book, our "victory culture," a deep social commitment to American military and economic power, was waning fast.[9] Cynicism had broken through on every side, in a disillusioned citizenry and in a visibly manipulative leadership class.

As fascinated as we sometimes seem by the Johnson-Nixon period (the sixties), our fascination is partial and blocked. Although several serious retrospectives have been published, more attention has gone to the genre of recantation and complaint about the era's excesses. There still seem to be more movies being made about the World War II era than about the Vietnam era. Music and counterculture gestures continue to be popular—who'd have thought there would still be hippies at century's end? But a sense remains that Americans have yet to come to terms with that time. That should not be surprising. It was too intense and complex an era to succumb to the analyses usually brought to it. Blaming youthful excess or Baby Boom demographics is a cheap shot that works only if one ignores the context. The era is hard to memorialize for the same reason its analysis remains obscure. It was a multiple, contradictory, yet also intense and focused time. It resists sense making unless one puts this matter of belief and cynicism at center stage.

The impassioned moralism of the civil rights and antiwar movements, even of the "love it or leave it" counterrevolution, is best understood as the concerted last gasp of a rapidly failing national consensus. The economic dissolution of the grand American consensus was then still hard to see, at least until the oil shock of the mid-1970s ended "the sixties." But the moral consensus that had accompanied this economic unity was in collapse, having failed to withstand the pressure applied by African Americans, war protesters, and women. It is understandable that voices of the Reagan-Bush counterrevolution would want to blame the dissolution on the protesters, but they were only messengers, if sometimes loud and disruptive ones. The grand American consensus had failed to solve its core problems, which included persistent racism, frequently disastrous foreign policy, ill treatment of women, and out-of-control industrialism.

Social trends, if largely unnoticed at the time, underscored the political transformation. By Johnson's administration, America was an urban society trying to shore up a quaint, oblivious, and pastoral self-image. The Beat poets set the stage for a much broader counterculture by exposing the dominant culture's absurdities. Fifties' television is still a hit on the cable channels — how could we have been so weird, so recently? To be sure, this effect is exaggerated, since television was just beginning to figure itself out. But the exaggeration puts the transition in sharper relief. In less than a decade, popular culture turned from the sullen, hillbilly, mamacentric Elvis, himself quite a shift from Peggy Lee, to the youthful exuberance of the internationalist Beatles.

The first political advertisement on TV ran in Eisenhower's 1956 reelection campaign. That ad featured a soundtrack jingle accompanying a simple Disney animation. Less than a decade later, Johnson ran the first televised negative political advertisement, the famous daisy-nuke ad that questioned Goldwater's impulsive attraction to nuclear warfare by juxtaposing a young girl picking daisy petals with a countdown to a missile launch. In the late fifties, NBC news anchors Chet Huntley and David Brinkley were still doing an amateurish fifteen minutes of nightly news with a toy Texaco truck sitting on their desk. A decade later, CBS news anchor Walter Cronkite had legitimized television news and then used that legitimacy to alter the trajectory of the Vietnam War. In a very short time the new grammar of sophisticated, lively, cynical culture was emerging and simultaneously being distributed to and learned by television viewers in even the most remote crannies of the country.

Change can now flash through political space at remarkable speed. It is quaint to remember that only a few years ago, everyone seemed to know how fast events should move. It made sense to argue that the civil rights, antiwar, and women's movements of the 1960s and early 1970s were trying to move too fast. A few years later, nobody told Eastern Europeans, in 1989 and 1990, that they were moving too fast — they just moved. The kids who wrecked the Berlin Wall played joyously to the cameras. The pace of Eastern European movement was fired by television's instant publicity and by then well-established ability to put intolerable pressure on outmoded systems.

The accumulating pace of events over the past half century was not only a consequence of television's new role. When intercontinental nuclear missiles were most fearsome, entire strategies were based on how quickly they could fly across oceans. First strike and second strike became concepts that justified unbelievable expenditures. And while the hotline telephone connection between Moscow and Washington received plenty of attention, little systematic thought went into the fast-strike new game. As political theorist James Der Derian has noted, this is a form of politics on the model of chicken, a game of nerves in which compressed time plays the major role. It is not too much to say that speed became a player in the process, much like missiles or geography. Speed became an agent to be captured, before an adversary could control it.

Some tactics that had been useful disappeared. It became hard to imagine that a president could ignore a letter from a foreign leader for more than two days in the midst of a potentially catastrophic confrontation. But that is precisely what President John Kennedy did during the Cuban missile crisis. By the 1980s, it had become much harder to buy time, to let events slide until better options emerged. The 1988 Dukakis campaign foolishly tried to ignore Bush's aggressively negative TV ads entirely and was trounced. In 1992, the Clinton campaign even responded to the released text of some Bush speeches before the actual speech was delivered, the better to arm those reporters with access to their fax machines with questions to ask. The circuit from action to response to political impact to next action all has been compressed, sometimes completing itself more than once in a single day.

Speed has the effect of limiting the number of stories television covers but intensifying the coverage of those chosen. This effect increases the sense of spectacle. A chosen story comes to dominate the news while it is happening, encouraging viewers to increase their perception of the story's importance. Daily print journalism followed television's lead. One veteran reporter for a major daily newspaper told me that his paper covers events as well as it ever did, but that now, the paper only covers one story at a time. Television accelerates events. Speed becomes a crucial part of decision making, further reinforcing the pace of change. The pace and focus of modern political events worked to the advantage of protesters in Eastern Europe and to opponents of apartheid in South Africa. But the pace of events sometimes retards our sense

of control. Events seem less governed by deliberation and decision. Events have a life of their own.

One consequence of this acceleration has been a widespread
sense of disorientation and disbelief. Cynicism has many causes,
but surely one of them is the pace of change. As television's role
developed, Americans were asked to reassess the cultural consensus. Could one believe Johnson on Vietnam? Advertisements on
television? The Warren Commission? The Pope about birth control?
Your father about sex, marijuana, or rock and roll? Bob Hope?

Any number of writers have explained that the consensus that
seemed to sustain American politics through the middle years of
this century has since eroded. As an example, consider the argument Robert Reich made in his 1991 book *The Work of Nations*.[10]
Nationalism, a key concept of the modern era, is a recent development that, Reich argues, is going away even faster than it arrived.

The demise of nationalism raises a host of questions. As the
economy underwent dramatic transformation in the last third of
the century, Americans no longer shared in economic outcomes.
The effect was so obvious that even the most gullible could no
longer believe that their economic future was inextricably linked
to the fate of the great national corporations. American corporate
enterprises had quickly made themselves into international enti-
ties with no definitive connection to place or constituency. Questions that would have been unimaginable a few decades ago now
are obvious; "Loyalty to place — to one's city or region or nation —
used to correspond more naturally with economic self-interest,"
Reich writes. "What do we owe one another as members of the
same society who no longer inhabit the same economy?" (303).

The old forms of social loyalty functioned, more or less steadily,
until recently. "Individual citizens supported education, roads, and
other civic improvements, even when the individual was likely to
enjoy but a fraction of what was paid out in the short term,"
Reich writes, "because it was assumed that such sacrifices would
be amply rewarded eventually" (303). An array of citizen roles supported such individual sacrifice, including civic boosterism, public investment rhetoric, and loud commitments to family, with its
intergenerational implications. In the post–World War II era, in-

creasing prosperity made the tensions in this arrangement less visible than ever, making it easier for citizens to resist opportunism. That resistance further increased the potential for social connection and investment. Reich argues that the economic connections helped induce habits of citizenship.

During the century's middle decades, this arrangement seemed so solid as to be permanent. In retrospect, it was a brief exception. Corporate internationalism tore economic nationalism apart more quickly than anyone had thought possible. As the economy went international, the game no longer reinforced the habits of citizenship. Reich poses the subsequent issue in appropriately dramatic terms, wondering whether the habits of citizenship can "withstand the centrifugal forces of the new global economy. Is there enough of simple loyalty to place — of civic obligation, even when unadorned by enlightened self-interest — to elicit sacrifice nonetheless? . . . How tight is the social and political bond when the economic bond unravels?" (303–4). Although Reich ends his book with the sort of standard call to citizenship that now marks most such books, the question he asks carries its own, different answer.

Although a small legion of believer activists advocates reconstructing citizenship, civility, and community, few face the question as squarely as Reich did. Almost nobody seriously proposes a significant redistribution of wealth. Even a redistribution of opportunity, a project much closer to the American mainstream, is blocked by attacks on affirmative action and equitably funded education. The presumption of shared economic futures is gone, and no gesture will bring it back. Adding urban amenities, convening neighborhood councils, preaching family values, escalating the symbolism of nationalism — all of these are regularly proposed. But all are gestures without an economic base. The old foundation is missing.

Dangers arise when social habits change rapidly. Reich emphasizes the peril posed by cynical leaders who try to maintain national identity through the creation of national enemies, perhaps by substituting the Japanese and their economic machine for the Soviets and their military machine. On the business page, as early as 1988, Peter Drucker expressed his fear of how the middle class was reacting to economic uncertainty: "The cynicism out there is frightening. Middle managers have become insecure, and they feel unbelievably hurt. They feel like slaves on an auction block."[11] The comparison to slavery, however misplaced, only underscores Drucker's discomfort.

If we better understood the cynical turn, we would know the peril of staking our future on reconstruction proposals, values sermons, and nostalgic appeals to community. Mostly, these approaches reassure those already predisposed to citizenship. Little is rebuilt. Calls to civility can in fact hide insidious and debilitating effects. The social theorist Benjamin DeMott wrote a scathing rebuttal: "Sold as diagnosis or nostrum, 'civility' is in fact a theater of operations — the classless society's new class war zone."[12] Believers tend to see most clearly the uncivil behavior of their opponents, while finding their class peers' misbehavior much harder to identify.

This effect is compounded, as DeMott notes, by the civility claim's imperviousness to debate: "In theory, it should be easy to counter [the civility] faith — but try it. Criticize a civility promoter, and you hear that you're a fan of rap lyrics about cop-killing, or that you're the sort of nutcake who tries to silence by boos any idea you happen to disagree with, or that you lack feeling for the glories of civil discourse in the public square." Applied by a powerful cynic, the civility diagnosis offers opportunities for mischief. It is more likely to exacerbate than to heal social division. The cynical turn resulted from a broad range of enormous influences, not a brief lapse of social manners. As the next chapters show, the conditions that produce Cynical America are deeply implanted in the American political character.

Chapter 6

Federalists and Liberals

Setting the Stage for Cynicism

> Surely, then, it is a remarkable force: this fixed, dogmatic liberalism of a liberal way of life.... There has never been a "liberal movement" or a real "liberal party" in America: we have only had the American Way of Life, a nationalist articulation of Locke which usually does not know that Locke himself is involved.
>
> Louis Hartz, *The Liberal Tradition in America*

Like other unwanted social phenomena, cynicism is often described with viral metaphors. Cynicism infects, spreads, and contaminates. Some wisdom is reflected in this figure of speech. Like a virus, cynicism can be surprisingly durable. It has carriers. But there are limits to the metaphor, too. Despite ever-improving scientific tools, the origins of a virus are often shrouded in mystery. But the origins of contemporary cynicism are accessible for examination and debate. The believer chorus misdirects our attention away from the roots of cynicism. Cynicism's vitality has precursors set deep in American political arrangements.

It is not surprising that Americans use viral metaphors for social phenomena. We live in a culture that regards its knowledge of itself, and of most everything else, as knowledge of *nature*. Our explanations and descriptions come wrapped in rhetorical devices that claim an organic certainty and universality. Americans of an

71

earlier age framed an ambitious government on the premise that it would tame human nature's destructive tendencies while also governing in the name of liberty and justice. These were audacious goals when they were formulated. Their scope has been broadened even further; the idea that we have civilized ourselves better than any other nation became a mainstay of jingoistic patriotism. A government founded on the ambitious hope that human nature's effects could be mitigated took on a powerful aura of its own. Most Americans now regard the government that has survived over two centuries as something itself akin to a force of nature.

This assumption would be intolerably pretentious if it were not simultaneously diluted. The nationalistic impulse is moderated by the pragmatic skepticism that came to pervade political culture. Americans acquired a deep distrust of politics, but they understood that distrust as a positive sign of nationalist faith, as evidence of social rationality. A grid of extraordinary stability can be built on this combination of ambitions and reservations. But there's a catch. If skepticism about government grows out of its assigned role, it can put the entire grid in peril. The certainty that we have captured nature itself pervades this grid of expectations, pragmatism, and pride. If we lose the confidence that government is well designed, it is almost as if we have discarded nature itself. Or as if we have discovered a grand manipulation, a con game that had taken us in completely. We feel burned, but we are not entirely sure who burned us. This gives American cynicism its bitter edge.

The tension between our skepticism of and reverence for government is so terrible a quandary that Americans seldom face it directly. Typically, we find ways to locate the pain in a specific sector of the public grid, rather than in more deeply rooted presumptions, institutions, and practices. We criticize the politicians or the media that tell us about them. We rail against corruption and disagreement. We wonder whether problems are now so difficult that the familiar political arrangements are overwhelmed. When all else fails, we recall Churchill's famous and mischievously cynical formula, that this is an awful way of collective life, tolerable only with the reassurance that it is so much better than the alternatives.

The seeds of a cynical culture were planted long ago, ready to flourish when the climate most favored them. Consider the first explanation of our political system, the *Federalist Papers,* and in partic-ular James Madison's *Federalist Ten,* a tightly written little essay that attempts to reconcile the forces of freedom with the need for order. Especially in this century, *Ten* has been widely studied. But I argue that it also has been widely misunderstood. If we press too hard to find evidence of an intentional conspiracy of landed wealth, we risk missing something else revealed by *Ten.* It contains a map of political concerns and governmental remedies, a map of the ten-sions and fears that dictated much of the Constitution's architecture.

Madison's *Ten* is so severely structured that it could just as eas-ily have been presented as a flowchart rather than an essay. The first paragraph begins by disclosing the terrible hazards of fac-tion, a "dangerous vice" that can issue forth in violence. "By a fac-tion," Madison writes, "I understand a number of citizens, whether amounting to a majority or minority of the whole, who are united and actuated by some common impulse of passion, or of interest, adverse to the rights of other citizens, or to the permanent and aggregate interests of the community."[1] Transposing this into flow-chart mode, into perhaps a quick bullet list suitable for Perot-style audiovisuals, we discover that a faction could be, in the ex-treme case, a united majority, acting on their common interest, in a way adverse to the "permanent and aggregate interests of the community."

Radical intellectuals of the early twentieth century thought that the enormous weight Madison placed on this phrase had revealed his otherwise hidden intent. Madison wanted to preserve the abil-ity of an elite class to veto majority proposals because he distrusted democratic versions of the public interest. But Madison believed that elite leadership was best suited to determine the community interests. His was a serious and specific proposal, grounded in con-fidence about leaders and elite institutions. Madison was not cyn-ical about government's potential to overcome the difficulties that democracy would foster. But it should not be surprising that at least a few of *Ten*'s contemporary readers cannot believe he was anything but a cynic.

Madison's essay shows how the stage was set for later cynicism in the design of the basic American institutions. *Ten* shows that promises were made that would later be converted into a hyper-patriotic commitment to democracy and American nationalism.

But the Constitution also blocked the fulfillment of those promises. The authors of the *Federalist Papers,* Alexander Hamilton and John Jay, along with Madison, designed a system that favored an elite class, one qualified to determine what was in the community's long-term interest. They instituted representation, which would later become the basis for American democratic pride, as a light check on that elite class. Mostly, representation was designed to filter out democratic demands that Madison obviously feared.

Madison's text now reads as a naïve, mechanistic plan. *Ten*'s third paragraph suggests two cures for the "mischiefs" of faction. One could remove the causes of faction or control its effects. Madison immediately dispenses with the first possibility. It would be unwise and impossible to try to get rid of the causes of faction. The differences visible in our politics reflect differences among humans. Remember, this is not only a tightly structured argument, it is also infused with a confidence that its topic is nature itself, applied to the task of governing. So government can be designed so as to control the effects of faction, which derive from nature.

Directing our attention to the tension between an inevitably factious liberty and the need for governmental control, Madison set the terms of the American debate forever. "There are two methods of curing the mischiefs of faction," Madison wrote, "the one, by destroying the liberty which is essential to its existence; the other, by giving to every citizen the same opinions, the same passions, and the same interests." Destroying the liberty that makes faction possible would be "worse than the disease." Madison knew he could not frame arguments about the new government in terms of limited liberty: America had just finished an armed rebellion conducted in its name. Dangerous as it was, liberty — or a passing facsimile thereof — had to be preserved.

"Liberty is to faction what air is to fire, an aliment, without which it instantly expires. But it would not be a less folly to abolish liberty, which is essential to political life because it nourishes faction, than it would be to wish the annihilation of air, which is essential to animal life, because it imparts to fire its destructive agency." Note that this connection between fire and air was news in Madison's day. This is force-of-nature stuff. The fiery political freedom that Patrick Henry had raised to the highest level in the fight against imperialist England was necessary in the way that nature's laws are necessary. So, thus, is the fight to control it in acceptable ways. If we cannot extinguish liberty, then perhaps the second alternative would work. We could nurture in every citizen, Madison postulated, "the same opinions, the same passions, and the same interests." But he knew that this was too much to hope for, especially given the limited government he had helped design. The fancy tricks enabled by electronic media and easy transportation were so unimaginable that Madison could openly ridicule the option of serious opinion molding.

But Madison was not only reminding us of his concern for freedom by raising his false, rhetorical option of unified interests. He was also introducing another important theme. The differences among people, including their differences of wealth, reflect differences in ability and interest. In one of the most eloquent and best-known paragraphs of *Ten*, Madison demonstrates that he has a more detailed and inclusive understanding of the contentiousness of society than did, say, Adam Smith, not to mention the current advocates for civil society.

> The latent causes of faction are thus sown in the nature of man; and we see them everywhere brought into different degrees of activity, according to the different circumstances of civil society. A zeal for different opinions concerning religion, concerning government, and many other points . . . ; an attachment to different leaders, ambitiously contending for pre-eminence and power . . . have, in turn, divided mankind into parties, inflamed them with mutual animosity, and rendered them much more disposed to vex and oppress each other, than to co-operate for their common good. So strong is this propensity of mankind, to fall into mutual animosities, that where no substantial occasion presents itself, the most frivolous and fanciful distinctions have been sufficient to kindle their unfriendly passions, and excite their most violent conflicts. But the most common and durable source of factions has been the various and unequal distribution of property. Those who hold, and those who are without property, have ever formed distinct interests in society.

Later critics of Madison's elitism fastened onto this paragraph's treatment of property. But there is more here than that. Governments can be arranged so as to encourage the disruptive differences among citizens, Madison believed, or they can limit the effects of these differences. One doesn't alter causes. In order to be real enough to be a basis of authority, nature, which for Madison is the source of causation, has to be immutable but still subject to efforts to restrain its effects. Madison wanted readers of *Ten* to see human nature as stout, authoritative, and contentious, with potential effects dire enough that we should accept constitutional constraints on its prerogative. He also wanted readers to see the competence of their leaders, men who could tame our unruly nature, much as similar men had, within Madison's generation, tamed fire by finally giving it a proper scientific explanation.

For Madison, constitution writing was an exercise in controlling effects and defending the needed coercion in the name of its causes. One can have freedom without direct democracy. Indeed, Madison felt this was the only way to have freedom without disruption and violence. Madison wanted a republic in which representation would be used like a filter to screen out the claims that would let disruption flourish. The remainder of *Ten* piles on arguments, often brazenly flimsy, for this alternative. The worst of these is the bizarre notion that a large state (which, in a time not yet enabled by rapid transport and communication, only representation will allow) will have better leaders, since it has so many more people from which to choose.

By means of the filter, we could have liberty while still controlling disruption. We can have political representation and stable government without the tumult of a lively political culture that would grow from the grass roots. Instead of politics, Madison argued we should substitute elite leadership and scientific expertise. Such are the costs of civilized life, given what nature has granted us as working material. The "freedom" call had been let loose by such extravagant advocates as Patrick Henry, and Madison's job was to rein it in. The irony is that Madison overshot his mark. And his exuberance proved central to the cynicism that would later feed on it. Cynics are keenly attuned to the opportunities and afflictions authority poses, especially when it is out of proportion to its justification.

Madison thought society would arc toward tyranny over issues of property. So he diluted popular rule. But even in his time, the issue he feared most, majority tyranny, was a false one. The mechanism of disruption never had a chance. The democratic energies Madison feared were chimerical. Insofar as tyranny has been constrained — an accomplishment that seems more real to some Americans than to others — it has been constrained through such mechanisms as social norms, the self-restraint of elites, and broad social consensus, not because the Constitution inoculated us. Madison feared that majorities would arise haphazardly, implementing unsound policies. Now we know that the majority does not even vote. We understand how little we matter.

Madison and his associates created constitutional rules that allocated privilege, determining which groups would enter the political struggle with inherent advantage and which would be weighted with handicaps. Political scientist Robert A. Dahl, whose 1956 reading of *Ten* remains among the most useful and influential, notes that the battle over advantage and handicap has been "bitter and even fratricidal."[2] Rather than minimizing such struggle, as Madison promised, his efforts at constraint set it off. No sooner had the states ratified the Constitution than Americans started undoing its intentions, seeking to democratize a system that was more democratic in name and symbol than in structure. Parties emerged almost immediately, as did interest groups. The franchise expanded steadily if too slowly, given the resistances embedded in those constitutional rules.

Madison's fear about majority tyranny was not his only misjudgment. Dahl's list of things the founders were wrong about is intimidating: "They thought the popular House would be dynamic, populistic, egalitarian, leveling, and therefore a dangerous center of power that needed restraint; they thought the President would represent the well-born and the few and that he would use his veto against popular majorities lodged in the House." The House is not the center of power. Most of the time, representatives have exercised their power to procure spending for their districts, and so fervently that we have added a new dictionary definition of the word *pork*. Insofar as there ever is a dynamic center, it has revolved around the presidency. "Today the relationship they envisaged is, by and large, reversed," Dahl wrote in 1956. "It is the President who is the policy-maker, the creator of legislation, the self-appointed spokesman for the national majority, whereas the power of Congress is more and more that of veto."

But this is barely the beginning of the founders' misunderstandings. They "misunderstood the dynamics of their own society," Dahl noted. The founders "failed to predict correctly the social balance of power that was to prevail even in their own lifetime. They did not . . . understand that in an agrarian society lacking feudal institutions and possessing an open . . . frontier, radical democracy was almost certain to become the dominant and conventional view, almost certain to prevail in politics, and almost certain to be conservative about property."

Dahl describes a thoroughly symbolic *Ten*, wrong on most of its empirical judgments, even the ones its authors are most vehement about. Dahl's post–World War II analysis still found utility in *Ten*'s distinction between democracy and dictatorship. Leaders have indeed been encouraged to be responsive through competition, either in (admittedly flawed) elections or through other political arrangements. So minorities rule, but they do so, most of the time, "within the bounds of consensus set by the important values of the politically active members of the society, of whom the voters are a key group." Dahl backed off this upbeat reading of communitarian democracy when the exclusions from this cozy system became more obvious. It is not that the arrangement is trivial; as Dahl points out, the consensus of elites does get us past some terrible problems, including the popularity of slavery only a century and a half ago. But the downside risk — the prospect of raging cynicism — overwhelms much of the upside accomplishment.

The opportunity for cynicism was set up long ago. A constitutional arrangement promised what it did not intend to deliver. A set of misjudgments consistently favored an elite class, one that could, eventually, become cynical about its privileges. Perhaps most important, Madison and his colleagues promoted a naturalism that eventually produced a false pride in the system. The stage was set for cynics, citizens and leaders, wigs and elites.

There is one more piece to add to the tangle of our cynical roots. It comes from the British philosopher John Locke, arguably the greatest single intellectual influence on the American founders. The philosophers read by the American founders made a variety of contributions. Locke's gift was to show us how to provide symbolic guarantees, or rights, but to manage them in such a way that these rights would not actually be much used. It was a lovely gift, much appreciated by every cynic who has followed John Locke to power.

Locke was a theorist of consent and its many possible uses. Consent can be a constraint, as Dahl explained and at least some of the founders hoped. But consent, as a political concept, can also be terrifically useful. It broadens and deepens the contract metaphor that is central to American political talk. When combined, consent and contract define a perfectly sensible, if limited, role for citizens. Government rules because a contractual agreement, not an external or sacred imposition, created it to do so. The agreement can be explicit, as when thirteen states voted on a proposal called the Constitution, or it can be tacit, as when we lend our agreement just by living here quietly. Tacit agreement is especially good. It combines agreement and passivity, and grants the resulting inertia high moral status. Inertia implies contractual fulfillment.

As useful as that idea has been in various political struggles, its main intent was reassurance: a contract can be broken; an individual can break the social contract by leaving; a contract can be rewritten; a legislature, not a monarch, makes and changes laws. At the extreme, the whole contract can be nullified, through revolution. Along with the edict that government be carefully limited to the protection of procedural rights, citizen property, and national sovereignty, these moves define liberalism in its eighteenth-century variant.

Soon after Locke set out the basics, other liberals added detail to his argument. Notably, Adam Smith introduced the notion of markets and automatic harmony. The market would take care of most any imaginable problem, he wrote, at least, within a given set of promises and limits. A nice side effect of this argument was to teach us how useful the market metaphor could be for politics, too. In a cynical age, leaders put consent to work. Rather than a hard legal mechanism with contractual status, consent starts to function more like a gesture. Or to put it more boldly, consent allows leaders of liberal societies to manage a paradox that would otherwise render their project hopeless from the start.

Contracts stipulate recourse, within limits. Manipulative leaders love to remind the consent-givers, the citizens, that they could revolt if things get out of hand. No politician worth his salt misses a July 4 celebration of revolution and freedom. "Inalienable rights" becomes a mantra phrase. The stray heckler at a politician's speech is neatly put down with a challenge to "do something—find out if anyone agrees with you!" We all internalize the grade-school lesson; the power of rebellion guarantees our freedom. The implicit opportunity for manipulation in that formula is easy for today's cynical citizens to parse.

Locke carefully studied the political dynamics set in motion by contractual promises. Starting with the capacity of the contract idea to conjure images of consent, he then made broader conclusions about the patterns of politics, its predictable ebb and flow. When a liberal society chooses, it can revolt. Governmental authority comes only from the people, Locke argued, and this means that as a last resort, they can revoke their approval. Locke's use of the phrase "last resort" amounted to a gamble, but he explained why he thought the odds were on his side. He was confident that the people would seldom use their right to rebel. Once legitimate government was established, there would be little need to invoke that prerogative. Only after a long train of abuses would people opt out of their contract. Leaders would appeal to citizen rationality and self-interest. And people would possess the reassurance that only their consent has let this power loose.

Most governmental responses to rebellion confirm the citizen-cynic's suspicion that the contract's promise is mostly rhetorical, save in the extraordinary and exceptional happenstance of, say, the Philadelphia Convention of 1789. If citizens take the promises too seriously, the repercussions are usually swift and harsh. In the United States, the militia movement of the 1990s elevated the Constitution to near-sacred status, taking seriously its guarantee of citizen recourse and reading the Second Amendment accordingly. When it is explained to them that no legal scholar of substance has ever agreed that the right of state militias to retain arms constitutes a literal right to rebellion, militia followers simply cannot believe it. Never mind the treason clause.

The seeming contradiction—that liberal society minimizes the potential for revolt by guaranteeing the citizen right to rebel—has long been the secret to the stability of the most highly developed Western democracies. When President Clinton stood at the edge of Tiananmen Square in the summer of 1998, just nine years after the terrible suppression that had happened there, television viewers saw him wipe a tear from his eye during the traditional 21-cannon salute. Who can tell what prompted his reaction? Had the booming cannons reminded him of the suffering that had happened there, at the hands of a Chinese military commanded by some of his hosts on this visit? Or was he feeling the frustration of trying to explain a basic Western truth: to minimize rebellion, brave and brilliant leaders must do the unthinkable and guarantee citizen access to the very rebellion that leaders fear most. Citizens yearn to do what is forbidden. What is guaranteed soon becomes boring or excessively risky. Locke understood this paradox, and the American founders learned from him.

The extent to which we have internalized Locke's message is hard to overestimate. Consider the historian Louis Hartz's famous argument that Americans simply are Lockeans: "the American community is a liberal community." More than any other American intellectual of the twentieth century, Hartz is credited for giving liberalism the reputation it enjoyed before it turned into "the L word" in the Reagan-Bush era. Hartz taught us to understand that, having skipped the feudal stage, the United States "lacks a genuine revolutionary tradition."[3] Never having had landed monarchs to overthrow, our own anti-imperial rebellion was of a decidedly different sort. Hartz explained how we had become a liberal culture, and his explanation was absorbed by generations of American elites, who understood themselves as the leaders of a liberal community. Nowadays, it may seem strange that so many American intellectuals once believed without much question that ours was a liberal society.

Hartz himself used terms of wonderment and surprise in his descriptions of how this liberalism had worked out in America. He saw liberalism as a font of paradoxes and dilemmas: "Surely, then, it is a remarkable force: this fixed, dogmatic liberalism of a liberal way of life. It is the secret root from which have sprung many of the most puzzling of American cultural phenomena." The components of this dogma — limited government, protected inequality, recourse defined in a carefully partial way, and so on — could hardly have been predicted to produce such durable social and governmental arrangements.

Hartz knew that Locke's argument could not simply be accepted on its own terms: "At bottom it is riddled with paradox."

Hartz even noticed the outlines of the symbolic argument. Lockean doctrine works metaphorically; it is "the symbol of rationalism." This then, strangely, lets that doctrine take advantage of the irrationality that so often marks political life: "In America the devotion to [Locke's scheme] has been so irrational that [the scheme] has not even been recognized for what it is: liberalism." Even as elites and intellectuals understood their society as liberal, this self-understanding did not extend far into the general populace. Symbols of consent and individualism have been deployed to generate agreement and conformity. If this contradicts the other premises Locke emphasized, including individualism, that is just an indication of how well the symbols have worked. Hence the peculiarly American social dogma promoting individualism that should, by any sensible definition, undermine dogma of whatever variety.

Hartz knew that American political culture worked through a sort of indirection by which political values come to be associated with their opposite. "At the bottom of the American experience of freedom . . . there has always lain the inarticulate premise of conformity." This is just one of the "paradoxes" Hartz notes. The paradoxes do not limit themselves, they multiply: "American political thought, as we have seen, is a veritable maze of polar contradictions, winding in and out of each other hopelessly: pragmatism and absolutism, historicism and rationalism, optimism and pessimism, materialism and idealism, individualism and conformism."

While civics classes teach the system in terms of the mechanics of contract and consent, actual politics has been moving forward through sleight of hand, indirection, paradox, and intended confusion of sign and substance. This is not to condemn that politics, but it does undermine simplistic explanations. American politics is paradoxical. Yet it is practiced in the name of straightforward, mechanistic forms of political authority. This gap between the process and its explanation has consequences. The most important consequence is that Americans avoid politics, refuse to become even minimally involved, and remain oblivious to the barest outlines of its workings. Americans are cynical because politics clash with pronounced values and the agreements they thought the culture had made. Citizen cynicism and ignorance of politics work to the powerful cynic's advantage. The cynical citizen has an excuse for avoiding political matters, and the powerful cynic, as politician, knows how to encourage citizens to let rulers rule. As a popular saying once put it, "Let Reagan be Reagan."

From time to time, Americans surely have experienced political culture in a context of belief, a sense of commitment that seemed palpably real. But cynicism, built on a heritage of paradox and manipulation, resides at the heart of American political culture. The idea that belief can be rebuilt or reconstructed is based on the fallacy that cynicism is a new and fragile phenomenon, a fleeting fad at century's end. But cynicism is not an attitude one generation or one group has discovered. The cynical spiral was traced long ago, in institutions, rules, and expectations central to American political culture.

Chapter 7

Why Americans Hate Politics

The Cynicism Trap

> Long after theocracy vanished, theurgy was a political
> institution. Even when disbelief was rife, few there
> were who would run the risk of neglecting the cere-
> monials.
>
> John Dewey, *The Public and Its Problems*

A long-standing dictum of American social manners advises that
on first acquaintance, two topics of conversation should be avoided
at all cost: religion and politics. What a pair. It's easy to make a
case for avoiding religion; spiritual beliefs are one's own business
and contention about them historically has been none too useful,
pleasant, or polite. But in a democracy, politics is by definition everybody's business. The cut and thrust of politics is discussion. Democracy presumes that citizens inquire, learn, and explain. The very
standard of democratic process is that citizens reshape each other's
positions by effective argument. A nation that teaches children it
is polite to avoid talking politics shouldn't be surprised that fewer
than half its adults bother to vote.

The truth is, Americans hate politics. We sit back watching our
fates being decided in Washington, D.C., and then change the channel groaning, "It's all just politics." We say the same thing about
any bad decision at our workplace. We dismiss politics as somebody else's game—a dirty, rigged, and inevitably unjust activity

that well-mannered people avoid. It's a spectator sport most of us don't like to watch, or, as Jay Leno said, it's "show business for ugly people."

The *Washington Post* reporter E. J. Dionne took a swing at explaining "why Americans hate politics" in a best-selling book by that title.[1] The first Clinton presidential campaign took the book seriously. Dionne became a favored Clinton insider, as well as an important *Post* columnist and a frequent guest on television talk shows. His analysis reflects much of today's conventional wisdom on its topic, a "common sense" that his book helped confirm. Refreshing the "vital center" analysis first articulated by Arthur M. Schlesinger, Jr., in a 1949 book with that title, Dionne argues that the idea of a vital, pragmatic centrism, so influential during the apolitical 1950s, could still apply to the 1990s.

Dionne's book tells a story of the left's failings, the right's opportunism, and the center's loss of authority and vitality. Dionne argues that cynicism results when politics strays from its remedy-seeking core. When politics and policy remedy lose their close mutual association, cynicism results among the citizenry, and among their leaders:

> The decline of a "politics of remedy" creates a vicious cycle. Campaigns have become negative in large part because of a sharp decline in popular faith in government. To appeal to an increasingly alienated electorate, candidates and their political consultants have adopted a cynical stance which, they believe with good reason, plays into popular cynicism about politics and thus wins them votes. But cynical campaigns do not resolve issues. They do not lead to "remedies." Therefore, problems get worse, the electorate becomes more cynical— and so does the advertising.[2]

For Dionne, campaigns should resolve issue debates. If they don't, citizens become cynical about politics. Campaigns then respond, cynically, by appealing to citizen cynicism rather than by generating support for necessary remedies. A spiral of cynicism ensues.

Dionne's argument coheres with a broad range of public intellectuals. Michael Walzer, Judith Shklar, Bruce Ackerman, Charles Taylor, Daniel Bell, Amy Gutmann, Amitai Etzioni, Benjamin Barber, and many others have offered centrist liberal or communitarian responses to our political problems that parallel Dionne's themes, in various ways and degrees. *Why Americans Hate Politics* serves as a stand-in here, and it is a capable stand-in. Dionne asked the right question, and his argument is compelling.

The irony is that Dionne's book, published in 1991, was very widely read but not as well followed. The early 1990s fairly bubbled with hatred of politics. Militias preached the hard line. Perot launched his own brand of antipolitics. Clinton began his presidency by pushing a dramatic health-care policy remedy but was checkmated by Gingrich Republicans who explicitly committed themselves to partisanship rather than centrist problem solving. That worked, producing Republican dominance of Congress after the landmark 1994 elections. Clinton's solutions became less centrist, as the Dick Morris-inspired destruction of welfare confirms. Policies became more symbolic and partisan. Nobody doubted the partisan impetus behind the Monica Lewinsky story. But about the only substantive story it pushed off the front pages in 1998 was the attack on Big Tobacco, an important story but hardly one that addressed our most important public problems.

I would argue that the effects Dionne criticizes are more predictable and more durable than his analysis leads us to understand. As reasonable as Dionne's argument seems, it contains several assumptions we should reexamine. To begin with, there is reason to question whether elections can be counted on to solve issue debates, including the most important and contentious ones. From the earliest days of the republic, James Madison was nervous about both elections and the democratic expression of citizen attitudes. Even serious defenders of American democracy acknowledge that elections often are not reliable vehicles for resolving specific policy debates. The landscape of American history is littered with elections that produced effects opposed to what the electorate apparently intended.

Nixon won the presidency in 1968 by promising (but not articulating) a plan to end the Vietnam War, which then raged on for nearly another decade. Clinton's 1992 campaign featured the need to reform health care, reforms that could not pass a Congress still held by the Democrats. Perhaps most famously, Lyndon Johnson won a huge majority in 1964 by suggesting that his opponent, Barry Goldwater, would get us into a war. Then Johnson did exactly that. In each case, these were issues of crushing importance. But the campaigns did not produce solutions, only winners.

Dionne's strong commitment to elections-as-remedy-producer also reflects implicit confidence that the public can identify what the root problems actually are. But this, too, reflects assumptions. It is a common joke to say, "one person's problem is another's opportunity." That little joke tells a significant truth. Every time we try to describe a neat little model in which political events identify problems, then pose solutions, we have skipped over an important element of the powerful cynic's work. In a democracy, political power derives from the capacity to define what is and is not a problem. Teenage marijuana use is a problem that has riveted the nation's attention, consumed billions of dollars, and bent the Bill of Rights out of shape. Poverty damages far more children than marijuana, yet it is hardly ever described as a problem because its solutions are less attractive to those in power than the marijuana "solutions."[3]

In common usage, we see a problem as something that needs solving, as in a math problem. But a problem may remain unsolved or might have to do with something we cannot solve. Some terrible difficulties may remain outside the domain of accepted problems. Dionne's argument presumes that problems require remedies. But some problems are helpful. Such problems persist. Cynics of every variety understand this. They know how naïve it would be to insist that politics simply be seen as the ensemble of attempts to deal with problems. The welfare example shows how partisan this business of identifying problems can become. Eventually, conservatives decided that welfare itself was the problem that produced rather than alleviated poverty. If we allocate such privilege to the problem-election-solution formula Dionne advocates, we risk missing the possibility that powerful cynics have manipulated the terms of debate, long before elections and their associated commercials commence. Dionne's proscription is clear and widely accepted; we should lower the level of contention in order to agree on remedies. As sensible as this is, it distracts us from other basic functions of politics, including the expression of the contentions Dionne wants to submerge.

Dionne is relying on a linkage that remains popular as a way to cut through the complications and deceptions that might otherwise dominate politics. Problems can be agreed on; then they can be remedied. When solutions succeed, citizens will have faith in the institutions that produced the remedy. But as obvious as this set of links seems, it has its own difficulties. The actual production of remedies is a much more complex and varied process than Dionne's model suggests. And the public reassurance he believes remedies will produce is always delivered via media that introduce yet more opportunities for interference and noise. Powerful cynics know how to use this remedy formula for manipulation. And plenty of receptive citizens await the powerful cynics' message. Both wigs and more sophisticated citizen-cynics are ready to spread the word.

For Madison, "nature" had underwritten the human potential for contentiousness and domination. Dionne, like other mainstream contemporary analysts, does not write as schematically as Madison does about human nature. A century of social science has managed to drive such talk underground in a small but notable accomplishment. Still, Dionne relies on a settled sense of what Americans think and how citizen opinions influence politics and policy. But citizen-cynics are hard to characterize.

When Dionne reconstructs an American character from aggregate polling data, he strives to document the natural depth of opinion, among American citizens, that supports the best themes of democratic rhetoric. Citizens tell any pollster who asks that they want solutions, moderation, and consensus. The problem with this characterization of American preference is that citizens quite often undermine it with their actions. A significant element of the voting public responds positively to the resentment strategies they say they dislike. If some public figure does provide a popular remedy, as President Bush did by employing American military might and President Clinton did by balancing the budget, their adversaries will increase the partisan heat, always afraid that major policy success will lead to domination in fundraising and elections. And the public will often respond more to the heat than to the popular remedy that prompted it.

Dionne's careful reading of polling data provides much to ponder, but polls remain a poor way to begin an inquiry into cynical politics. Cynicism sits at the edge of those polls, mocking them. Polls require their respondents to say what they think. But cynics lie, grow bored easily, or anger quickly. They make poor polling subjects — an aspect of the polls' volatility in recent election cycles that has been largely ignored. A cynical reading of the polls is always more accurate than a pious one. Americans have long loved the rhetoric of the center, as we were taught to do. But love of a center does not well survive when a firm cultural consensus begins to fragment. Apolitical centrists can be manipulated. They can begin to see centrist remedies as the outcome of a deal rather than an expression of the center's vitality. And an apolitical citizenry doubts its interests were considered in the deal making.

Dionne lives in the remedy-seeking world that risks taking citizen self-descriptions a little too seriously. In his story of American politics, citizens demand remedies, but activists and organized interests frustrate that demand: "Politicians engage in symbolic rather than substantive politics [because] liberals and conservatives alike are uncertain about what remedies they can offer without blowing their constituencies apart." The major political coalitions — Democrats, reaching out toward liberals, and Republicans, reaching toward conservatives — "have become so unstable that neither side can afford to risk very much. That is because the ties that bind Americans to each other, to their communities and thus to their political parties have grown ever weaker."[4]

As Dionne understands, coalitions, those staples of contemporary political analysis, provide a possible way to finesse the remedy and problem tension. Cynics understand that someone has to *assemble* a coalition. The assembly project takes place in a political world rife with opportunities for manipulation. The weaker ties to community Dionne correctly identifies as posing difficulties for an honest coalition politics arise in part because cynics of all varieties just don't believe in the precepts of community. Believers still hope that an overlay of values can protect such pragmatic political projects from the cynics if decisions are made openly and deals are made responsibly. Coalitions need deals and pragmatic bargaining. If those potentially cynical moves were somehow unnecessary, coalitions might also be irrelevant, but enough of Madison's governmental structure remains to prevent this outcome. Believers nonetheless argue that the dealing can be constrained by values and commitments. The dealer can yet become an honest person.

The cynical citizen, watching Congress, doesn't believe that coalition building can somehow redeem the cynicism of everyone involved, citizens and decision makers alike. The desperately low esteem with which legislators are held, as a class, undermines Dionne's argument. His remedy focus leads inevitably back to Congress, from which most remedies must emerge. Even if Americans love their democracy in the abstract, they deeply distrust Congress, which was designed as our central democratic institution. To trust and respect Congress, citizens must believe that legislators could do their coalition building in line with Madison's idea of the permanent and aggregate interest of the community.

Doubting that legislators can do that, Americans turn almost inevitably cynical about Congress and its legislative product. These endless, gridlocked tussles between Congress and president are simply a succession of cynical games. If voters keep returning their legislator to the fray, they don't look less cynical—less worldly, less sophisticated, or savvy—than voters in other districts. In a cynical society, it is useful to rail at things in general, while still taking care of the local business. Don't leave any money on the table, as the overtly cynical saying goes.

Some congressional representatives, by definition drawn from an articulate and persuasive population, can actually deploy a compelling explanation of their role as the operators of representative government. But there is little evidence to suggest that their articulate justifications make a difference. Most of our incumbents and challengers have too much on their plate to also be effective champions of Congress and the remedy-producing process. There are funds to raise, coalitions to foster, and partisan fires to feed. Instead of sophisticated explanations of congressional proposals, we get patriotic symbols and staged photo ops. Everybody knows that the actual qualification for potential congressional candidates is the ability to "schmooze" wealthy contributors. Cynics, with much good cause, have gone too far beyond belief for the political ceremonies to be taken at face value. There are too many deals, too few solutions, too many reasons to lose faith, too little incentive to actually learn how a bill becomes a law. Who could care? And why?

Dionne correctly understands the problem any policy specialist faces. Policy smarts aren't enough. Remedies must appeal to a constituency if they are to succeed. When Jimmy Carter tried to assemble an energy program (which he said was his "highest priority"), Dionne thought the result "was a classic technocratic program put together with little regard for constituency interests." Carter's program was coherent and sensible, criteria that are always important for the wonks, but it failed to appeal to a constituency sufficiently broad to get it implemented. Then the plan was oversold: "Perhaps the most fundamental error Carter made was in his claim that the struggle for energy independence should be seen as 'the moral equivalent of war' " (134–35).

Carter had made the mistake of unconvincingly mixing his modes: the rhetoric of war clashed so boldly with the rhetoric of expert policy solutions that his adversaries could begin to make fun of him, encouraging citizens to become cynical about his simultaneous love of narrow details and broad preaching. For Dionne, Carter's heated rhetoric, which undermined his cool, technocratic style, covered a failure to gather a coalition. Just as easily, it could be evidence of a cynical strategy or of an inept initiative that opened the door for cynical adversaries. At the time, Carter's poll ratings were slipping. Neither he nor anyone else could decisively separate those poor ratings from political attempts to produce a remedy for the energy problem. Carter's southern Baptist-style call to action contained no sufficient defense against charges that his overwrought "moral equivalence of war" talk was a clumsy attempt to cover for a trumped-up crisis. Cynicism — from citizens, partisans on both sides, and the journalists who told the story — blocked the formation of a coalition strong enough to repair the mess.

Dionne's advice is more cynical than he can acknowledge. Energy and environmental policy required sacrifices from most Americans. Carter seemed to believe that the sacrifice itself would improve the national character and make the nation governable again. But a public good worthy of our sacrifice, Dionne understands, needs to be built on a constituency, on perceived interests or general partisanship. And when interests and partisanship are in play, cynical manipulation, or the perception of manipulation, has a special opportunity. Dionne's proposal to reinvigorate the "vital center" does not adequately address the contradictory structures that confound a politics of remedy. What else is the omnipresent criticism of special interests but a display of the defenses arrayed against any attempt to build a sense of the public good? The steadfast conviction that special interests wield too much influence, a conviction shared by right and left, even though they identify different specific culprits, is itself a reflection of how hard it will be to reassemble the centrist consensus.

A public good, by definition, must have consensus support. A public good would be "above politics," as Americans say. It would be shared, providing a base for action. But the only way to create that public good is by generating a constituency. Madison believed that an elite class would identify an enduring public interest, formulate appropriate policy, protect the public good, and reassure the citizenry. But the American founders did not assume that the masses would be allowed to vote. Indeed, it has only been in the past quarter century that the public finally captured direct voting control over party nominations through primary elections. The electorate's power had to expand to allay citizen cynicism about false democratic rhetoric. But once the voting franchise was expanded and elections (rather than caucuses or machine politics) really determined who won office, this arrangement proved quite susceptible to cynical manipulation and then citizen skepticism.

Dionne cites Nixon as a key milestone in the cynical collapse. But this example also shows how systemic cynicism has become and therefore how resistant it is to the solution he proposes. Many of Nixon's policies moved to the left. But the crucial move was the political one, and by that measure, Nixon moved hard to the right, practicing a divisive "us against them" politics that obviously suited him. Nixon's associates even coined the term *positive polarization* to name their strategy. Thus, given the chance to assemble what Dionne calls a "modern Republicanism," Nixon took the cynical turn, disconnecting politics from policy. And once Nixon had discovered the techniques of resentment politics, the lesson survived his downfall. Indeed, with Republicans feeling vulnerable to a seemingly hegemonic Democratic Party after 1974, they had yet more incentive to deploy the backlash tactics they had developed.

Backlash and resentment are keys to contemporary cynicism, a subject I return to elsewhere in this book. In the post-Watergate run-up to Reagan's 1976 and 1980 campaigns, Dionne reminds us, Republicans completely gave up on the rhetoric of broad community. The party that, as late as 1960, could count on a substantial black vote, and had Jackie Robinson's endorsement that year, as well as the endorsement of the African American newspaper in Atlanta and many other influential voices, turned in a different direction. The self-appointed carrier of Lincoln's tradition took a lunge in a direction Lincoln may have made possible, with his creation myth of American moral purpose and unity, but which he probably would have thought remarkably bold.

Dionne's book attempts to reclaim ideology as a way to read American politics — in service to a principled center. "For three decades, the United States has gone through a harsh but necessary debate over first principles," Dionne argues. "In their different ways, the New Left, the neoconservatives, the Buckley right, and the libertarians all understood that old Vital Center of the 1950s needed to be shaken up" (326). The old "vital center" was too exclusive, the left claimed. The right countered that it was also ineffective.

For Dionne, these are temporary conditions, the sort of troubles any lively system will encounter as it grows. Ideologies inject corrective doses of criticism into an organism that likely does not know it needs correcting. We should act to reduce the ideological dosage, he suggests: "The time has come for a settlement. Ending popular hatred of politics demands a new politics of the middle class, an approach that represents the ideals and interests of the great mass of Americans in the political and economic center. It is the politics of the restive majority" (326). Dionne's project involves "curing the mischiefs of ideology," the title of his concluding section and a direct homage to Madison, whose *Federalist* essay sought to ameliorate the mischiefs of faction.

Dionne does not dismiss the need to conduct ideological debate over first principles. If ideology has become troublesome, it is time to set the debate aside and move to solving our problems. But Dionne's argument risks missing that this position contains its own ideological commitments. Political life, he argues, needs to emphasize problem solving rather than conflict and debate. Unanimity, or at least acquiescence, is thus mandatory. Partial, special interests diminish the general perspective necessary to our common tasks. Community still can be assembled, much as Madison intended. Democracy, in this view, is something like the prelimi-nary discussion that leads to a plan or an agreement.

Dionne's view is rigorously centrist, although his argument has been more attractive to the center-left or, more precisely, to the right wing of the Democratic Party. To make his centrism credi-ble, Dionne has to stage a battle in which both left and right have been excessive in their demands. In his scenario, "the Sixties Left and the Eighties Right" create a paradox: "Their elevated aspira-tions drove both left and right further and further away from the practical concerns of the broad electorate and blinded both to the challenges facing the United States at the end of the century" (330). To stage this battle, Dionne has to describe the combatants on all sides as excessive and, thus, blocked from producing a compelling vision of the public good.

Dionne furnishes a lengthy list of misunderstandings each side has about the other. Threaded throughout this list is the presump-tion that a recognizable center still exists, that there has been no transformation of the entire political enterprise. In Dionne's Amer-ica, "middle class anger" has "legitimate sources. . . . Anger at ris-ing crime rates was not a covert form of racism but an expression of genuine fear that society seemed to be veering out of control" (330). Dionne does not explain how he knows that this wasn't "a covert form of racism." His form of proof is to balance this judg-ment by making similarly general comments about the targets of right-wing moralism. So he invents centrism: "Gays demanding tolerance were not looking to insult the heterosexual world; they were simply asking that they not be picked on, ridiculed and dis-criminated against" (331). Clearly, many gay activists, and espe-cially many AIDS activists, would not recognize that portrait of their tactical choices.

For Dionne's story to make sense, the left has to be pictured as a force that painted itself into a corner when it "increasingly stopped trying to make its case to the voters and instead relied on the courts to win benefits for needy and outcast groups" (332). This last will, no doubt, be a surprise to feminists, for whom the courts have been a continual threat for many years. Labor, a key element to any imaginable American left, has simply been debilitated from effective legal, economic, or political advance. Environmentalists have emphasized precisely the projects Dionne prefers: building mass organizations, passing legislation, and articulating a community-oriented vision of their goals. The other possibility—that objection has been fair game for demonization and suppression by sophisticated means—doesn't fit the picture that Dionne paints.

Dionne's argument requires a mainstream citizenry that has been frustrated by activists who are more extreme than their constituents. We could produce a public good if the extremists would yield to their moderate constituents. Dionne supports this argument with evidence that inactive citizens who are steadfastly suspicious of extremists describe themselves as moderates. Americans continue "to hold with our republican forebears that there [is] such a thing as 'the public good.' Americans hate politics as it is now practiced because we have lost all sense of the public good" (332). For Dionne, the human subjects of his inquiry ("Americans") are stable. What is at blame is the extreme moralism of fringe activists, which interacts with institutional conditions that make coalitions hard to form. The contentiousness of politics is an obstacle.

As an observer whose sympathies run to the mainstream left, Dionne should have understood that the offenses of left and right activists have not been symmetrical. The right has been better funded and, as a consequence, more focused. There is no left equivalent to the Coors family, the Heritage Foundation, and Richard Mellon Scaife. The right inevitably defends privilege while striving to portray the left as itself privileged. Pushed by such asymmetrical pressures, the "middle" has shifted accordingly. Dionne sees excessive activism that frustrates the production of a public good. From a slightly different angle, we might perceive an ongoing tug of war over where the middle will be located. If this is the case, a move to the supposed middle begins to look more like a concession to manipulation than a recovery of the public good.

Dionne's claim that Americans hate politics because of poor policy remedies ignores too many contrary signals, perhaps because he takes at face value the pollsters' reports that the citizens polled dislike government because it does the wrong things. But Americans' hatred of politics is both stronger and more complex than that measure suggests. This American suspicion builds on perceived abuses and manipulations, on vain hopes that we can live innocent and apolitical lives, and on the contradictory impulse to a worldly, sophisticated cynicism about institutions that have violated a trust. Even before this hatred of politics became evident, and before most of the ideological excesses Dionne catalogs, Americans had already begun to accommodate themselves to persistent cynicism.

John Dewey, the great American philosopher and activist, identified this sense of conflict earlier in this century. Amid the entertainment diversions of the contemporary world, politics is "crowded to one side," he said. Political conversation becomes "hard work" to sustain, "and once initiated, it is quickly dismissed with a yawn."[5] Dewey's point is confirmed almost everywhere. Education in politics (or, worse, "civics") is stunningly timid, earning the complete disinterest of most students, especially the bright ones. Partisan publications and organizations are in decline, except for those that deal best with the apolitical world of public relations and mass mailing. As a new generation of postmodern Lacanian intellectuals explains in a lively and diverse scholarship, politics was never about opinion and contract, as much as it engaged desires and fears. Avoidance of politics is more a condition than a response or exception.

I can think of no other developed country in which the major political newspaper, the *Washington Post*, is not even available to most of the citizenry. For most Americans, Washington is a destination to visit for its museums and monuments. This is a country that despairs of politics. Our hatred of politics is the kind of intimate love-hate that comes not from a run of bad legislation or overeager activists but from a long-term double bind. Assuming that politics cannot actually repair our injuries, we learn to love the system and hate everything it does. In our cynical age, this despair is out in the open, easily accessible to both manipulation and perception of manipulation.

Even if Dionne missed it, Americans hate politics because they are *supposed to*. Americans have internalized Madison's lesson — to be dubious of what could be accomplished by citizens acting in the political arena. Better to leave politics to the elites. But Americans have also absorbed Lincoln's lesson, redoubled by the Cold War and the grinding, half-century experience of living with the bomb. The price of not having a fierce, nationalistic pride is too high to bear. We are supposed to love this system enough to defend it, to tolerate it, to pay for it. But that intense pride does not alter the basic political arrangements, which become more adroit than Madison ever imagined at stifling action, and making any action susceptible to cynical reinterpretation.

The American founders produced a conflicted system capable of tolerating the contradictions inherent between the public good and the dictate that society be governable. Cynics then adopt the language of public good and centrism as the necessary accompaniment to control and governance. This is not a conspiracy. Especially after Hillary Clinton was so roundly criticized for blaming her husband's troubles on a "vast right-wing conspiracy," savvy citizens know better than to use that word. Think of our predicament as a largely inadvertent design, built incrementally:

- An ideology of individualism emerges but is continually undermined by contradictory developments. A highly interdependent, utterly networked, and disciplined society comes to think of itself as a collection of cowboys.

- That society also learns to reconcile its tensions by imagining that its government possesses almost supernatural legitimacy at the abstract level of democratic values. At the same time, Americans learn to worship pragmatic, rational problem solving, an activity that crowds out the contentiousness of political struggle.

- Mass media emerge as a safety valve, placed precisely as the mechanism by which we acquire most of our knowledge about government. We are critical of the media, but we are also utterly dependent on it.

Combine these elements and you produce the ingredients for a cynical cocktail. Contemporary individualists, acting in the name of problem solving, will spin out resentment much better than they make cars. Believers will turn cynical at the drop of a dime. They can still live, work, and function as cynics in this society. Nothing ever tests their cynical faith. And powerful cynics have learned to manipulate cynical citizens. A society built to this design is set up for self-destruction.

But if the sources of cynicism are sometimes surprising, so are its vectors—the practices, institutional arrangements, and communications media that move cynicism through a culture. Perhaps the most obvious of those vectors, the pervasive and evolving technology and culture that surrounds one of the central elements of our time, is television.

Chapter 8

Medium, Media, Mediate

Television and Cynicism

> Turn, now, to politics. Consider...a campaign for the
> Presidency. Would it be possible to imagine anything
> more uproariously idiotic—a deafening, nerve-wrack-
> ing battle to the death between Tweedledum and
> Tweedledee...—the unspeakable, with fearful snorts,
> gradually swallowing the inconceivable?...What did
> Harding say in 1920, and what did Cox reply? Who
> was Harding, anyhow, and who was Cox?
>
> H. L. Mencken, *The American Scene*

Journalists are our archetypal cynics, having been given the professional responsibility of going to work every day knowing they
will doubt the word of nearly everyone they contact. But there is
more to cynical journalism than the old movie archetype of the
ink-stained, doubting, and wretched reporter. News media have
become so crucial to the public world that the two share and rein-
force each other's stains.

There is no better place to mark the beginning of contemporary
journalism's cynical slide than with Mencken, the high-school graduate turned prominent Nietzsche interpreter turned colorful and
angry critic. Before his fall from popularity, Mencken was an enormous figure. By the mid-1920s, the author and commentator Walter Lippmann called Mencken the most powerful influence on a

whole generation of educated Americans. Early in his career, the essayist and critic Edmund Wilson praised him as the "civilized consciousness of modern America . . . a genuine artist" of great honesty and courage. As Fred Hobson put it, Mencken was "hailed as a phenomenon unprecedented in the nation's cultural life. . . . Perhaps for the first time in American life a critic, rather than a novelist or a poet, was the most famous and most influential American writer."[1]

In some ways, Mencken followed Mark Twain by ridiculing the absurdities of American culture while also loving the American language; sharply preferring a pragmatic realism to the romantic excesses shared by much culture high and low; and delighting in the exposure of sham and pomposity. But Mencken differed from Twain in important ways, and those differences mark him as our first well-known public cynic. Mencken was urban and urbane. He traveled with the literary and political elite of America's great eastern cities. Twain loved the American outback. Mencken loved the salon, the saloon, and bright lights. Mencken's suspicion of America outstripped Twain's critique. Even in the face of considerable criticism, Mencken durably preferred Europe to the United States, and his favoritism toward Germany eventually scarred his reputation.

As a columnist, editor, and author of books, reviews, and articles, Mencken punctured hypocrisy and moralism. His targets were politicians, reformers, boosters, puritanical religious crusaders, and preachers. His greatest story was the 1925 Scopes trial. This first American "trial of the century" pitted the modernist against the fundamentalist and the provincial in a courtroom drama of enormous interest, much of it engineered by Mencken. Forty years later, Scopes would say, "In a way, it was Mencken's show."[2] More intimately involved with the case than his journalistic successors would be with the O.J. spectacle, Mencken suggested that the defense call the former presidential nominee turned fundamentalist crusader, William Jennings Bryan, as a witness, making him the issue. The great phrasemaker, who coined the phrase "Bible Belt," then gave the trial the name now universally attached to it, the "Monkey Trial."

Mencken's critics always thought he was secretly a believer (perhaps for Germany, perhaps against Jews), and the character of his prejudices is still debated by biographers and scholars. His critics thought American values had been confirmed by Mencken's fall from popularity. But that judgment misses the point. Mencken's legacy is not found in his specific stands but in his modern, secular, and purely cynical attitude. His ultimate failure says less about American cynicism than it says about the way mass media have changed during the century that Mencken helped change. It wasn't that his cynical criticism of pomposity and official absurdity was misplaced or corrupt so much as that he couldn't quite foresee his opportunity.

By Mencken's time, the partisan, diverse press had already well begun its corporate consolidation into what we now call the media. No longer premised on ideology, newspapers and magazines began to promise an authoritative, independent view of all the news that matters. As print distribution patterns changed, Mencken was the first great national curmudgeon. He modeled the attitude that would flavor journalism's New World. Soon, electronic means of distribution would bring that world to a massive audience the newspapers never acquired. Universal literacy had only begun to take root when Mencken was a boy. By the time he died, ubiquitous television was "on the air."

George Will's ideas are as extreme as Mencken's ever were—his cruel dismissals of Bill Clinton just as irrational as Mencken's attacks on Franklin Roosevelt, for example. But Will takes more care to appeal to certain conventions even while he is cutting loose enormous prejudice. Will seems to understand his power. Mencken didn't quite appreciate that he had the influence to make the country resemble him—a neat solution for the cynic who can manage it.

Politicians, reporters, and audiences know that images rule and that those who generate images can and do misuse them. Television, the medium that grew up in Mencken's wake, is no longer a secondary "tool" delivering culture and politics. Society and television infuse each other. We fear, distrust, and love TV. It energizes us, but the energy jangles. More than it is false, censored, biased, or annoying, TV is cynical. Viewers have learned to criticize television in terms of its bias or objectivity. In turn, television insists on a realistic, naturalistic perspective. Talking to the lens, every talking head strains to conjure belief. Television insists that the central question is whether it is real enough, an adjunct to its main goal—to be watched. We learn to criticize it in terms of its self-defined project of appearing objective and natural.

This is an enduring puzzle. People are suspicious of television; to be a TV viewer is also to be a TV critic. But our criticisms paint us into a corner. Ideological conservatives are convinced that TV's bias favors the liberals. Liberals are likewise convinced that it favors the right. Asking television to be more accurate or less biased misses the point. Because it produces so many images, TV allows for myriad interpretations and thus turns this puzzle to its advantage. All are irrelevant to its real objective—to portray itself as reliable and to keep you watching. Television is, by its own design, a matter of desire and habit. And to test an issue of desire by the counterevidence of the facts, the way believer critics test television, is to miss the game entirely. Television is a refuge almost every American visits; it is the dark star of a cynical culture.

When Mencken wrote his columns, there was never much doubt that he intended to rile his readers with clever, witty reports on the foibles of American life. But by the time Walter Cronkite, the pioneer of the anchor role, was ending his newscasts by saying, "And that's the way it is, April 13, 1980," he meant exactly that. The force of this realism is so strong that even Cronkite, who angrily criticized the news business after his retirement in 1980, could not stop it. ("My lips have been kind of buttoned for almost twenty years.... CBS News doesn't really believe in commentary.")[3] As viewers became more sophisticated, Cronkite's successor, Dan Rather, could use a more self-conscious signature tag line: "That's part of our world tonight," or worse, during one brief experiment, "courage." Television promises so much that such absurdly false promises become its signature.

TV's form allows it to make such promises. Television combines the realism of the still camera, the motion previously only seen in the movies, and the immediacy of instantaneous delivery previously experienced via radio or telephone. But realism is not always what it seems. Television selects which scenes will be covered, and this fact renders this most realistic medium perversely unreal.[4] Television's capacities, which remained unique until the Internet began to take shape, amount to a claim that TV represents reality. This claim persists even after viewers' experience continually denies it.

Television labors continuously to maintain this cynical tension. TV promotes itself as unique and universal, a sort of electronic form of air, food, and water. It is always on and always scheduled. As the media theorist David Ross explains, TV's ubiquity may be its most important feature: "The unstoppable character of television [rates] right up there with the earth's rotation in terms of natural phenomena. Television's velocity was constant—it kept its pace whether you were watching or not, whether you were eating, sleeping, studying, playing, or paying attention."[5] Like the pink rabbit on the battery commercials, it keeps going and going. Ted Turner gave a roguish expression to this inevitability when he launched CNN in the early 1980s. He noted that the network wouldn't own a copy of "The Star-Spangled Banner" since it would never sign off or, rather, would do so just once, "when the world ends." Find a powerful rogue, and you've found a cynic.

Mencken's career was sometimes lamented as having been absorbed mostly in daily editorializing. But that's the point—this happens every day at predictable intervals. Like the "reality" of daily life, TV shows up every day, without fail. But television pays a price for this persistence because it also requires a high degree of comforting familiarity. We know that the sitcom M*A*S*H is about a war, but cynics also know the regulars will be back next week; it is a fake war. The plot may promise tragedy, but before the program ends, viewers know there will be a happy story told in the same tone of voice with the same camera conventions and a familiar reporter. The tragedy is contained.

Mencken, too, found it hard to continue surprising his readers. Eventually, he lost the edge between cranky observation and persistent good humor, as represented by his witty language and joyful outrage. Television soon faced its own limitations. But unlike the solitary writer, television had remarkable capacity to change its form. The requirement of daily and weekly predictability would seem to undercut TV's ambition to keep us watching; after all, most of TV lacks suspense. The star will return next week. So television compensated, emphasizing movies and sports broadcasts, both of which can still display some surprise. Newscasts became crucial, since news provided opportunity for story, suspense, and seriousness. But television, with its restless urge to keep us watching, needed more. It developed an attitude.

Characterizing that attitude, the media scholar Mark Crispin Miller writes that TV flatters us "by condescending broadly... as if to wink at us and say, 'We know this is all pretty stupid, don't we?'" This attitude is most obvious in advertisements: "TV protects its ads from mockery by doing all the mocking, thereby posing as an ally to the incredulous spectator."[6] This is a long-practiced advertising technique, but in television, the posture persists after the commercial ends. TV's attitude permeates its programming and its audience. Everyone involved is protected by what Miller calls their "sense of their own knowingness." Actor John James, a regular on the *Dynasty* series, summarized it neatly: "I call it talk-back TV.... You turn on the set, sit back and, between scoops of Häagen-Dazs, you say, 'Do you believe he said that?'"[7] James could have been quoting the condescending Mencken, except that the latter never imagined how pervasive his attitude could eventually become. Today, Miller explains, viewers constantly reestablish their superiority to TV "not by criticizing or refusing it, but by feeding on it, taken in by its oblique assurances that you're too smart to swallow any of it."

Television promotes individuality while also undermining it, by ignoring or ridiculing real individuality in preference for the oddballs on *Geraldo*. Mencken had a well-practiced literary sneer, but television can model this attitude far more effectively than he could have imagined possible. Television, with its far greater and more malleable capacities, adopted the cynical sneer as a condition of its continuing prosperity. TV could invent a cynical culture that continually reinforces itself in a tight circle of pattern and response. On every type of show, Miller notes, characters "participate in this reflexive sneering, and such contemptuous passivity reflects directly on the viewer who watches it with precisely the same attitude."[8] TV flatters its audience, but this flattery has a debilitating and vicious undertone. It insinuates that anyone who tries to rise above this muck of contempt will be attacked. In effect, TV reminds us that it could just as well be deriding us personally.

Television's cynicism, its ironic appeal to (and simultaneous destruction of) individuality, is always ready to fend off attacks. Call it Mencken's revenge: even criticism now reinforces television's role. Humanist critics like Neil Postman seem stuck in a rut of moral judgment, like a Roman emperor doing thumbs up, thumbs down — Siskel and Ebert style. The world doesn't change except to accommodate TV's cynical lesson. The most popular criticisms of television's impact have long taken the form of appeals to values and belief. We hear that TV should be more responsible, that campaign advertisements should be limited by law, and that citizens should be more critical of TV and should read or even do more. Excessively attached to moralistic condemnation, this kind of critique fails because it misses too much of television's liveliness, as well as its inevitability and importance. Critiques presume that there is something genuine or real that would emerge if television were better. Imagining that real nugget, the critics risk missing what is happening in plain view. Television is constructing realities, and a struggle is on over those constructions.

Even very recently, television was the dirty secret of American intellectual life. Social scientists hardly studied it at all. When they did, their efforts were often just this side of ludicrous. In various experiments, subjects wired with electrodes watched violent or sexually explicit videotapes. It is not easy to design a research project that studies human subjects' interaction with a ubiquitous instrument like television. Opinion polls studied a populace that was already uncomfortable about its intimate relationship with "the tube" and thus could scarcely report honestly or accurately. The studies by various academics were hardly any better. A very few writers tried to chronicle the way candidates interacted with television. But the entire enterprise produced very little "knowledge" except to report what we already knew. Americans were watching a lot of television and told pollsters that TV was their primary source for political information.

As literature or culture, television did not fare any better in serious intellectual circles. Popular culture became an academic subspecialty, but one with a persistent credibility problem. A tired hunt for stereotypes, a search that begged the tentatively abandoned class analysis, lacked the sophistication required by the new media. Television even failed at its obvious strength, pedagogy. Colleges that would not think of having chemistry classrooms without sinks or astronomy labs without telescopes still have very few classrooms equipped for effective use of television. When television was employed, it was used ineffectively: to show taped lectures or documentaries when the professor had to miss a class. Long after the videocassette recorder was commonplace in the American household, it was still rare in higher education classrooms and almost never found in faculty offices. Every professor needed a typewriter and then a computer, but nobody needed a television set.

This is changing. Although a conservative old guard fights against the deep interest in television that now flourishes in academe, it is too late. It is no longer possible to think about political or social life without understanding television. An effective understanding of the tube will have to be a cultural understanding, deeply interpretive and attentive to the variety of ways culture is being created. And if we pay such close attention, we will discover that TV's secret is a very open secret. Television parallels American politics. Seemingly natural, both work hard to enforce conventions that are cynical and naturalistic. Huge efforts are made to maintain an emotional link. While "everybody knows" that both TV and politics are something other than real, they still work.

TV is an unusual friend, one its audience fears, distrusts, hates, and loves. The television experience, so realistic and emotionally engaging but also so private and safe, is more than anything else, cynical. Often, it serves the interests of powerful cynics. On occasion, and more often recently, TV serves cranks and outsiders, wig cynics who know how to play television's game. Always wanting to shore up its legitimacy, television gives plenty of airtime to believer critics like Kathleen Hall Jamieson who tell the tube how it should behave. But both television and its audience have already discounted such lessons. We suspect that television is actually serving a different master than the ones it ostensibly promotes, but we keep watching. Everybody knows the tube is cynical.

Try this: borrow a video camera and a tripod; set them up in your living room; and suit up in your "dress for success" best. Turn the lights up, bring in another lamp, and make the lighting intolerably bright. Now look straight at the camera lens and say something wise about the world. Take about thirty seconds, but don't glance at your wristwatch, and remember to smile. Move your head and shoulders as if you were talking to a person, but don't move so much that the camera has to move; it stays where it is. Don't be tense.

Replay your performance on your video player, imagining that millions of people are watching you. This dance with the lens is difficult and unnerving. It is not the same as looking into a mirror, although the lens might reflect back a little. It is unlike talking to a person or a group. TV's central ritual, necessary to every newscast or presidential address, has a shape of its own. It is not like talking on the telephone, itself a strange and disembodied way to communicate. It is more like talking to a telephone answering machine — a performance that still unsettles many callers. This is communication in a bottle, with no response. The people with whom television presumes to communicate cannot answer back. The conventions of conversation are followed ("Hi, I'm Wink Martindale"), but there is no conversation. When the audience does get to ask questions on the popular call-in shows, the communication is simulated. Call-in shows are power trips. The announcer interrupts and can hang up, canceling the caller altogether. The producer screens callers. If all else fails, there is tape delay.

Talking to the lens, TV talking heads strain to conjure belief; the lens stands in for people. Television inherited the rhetoric of realism from photography, adding motion and sound and a distribution of viewing instruments in every home and many public spaces. Television actively produces this sense of realism. TV journalists learn verbal and visual vocabularies, rules, and syntax. Other media have avoided realism or have used it as one possibility among others. The effort to convey itself realistically consumes much of television's energy and concentration. Tube culture forms around the effort to be realistic as well as attractive. That culture infects the journalists who work in television. The cynical reporters, and less visible but still cynical producers, writers, and executives, are no historical accident.

As the media scholar Robert C. Allen suggests, television has discovered a cagey way to hide its secrets. It puts them out in the open, for everyone to see. TV works through an "apparent naturalness.... After all, no one had to teach us how to 'read' television programs. But the naturalness of our relationship with television is illusory. Television, like the cinema, painting, or photography, does not simply reflect the world in some direct, automatic way."

Instead, television gathers its representations of the world according to "complex sets of conventions — conventions whose operations are hidden by their transparency." Contemporary viewers are easily able "to make sense of television," Allen notes, but that ability "is, in fact, a result of our having learned those conventions of television reading — even though we are usually not conscious of their operation, nor can we remember having been taught them."[9]

The visual style of TV news, which differs significantly from that of the movies, underscores the realism in ways that viewers might not consciously notice. The news has to be even more real than the rest of television. TV news cameras move sparingly, whereas movie cameras move incessantly. Whether on the news or the sitcoms, TV uses few tracking shots or pans, and almost no zooms. (Such shots appear primarily in "on the scene" coverage taken from helicopters, when TV's opportunity to boast of its immediacy and its resources overwhelms its careful observation of the stylistic conventions.) In the movies, the perspective of a disembodied eye, floating around, zooming in from great heights, is a familiar trick. This is how movies, ever since *Citizen Kane,* a cynical thriller, show their artfulness and mastery of craft. TV cameras stay at eye level, the better to imply one master viewer. You.

CBS's marketing of Walter Cronkite as trustworthy might have seemed unusual to someone unfamiliar with television culture. His work was visible on the screen, available for anyone to assess. Who cared if you could trust Walter? But CBS knew the game. Teaching its audience that Cronkite's trustworthiness was the crucial variable, CBS was saying, in effect, *watch us . . . every night . . . otherwise you might miss something . . . but if you watch Walter, you won't feel left out.* When television (and society) loosened up in the 1970s, the anchors became more overtly sexual—with first Tom Brokaw and Peter Jennings, then, finally, women. The point was to keep us watching.

This is no deep secret. You can see it all. The anchor is the most important person on the news. He or she has mastered the strange act of staring into the lens — looking you "in the eye" and with the aid of the TelePrompTer speaking without pause or error. Until ABC's *Nightline* broke the pattern a few years ago, everyone else was required to look away from the lens. They looked shifty, indi-rect, subservient, or perhaps not quite "with it." The camera shoots the anchor in a tight close-up, implying "touching distance" fa-miliarity. Correspondents appear in longer shots, farther from the viewer. They speak through the anchor and hold bulky micro-phones that, miraculously, anchors do not require. Anchors (the label misapplied to news readers who hurtle around the world, no longer tied to a New York set, only to a satellite uplink) consume precious time introducing—summoning—each correspondent.

The anchor is supposed to serve as your eyes, as the trusted seer of events that might be of interest, even though they are re-mote. The reporter answers the anchor's questions, then takes more precious time mentioning his or her employer and where the seg-ment is being broadcast from ("reporting live from Beirut for CBS News..."). It is a ritual of connection to the anchor and a prideful boast of the wealth spent to put someone trustworthy at the scene to witness events for you. Notice the human-interest spot at the close of the news program. Isn't it reassuring to know that the all-seeing anchor has a sense of humor? But it is always a par-ticular kind of humor, one we recognize as belonging to the cynic. The anchor has been there before, seen it all, and knows the human foibles. The anchor is media—the intermediary between viewer and news. If you cannot identify with the anchor's seeing and sto-rytelling, you are blind and voiceless. You must love your anchor.

Television wants to make sense to even the most casual viewer. It must be intelligible in ways that draw little or no overt atten-tion to itself. The media theorist John Ellis explains that each image on TV contributes to this project of sense making. Each image is "held until it has been used as information, then cut to another image." These images rigorously use "conventions of sound/image relations (the voice-over, and synchronized dialogue both with as-cribed sources)." The seemingly transparent handling of transi-tions, sound, and visuals contributes to the same project. Televi-sion makes itself central to its viewers' lives. Increasingly, television looks to cinema mostly for innovation, here and there, because its own tendency is conservative.[10] More recently, pop culture also con-tributes some innovation, although TV's handling of emotional material, especially, is distinctively its own. Television has learned how to make sense in ways so natural that the line between TV and the world blurs. Like every powerful cynic, television became a seductive recruiter to its cause. It pulls us in.

This chapter has mostly emphasized television's form, style, and culture. By now, you might well be asking, to paraphrase Walter Mondale's complaint to the telegenic Gary Hart, where's the substance? It turns out that while television has been staking a claim as the best representation of reality, it has also convinced the substantial players, the officials and candidates, as well as the regular audience that television itself is the crucial reality. Some of those players were reluctant at first. Their awkwardness showed, and they were punished. Remember the awful TV presence of Johnson, Nixon, and any number of that generation's lesser public figures. But in time, either education or natural selection worked, and the stumblers gave way to a new generation. First there was the improbably elderly Reagan, then Clinton and the rest of the Bob Foreheads so well caricatured by the cartoonist Mark Alan Stamaty.

If television were simply a toolkit of techniques, no matter how powerful, it might still be possible to stand back and criticize it, perhaps to form an anti-TV culture or movement. But television has proven itself so powerful that it has become the very arena in which events happen. Capturing territory is easy once the airwaves have been managed. Before television matured, leaders and strategists would watch the front page of major newspapers to see how their actions were being represented, the better to judge what their next step would be. Now players and citizens alike are watching CNN to determine the next step and to see the steps that other players are taking. Colin Powell, the top military officer during the Gulf War, found out it had actually begun the same way the rest of us did: he watched CNN and listened to Peter Arnett, the veteran war correspondent who reported the U.S. attack, live from its target in Baghdad.

Those in power were initially reluctant to admit this new player to a game that jealously guards seats at the main table. Lyndon Johnson, who as a TV station owner's spouse had some sense of the medium's force, even if he couldn't figure out how to use it, took some ribbing for his preference for having three TV sets in his office, the better to watch all three networks at once. (As Graceland's tour guides proudly note, Elvis Presley's mansion also included a room with three sets — gifts from Johnson, who was charmed that Elvis shared this hyperactive viewing habit, although in his case it was for football season.) Eventually, the remote control would make the three sets redundant, but no player now underestimates television's importance. Traveling campaign professionals carry battery-operated sets, and government offices everywhere are wired for cable.

Under George Bush, American military planners added a new criterion for the use of force: such ventures would have to expect quick success. An elaborate effort, building up support and troops as a war spread in an extended, incremental way, no longer made sense. In some ways, this sided with the military preference for massive force applied with an element of surprise. But the reasons for the shift were entirely political. Rather than building support and force slowly, together, military planning assumed support in an action's early phases and sought to complete the action quickly, before protest could grow. Military planners take television into account as opportunity, exemplified by the Gulf War, which was staged as a TV spectacle, or as potential problem, if a military action went on too long. As later reports would reveal, the Gulf War stopped almost instantly when leaders started to contemplate how awful the "highway of death" would look on the evening news.

As self-confident as he was, Mencken could not have imagined this kind of influence. The preachers, politicians, and profiteers he loved to lampoon could be made to play by his rules on turf of his choosing. Mencken's successors would discover how to model the attitude their medium required. America really could be an urban, hip, sophisticated, wired — and cynical — nation. Then we would teach the rest of the world how to do it. That would be another surprise for Mencken, who wanted America to become more like Europe. Instead, the reverse was required.

I am not simply bemoaning television's role. Indeed, I think the bemoaners have it wrong. For good or ill, television has played a significant role in transforming us into Cynical America. TV is an important part of the explanation of why we are more cynical now than we could have been in Mencken's time. Likewise, I would have us wait before rushing to judge too broadly whether this is good or bad. But this much is obvious: it is. Television's world, a cynical hothouse, has become as important as any other factor we can yet fully imagine. This is where we live.

Chapter 9

Bush, Burned

The Patterns of Televised Politics

> It has been said by some cynic, maybe it was a former president, 'If you want a friend in Washington, get a dog.' We took them literally—that advice—as you know. But I didn't need that, because I have Barbara Bush.
>
> George Bush

The day after the 1988 presidential vote, ABC's *Nightline* aired a special review of that extraordinary election. Campaign professionals, top journalists, and a few commentators from outside the usual circles gathered on an elaborate set. Instead of the two or three guests usually featured on *Nightline,* this show had dozens of guests. By all accounts, it had been an exceptional election. George Bush, Ronald Reagan's loyal vice president for eight years, had appeared unelectable early in the year, due to the Iran-Contra scandal and Bush's own public image, somehow poorly developed after a lifetime in the public spotlight. The Democrats nominated Michael Dukakis, governor of Massachusetts, a successful state, and a champion of "competence, not ideology," as his campaign had constantly reminded the electorate.

When Bush drubbed Dukakis, there were some questions to ask. Most of the commentators on *Nightline* that evening thought the Dukakis campaign had been sluggish and, almost in defiance of the candidate's stump speech refrain, incompetent. Bush's campaign, in contrast, bristled with competence, but several of *Nightline*'s guests made mention of the dark edge to the Bush victory. Bush had manipulated the debates, effectively spun Dukakis's successful convention into oblivion, and had turned liberalism — the posture Harvard political scientist Louis Hartz had convincingly argued belonged to us all as Americans — into "the L word." It had been a mean campaign. And the commentators' attention that evening focused on a few of Bush's most egregious television advertisements, finding in them the handle on the campaign's dark spirit.

The question was whether television had fairly covered this aspect of the campaign. That would be a tough question to answer in the affirmative. The Willie Horton advertisement had been, all acknowledged, a wicked instrument. One widely shown version of the ad had dozens of ethnic prisoners filing through a revolving prison door. This was an attempt to symbolize the futility and danger of any prison furlough program, including the one Dukakis sponsored and Horton had taken advantage of to commit more violence. Then a mug shot of Horton appeared, making him as wild a vision of black violence as anything ever dreamed of by the swing voters Bush's campaign was targeting.

The problem with the ad was that it was false, several times over, in terms of the rules television uses to define truth. Almost every implication offered by the ad had been twisted in the direction of emotional, resentful motives no American would publicly suggest should drive a presidential campaign. The ad implied that hundreds of murders had been committed by prisoners on furlough, which was not the case. As vice president, Bush had also spoken for and presided over (albeit from a distance, as was also the case with Dukakis) furlough programs more dangerous than the one in Massachusetts. And the overcrowding in federal prisons was in large part a consequence of a punitive and arguably racist war on drugs during the Reagan years, before which criminal prosecution had been mainly a state and local duty, not a federal one.[1]

Perfectly positioned to understand the falsity and wickedness of the ad, the people who run television had debated how to respond. Afraid of the liberal tag, Dukakis had been paralyzed by

the ad and failed to play his appointed role. He avoided comment-
ing on the ad in a way that would draw attention until very late in
the campaign. This made TV's job easier. It could pretend that the
odious Horton ad was somehow a nonissue. Some news organizations ran a story about the ad, but none of them followed up. The
Horton ad ran for as long as twenty-eight days, mostly at a high
saturation level, in states Bush's campaign thought susceptible to
its backlash message and style. The saga of the Horton ad was not
a pretty story, and it was a known embarrassment to those associated with television news. So, again, did television handle the Horton affair properly?

After a few false starts by other commentators less bold than
ABC's Sam Donaldson on that postelection *Nightline,* Sam answered the question. He said that candidates had a right to lie as
long as their competition failed to stop it. The story, in such a
case, was the victim's reticence, and television had reflected that
story in its own, complicit reluctance. This was an accurate and useful answer. Within television news' self-defined rules and its self-
image as objective, this answer fulfilled the important requirements.
But Donaldson's answer had a problem, too, and everyone in the
room that evening knew it. The uncomfortable pause after his statement left no doubt that something of considerable significance
had been disclosed and that those assembled were embarrassed at
the revelation. The problem is that television constitutes itself not
only as objective but also as truthful and reliable.

Television promises truth but reneges on its main premise, which
is communication. This leads its viewers to perceive it, accurately,
as cynical. In a similar way, television promises objectivity but cannot fulfill that promise, and it therefore produces a cynical audience as a result.

Any presentation that relies on naturalism, as television does, will
be judged by whether it is using realism to convince or report. TV
viewers are familiar with both types of effort. Commercial advertising always tries to convince, and news shows promise that they
are reporting. But a host of problems arise along with the journalists' promise. Among the problems of television objectivity are
these:

- Even when television shows two sides of an issue in a single newscast, it tends to subordinate the conflict to the unifying, narrative voice of the anchor. Or it turns one side (or even both) into caricature to feed the spectacle that makes the news attractive.

- Even when two sides have been presented, other positions are routinely excluded on the basis of a hazily defined news judgment that mostly refers to what other media outlets are already doing.

- The "two sides" form of objectivity (as unbiased) is not the only kind of objectivity possible. We could also demand objectivity-as-truth, which might require that one candidate be treated more harshly than her opponent.

- More likely, objectivity usually refers to an ebb and flow, an evening of advantage over time. This evening requires sympathetic and sophisticated viewers who understand that something they dislike will be countered in due course, whether or not they are there to see it. But television's immediacy and cynicism are generally inconsistent with the development of such sympathetic viewers.

- There is so much television and it so radically invites the viewer's interpretation that TV puts itself in the position of constantly being accused of bias by almost everyone. This is the cost of producing emotional, spectacle-filled shows, and it is a cost TV has learned to live with, if cynically.

Carl Bernstein, who as a young reporter broke the Watergate story for the *Washington Post* in the early 1970s, wrote about this issue just before the 1992 election. He took note of the background for that election. The awkward *Nightline* broadcast had indeed provoked four years of self-examination by the media: "After the [1988] election, the press underwent an unusual amount of soul searching about its coverage — its focus on flag burning, the Pledge of Allegiance, Willie Horton. The real story, lost in all this, had been the conduct of Bush's campaign and its reflection on the candidate's character and agenda."[2]

The horizon of objectivity — its time frame or scope — was at issue. There were accounts to settle, and the debts due were not all twenty-four hours old, since the last edition of the nightly news. As Bernstein put it, "In a way, Bush is being held to a higher standard than either Ronald Reagan or Richard M. Nixon. For one thing, he is paying for the press' lapses during the Reagan years — when the media cowered before the President's popularity." After the election, Clinton would experience some of this debt settling, too. After a honeymoon that lasted days rather than the usual period of several months, the press came after him with a vengeance, unlike anything Bush or Reagan experienced, evidently so that the errors of journalists through those years would not accumulate to such a large debt again. But in 1992, the debt was Bush's to pay.

Bernstein explained that the press's understanding of Bush had finally settled into a suspicious, anxious mood. Objectivity — a tough standard, we are starting to see — might demand more from one candidate than from another. "Bush is viewed by many reporters and commentators as someone who has made a political career by fleeing principle: courting his patrons, and endorsing whatever their causes of the moment were, to advance his own future, shedding his stated beliefs like a snakeskin."[3] The Reagan-Bush years had leaned hard on the rhetoric of principle, but they also produced a policy record open to interpretation as partisan for the wealthy, oblivious to the poor, and heavy on patriotic manipulation. When Bush picked up the old Reagan vocabulary to secure his second term, the line of succession had finally stretched too thin. Cynicism was too visibly a possibility to be ignored any longer. Nobody would suggest that objectivity required that a reporter give utterly equal balance in a contest somehow radically unbalanced by its character.

Fortunately for Bernstein's argument, the press was able to cite some rough treatment of Bill Clinton and Ross Perot, too. Having admitted that "the tone and urgency of U.S. press coverage in the past year" bordered on what was once called advocacy journalism, Bernstein could still claim fairness in terms of the usual standard. Even if the press has been "going out of its way to controvert the Bush rhetoric and reveal his neglect of the nation's problems," the standard of fairness may still have applied. "That is not to say that coverage has been unfair. Rather, it has moved toward the ideal of what good reporting has always been: the best obtainable version of the truth. Moreover, the same rigorous standards have been applied to Bill Clinton and Ross Perot." Bernstein noted that conservative journalists like George Will led the charge against Bush, mitigating against a simple, ideological interpretation of the press's renewed vigor.

Bernstein was trying to adopt the objectivity-as-truth model while also keeping the objectivity-as-unbiased model together. He knows that both models are included in the sweeping expectation the media has taught its audience to demand. But journalists had wandered into a bind in this double promise. To keep hitting Clinton on an old draft record (that was not so different from many of theirs) and on Gennifer Flowers would be to risk repeating the Willie Horton manipulation. Besides, Clinton had responded to those attacks somewhat more adeptly than Dukakis had handled Horton. But quieting those assaults on Clinton would make the continuing attacks on Bush seem unevenly applied. Which, in the sense of the "bias" definition, they were. It was George Bush who had to pay off twelve years of Reagan-Bush media debts, not Bill Clinton.

We have so often had roughly equivalent candidates — middle- or upper-class white guys, policy centrists, of modest or compromised capability or charisma — that the tensions in the promise of objectivity have seldom emerged so vividly. Imagine a race in which one candidate is thoroughly mediocre. The other candidate is a manipulative dark genius, gravely flawed by personality and policy, a powerful cynic. A journalist would be obliged, under the objectivity-as-truthfulness model, to reveal the second candidate's actual character, even though that candidate would probably be better equipped to hide that character by manipulating the coverage. To make matters worse, the second candidate would also be skilled at aiming resentful attacks at the press, to gain support in a constituency also fueled by resentment. That candidate would launch biting criticisms of the press on the basis that they were not being objective because they were biased.

I do not believe this is such an absurd hypothetical. And such a race can't shore up the kind of consensus position that has often characterized American politics. As resentment and cynicism become increasingly systematic, there will be more campaigns like this hypothetical one, not fewer. The angry, expressive partisans for the second candidate would not be satisfied to hear that four or eight years ago, the media had actually been much more helpful to their party's candidate.

Bush, in short, stumbled into a time warp of crossed objectivity standards and mixed horizons of judgment. He ended up paying for other people's debts, but he also was an easy mark, the sort of client a bill collector loves to dun. The debts dated back to Ronald Reagan, who with aides like Michael Deaver first exploited television's cynical potential. Not to say that this is necessarily an evil thing. One can imagine that Reagan's "reverse chameleon" capability, as Garry Wills called it, his ability to make others take on his ideological and political colors, would be a useful, even necessary thing in a wartime president, for example. But Reagan's supporters seldom preferred this kind of praise.

There are political sides, and each has its believers, powerful cynics, and wigs. Sometimes one or another of those sides actually is dangerous. Throughout the political world, some media experts are smart and talented. They are analyzing television as acutely as any of the scholars cited in this book. The media experts are constantly figuring out maneuvers that will make the journalists' jobs ever harder. We can never be assured that the various sides in a political campaign are equivalent contestants. This complexity gets in the way of television's promised objectivity, multiplying the problems contained in its culture and style. Actual political events, the things that happen when there is actually something at stake, some definition in flux, resist characterization, even if the news must always be characterizing them.

Using a strong sense of narrative, television news doesn't respond to questions of its ideology so much as it subsumes them in a flow of narrative, driven by a strong impulse to make itself attractive, even indispensable. When questioned about all this, TV journalists often respond by invoking the "ebb and flow" of coverage.[4] TV sees itself as evening things up, over time. More recently, this explanation has been invoked regarding Bill Clinton, who is alternatively loved and hated by the tube folk. The ebb-and-flow model of objectivity suggests that errors even themselves up over time. Since no competing candidates ever commit their gravest errors (or sins) simultaneously, a journalist has to depend on the likelihood that coverage will also even out over time.

The inconsistency implied by the ebb-and-flow argument goes against TV's avowed reliability and fails to suggest much media self-awareness of its role. An ebb and flow over time is hard, perhaps even impossible, to monitor. And without a way to confidently assert balance, the self-announced objectivity of TV news becomes an empty promise — always an invitation to cynical critique. The very configuration of this argument means that journalism will constantly be open to charges that it is biased or even conspiratorial. Still, the ebb-and-flow argument does make sense, even if it is a kind of sense that complicates matters that were supposed to be made simpler by the commitment to journalistic objectivity.

Politics, in an important sense, *is* ebb and flow. The political world unfolds as events unfold. Not every political answer arrives in time for that day's newscast. Some accounts wait years to see a balance. In retrospect, ebb and flow helped send Bush out with the tide. The problem is in television's use of the argument to justify its arrogance and power. As long as objectivity takes the form of apology and self-justification, the promise itself will retain a cynical edge. The powerful cynic is adept at apologies. After each such apology, the cynical ruler shows up to work again the next day, ready to manipulate again.

The unfolding, contingent arena for public life includes the media as well as the political participants. The players interact with the medium of their play, sometimes pushing both sides to develop new approaches before the old objectivity debts have been repaid. This would be a positive strategy for a presidential administration. It was employed successfully by Ronald Reagan, at least in the first six years of his presidency. This is to say that the cynicism of Bush and the TV actor impulses of Reagan should not push us to lodge our complaints only with them or with their party. Reagan and Bush just pushed a game further along, more quickly than their predecessors had. Indeed, Jimmy Carter's (arguably) opportunistic use of the Iranian hostage situation, boiled up to "crisis" level and hyped in the face of the perilous 1980 election, could have been the first move in this direction.

Reagan and his staff understood how the media game was moving and pushed it to their advantage. Politics is marked by contentiousness. If the Republicans of the 1980s were much more adroit than the Democrats or the media in staying ahead of developments in the game of televised politics, we should not mistake that for simple evil. To be sure, there were cynics on the scene, but this does not distinguish the Reagan era from others. It may be that they managed to push cynicism to crisis level, a public service of an unusual sort.

Television usually responds to challenges against its objectivity with defensive self-examination, a critical mode now regularly adopted on all those journalist talk shows. That defensiveness can also lead to changes in media coverage, as was evident in the difference between the 1988 and 1992 campaigns. But the objectivity problem, like the realism problem discussed in chapter 8, is too deeply settled in. Any attempt to "do better next time" is already embroiled in its own controversy, its own set of charges and countercharges.

A better response would be for television to change its ways. And an argument can be made that it is doing just that, albeit more slowly than many of us would like. By 1992, the networks had largely ceded to cable the coverage of the conventions, a move Marc Miller had proposed eight years earlier. Although cable news is subject to most of the same problems that afflict the networks, the dispersion of news coverage is probably helpful, especially since two of the cable channels, Fox and MSNBC, seem to be adopting self-consciously different ideological bases. The debate show, an innovation of recent years following the success of CNN's *Crossfire,* is an ambiguous development. TV had long avoided real, face-to-face political contention. The debate shows bring some sense of political struggle to the screen. But these shows often feature a narrow spectrum of views. Many debates on serious issues decompose into coarse shouting matches, as the veteran commentator Jack Germond complained when he left the *McLaughlin Report.* It is as if television wanted to show the very worst kind of political debate.

If TV would feature criticism of its role — criticizing the political ads that run amid the news, for example — that would address its omnipotent façade. And TV has begun to do that, too, if incompletely. Kathleen Hall Jamieson's campaigns to get television to frame the commercials it shows on the news and to run regular "ad-watch" features during campaigns are both helpful. If it someday became possible to limit campaign advertisements, that might help shift more emphasis to the other kinds of shows that are emerging. But Perot's arrival and the recent undermining of all rules on the use of so-called soft money deferred any immediate opportunity to seriously restrict these ads. Widespread understanding about how Dukakis helped destroy his campaign by not responding in a timely way to the Horton advertisements probably does more to moderate the effect of such ads than anything else.

Despite all the groaning about negative campaigning, trying to make campaigns positive is no solution at all. The negative/positive distinction in political campaigns is too broad to be meaningful, which is why Americans can *both* say they dislike negative campaigns *and* still react to them, deflecting their voting behavior in directions the ads intend. Too many kinds of campaigning are lumped together as negative than can easily inhabit a useful category. Some negative ads are clearly oriented toward issues. Republicans routinely call Democratic appeals to class "negative," but a major difference between Dukakis's failure and Clinton's success was that Clinton used social class (and finally, gender) to rally his constituency — an elementary political move. On the other side, Clinton decried Bush's "character" campaign as unfair, even while he was using any number of character issues — most important, obliviousness — as his central campaign themes.

The categories "negative" and "positive" too easily reverse positions or collapse into each other. Politics is about contention, and where contention happens, negativity must surely follow. Negation is the mark of differences worth struggling over. What would a positive ad campaign look like? Ronald Reagan's (and Ed Rollins's) "Morning in America" ads from the 1984 campaign? It is hard to see how that ad contributed to the public store of knowledge and opinion. It is easy to reverse the interpretation of the ad, to portray it as a wily attack on Mondale's "un-American" connections to organized labor, environmentalists, and, hence, socialism. With a platform such as television and an audience it has trained, cynicism is hard to police.

A similar problem attaches to the familiar argument that issues should be at the center of our campaigns and their ads. In the compressed format required by television, issue talk is still heavily encoded and open to manipulation. President Clinton's talk about Social Security and Medicare cuts during the 1996 campaign was issue talk, but it drove Jamieson to repeated complaints that his statements manipulated the truth, a charge Republicans continued to make after Clinton's reelection. The president's campaign staff defended their behavior, but in the end it was hard to see 1996 as a new kind of campaign. The complaints shifted as the tactics shifted.

Perhaps in response to the problems of the negative category, some commentators now aim their criticisms at attack ads. That is, at least, a narrower category, referring to those wildly assertive, aggressive, maybe even dangerous ads, the ones that raise taboo topics directly enough to bloody an opponent. This is Willie Horton territory, the wig precinct where Jesse Helms used his anti-affirmative action "white hands" ad to defeat Harvey Gant in a 1990 Senate race in North Carolina. The anti–National Endowment for the Arts (NEA) ads Pat Buchanan ran against Bush in the 1992 Georgia primary were classic attack ads. It is much easier to oppose attack ads than it is to be against negative campaigning in general.

If television could renovate its commitment to objectivity as currently defined, that would undoubtedly be a good thing. But this will not take the shape of a return to the nineteenth-century press, with advocacy newspapers from every angle. More likely, television will continue to develop different kinds of forums for political commentary. As the CNN-fueled expansion in the amount of political programming continues to diminish the importance of the nightly news, the combined effect is positive, if also limited and fragile. There really is no chance that television will forfeit the universal news voice so central to its own sense of itself as attractive and effective.

The talk-show campaign of 1992 received much attention as some kind of alternative, but it generated little commentary describing how this would be different and why such an alternative might emerge. Television's channel broadens as it finds ways to vary its presentation. It remains a matter of interpretation and argument whether or how this might be a positive or negative development. On the one hand, this is a powerful cynic's move — promoting the appearance of politics (all those candidates, all over the tube, all the time!) without the contention of politics. This is simulated activity, repeating campaign themes without paying for the ads, answering mostly softball questions, either from Larry King or his callers, most of whom do not know how to ask a question that makes a campaigner nervous. It's what the powerful cynic would design if given free rein.

On the other hand, however, even the cynic's move can be used against him or her. The algebra of television impact has never been a matter of simple weighing, a calculation of who got more minutes or of how many of those minutes were scripted or boring or interesting as news. TV's math is always exponential. One little moment, replayed as sound bite, can dominate an hour or a week. The second "town hall" presidential debate with Bush, Clinton, and Perot showed how this new TV math works. In three questions, Bush lost control.

First, a family therapist (a male with a ponytail, as he was usually described in subsequent reports) kept the president from using his campaign's main theme, which was "character." In the code of 1992, character had come to stand for Bill Clinton's marital problems and draft status, not for the questions about Bush's own character—his tendency to sacrifice principle, for example. All it took was one challenge from one citizen to put the "character issue," a cornerstone of Bush's paid media, off limits for the duration of the debate. A few minutes later, an African American woman asked Bush about his personal experience of economic downturn. That got Bush somehow musing about having read about teen pregnancy in the bulletin of a black church. After the debate, most commentators were remarkably kind to Bush, suggesting that he seemed a bit confused.

The proliferation of debate formats was, in part, a Clinton strategy, which may help illustrate a change in how campaigns see themselves and how we should view them. The field of campaigns becomes more like a continuing, strategic struggle rather than a set of events and things, each of which can be interpreted in the context of a relatively settled set of judgments ("appearance counts in debates"; "the challenger can establish himself as credible in a debate," etc.). Television does engage in self-examination and it does change its techniques. But this change is incremental, and other problems spring up as quickly as reforms are instituted. Politics is about struggle, and the operatives who have survived the past few decades are those who move fast, exploiting opportunities and staying ahead of the curve. Politics is not a fixed field of good and bad values, issues and ideologies. It is a shifting arena in which events build on precedents, sometimes very new precedents.

Bush's loss in 1992 did not somehow prove that cynicism is on the wane or that it always loses in the end. Both judgments underestimate the political game and its new variants — falling back onto the grammar of physics or biology, where "natural laws" sometimes seem to confer a determinism on the events they address. No such confident basis for judgment presents itself in the realm of politics. In fact, Bush's loss may suggest that there are countermeasures to his brand of cynicism. The media can adjust. These adjustments may indeed redress grievances, not in one broadcast but over time. This is not a reliable effect either, but it might be at least slightly reassuring.

At the same time, the difficulty the media exhibited, during and after the 1992 campaign, should tell us that it has not entirely absorbed this new redefinition they have imposed on themselves. This should not be surprising. Cynicism is wild. It seldom promises evenhandedness the way liberalism, market ideologies, or humanism does. There is no guarantee that each candidate will be equally cynical, at the same time, for a similar duration. The cynical candidates, to make matters better for their side, exploit that fact, crying out when they think they might gain advantage from an appeal to resentment. Thus "nattering nabobs" enters our vocabulary, and we get "annoy the media" bumper stickers in our neighborhood.

The cynic just doesn't care. About anything, but especially about the journalists' objectivity and fairness problem. It is never the cynic's job to make life easier for journalists. Their problem is the cynic's opportunity.

Chapter 10

The Uses of Backlash

Applied Cynicism 101

> You cannot be president of the United States if you
> don't have faith. Remember Lincoln, going to his knees
> in times of trial and the Civil War and all that stuff.
> You can't be. And we are blessed. So don't feel sorry
> for — don't cry for me, Argentina.
>
> George Bush

In the months following Vice President Dan Quayle's 1992 attack
on the television character Murphy Brown, Quayle tried to distance himself from the controversy, suggesting that overeager
media had fastened on a trivial aside from a single campaign speech.
But his distancing was evidently strategic. For Quayle's staff, the
conservative "family values" issue had been moved up, and their
hope was that the VP's visibility would quiet rumors that Bush
was considering dumping him from the ticket.

The day after Quayle's speech, the *New York Times* gave his remarks serious coverage, complete with a photo and excerpts from
the speech. The page one article had the look of a well-spun event,
aided by sources who helped point out the significance of the speech
to any journalist who might have missed it. This was no side comment at a regular stump speech. As the *Times* reported, Quayle
delivered "the sort of tub-thumping message that conservatives,

including some of the Vice President's supporters, contend is lacking from Mr. Bush's oratory."[1]

The entire speech, not a throwaway paragraph as Quayle later claimed, involved the culpability of poor family values in creating the conditions that produced the Los Angeles riots that had occurred just a few weeks before. While he said he could "understand how people were shocked and outraged by the verdict in the Rodney King trial," his explanation had nothing to do with police work, criminal-justice system machinations that moved the trial to Simi Valley, or even Rodney King. "I believe the lawless social anarchy which we saw is directly related to the breakdown of family structure, personal responsibility and social order in too many areas of our society."

Given that context, it is clear that Quayle attacked Murphy Brown as a convenient foil for the target he actually had in mind, namely African American culture. When Bush visited Los Angeles two weeks earlier, he also had criticized "wanton lawlessness" (presumably the rioters', not the police's). But Bush had painted a far more evenhanded context: "We are embarrassed by interracial violence and prejudice. We are ashamed. We should take nothing but sorrow out of all of that and do our level best to see that it's eliminated from the American dream."[2] Never mind his suggestion that the American dream contains violence and prejudice. Quayle had a sharper correction in mind.

By attacking television, Quayle could have his right-wing response to the riots without focusing directly on the blacks and Hispanics whose presence was so visible in the burning and looting. The initial *Times* story reported that Quayle "called for 'social sanctions' against women who bear children out of marriage 'irresponsibly' and at one point even lashed out against a popular television program, 'Murphy Brown,' in which the title character, a single woman played by Candice Bergen, bears a child." Quayle's line was, "It doesn't help matters when prime-time TV has Murphy Brown — a character who supposedly epitomizes today's intelligent, highly paid, professional woman — mocking the importance of fathers, by bearing a child alone, and calling it just another 'life choice.'"

One reason this story stirred up such a furor is that Quayle's targets responded quickly and accurately. In the very first *Times* article reporting his remarks, the TV show's creator and producer,

Diane English, fired back: "If the Vice President thinks it's disgraceful for an unmarried woman to bear a child, and if he believes that a woman cannot adequately raise a child without a father, then he'd better make sure abortion remains safe and legal." English's refusal to be quiet or even deferential in the wake of the vice president's attack seemed to frame all subsequent discussions. Usually, backlash draws attention away from itself, letting indirect codes and subtexts carry the political weight. This time, the backlash itself became a significant part of the story.

The *Times*' page one treatment emphasized the implicit differences between Bush and Quayle on this issue but revealed a host of incongruities along the way. Bush's spokesman, Marlin Fitzwater, "heartily endorsed" Quayle's remarks early in the day, when he said, "The glorification of the life of an unwed mother does not do good service to most unwed mothers who are not highly paid, glamorous anchorwomen," as is Bergen's character on the show. Nobody seems to have asked him whether Quayle's attack on their character would "do good service" to these women.

Fitzwater then "returned minutes later to pacify the 38 million people — some of whom vote — who saw the fictional Ms. Brown deliver a baby boy on the show's season finale [earlier that week]." But Fitzwater later declared Candice Bergen to be his "personal favorite," adding, "I'm willing to meet with her any time, any place to discuss this." He also got his line straighter on unwed mothers, noting that the show's plot exhibited "pro-life values which we think are good." Quayle also joined in, confirming that he has "the greatest respect for single mothers. They are true heroes."[3] This seemed to signal a major shift from the previous day, when they were blamed for the LA riots.

In a day's time, the symbol, Murphy Brown, had spun completely away from the social breakdown it supposedly symbolized. Quayle soon tried again to keep his issue alive without taking on a popular TV show. Borrowing a favored feminist slogan, he said, "Hollywood doesn't get it. Abortion is not the reason we have a poverty of values gripping our inner cities."[4] That statement is sufficiently nonsensical that it should probably be read as evidence of the pressure the whole episode was causing.

For his part, Bush reacted by making jokes about how a crazy media was once again focusing on side issues. Appearing at a joint press event with Canadian prime minister Brian Mulroney, Bush told his visitor (who the *Times* thought "looked bewildered"), "I told you what the issue was. You thought I was kidding." Bush was no doubt trying to distance himself from Dan Quayle's antifeminist crusade, knowing that the abortion issue could not help Republicans in 1992. Bush's inability to neutralize women's rights persisted through the campaign, especially in the staging of the Republican convention, which featured a prime-time speech by challenger Pat Buchanan declaring a new offensive in the culture wars.

Quayle's political opponents, and comedians everywhere, treated this as another of the misstatements that seemed to characterize his attempts to do ideology. (A few weeks later, his place on the Republican ticket safe, in part because of Murphy Brown, Quayle helped the comedians again by assertively and plainly misspelling the word *potato*.) But ridiculing Quayle no doubt veiled ideological disagreement, just as Quayle had probably intended to find a code that would allow him to stake claim to an issue that would appeal to his party's right wing. Quayle wanted to find a cynical sequel to the Willie Horton episode that had been so useful four years before, this time to cover the Los Angeles riots, an event for which he really had no explanation, at least none that was direct enough to work politically. Perhaps Murphy Brown could be enlisted for the 1992 campaign.

As old and familiar as American political resentment is, opportunities to wage it as a tactic proliferate in the television age, confirming and reinforcing our culture's cynical turn. The discovery and development of the backlash strategy is a crucial landmark of our cynical age. Voters must be presented with understandable codes. Television possesses a characteristic voice, and that voice is dug deeply into its way of representing the news. The Murphy Brown affair demonstrates precisely where many of those codes will be found. Both the opportunity for and the desirability of backlash politics expand as rapidly as TV's influence expands and the society's turn toward cynicism consolidates.

The Murphy Brown case also illustrates that backlash needs to be understood as an aspect of politics rather than a characteristic of voter psychology. No budding movement against Candice Bergen preceded the Brown affair. This was an overt strategy, a response to urban rioting that Quayle and Bush had no intention of solving, both because of the expense and because a demonized black urban class was just too useful for their political position. The reasoned and reasonable remedy talk so beloved by communitarian believers finds its double. Enjoinders to be guilty (about distant riots) or to claim responsibility or to properly understand sociological relationships meet an opportunity too attractive to leave alone; the preachers' messages can be turned against them.

Quayle's choice of Murphy Brown is intriguing. At one level, her individualism fulfills several American dreams, including independence, professionalism, sexuality, and gender equality. But the combination can cut two ways. Feminist claims that the personal is political meet a backlash response. The fact that Brown is a fictional character helps. What has changed in the TV era is the ease with which backlash can be applied across the whole landscape. Resentment goes better with television. Distance is its advantage, not its handicap. The codes are clearer and better known than they would be for most real persons. What complications exist in the Brown character are useful, too. Her financial independence provides a target for resentful attacks on affirmative action, a genre of coded politics used two years earlier by Jesse Helms in a hotly contested Senate race. Murphy Brown is what conservatives call a "limousine liberal," a person of privilege whose liberalism they suspect because it is not grounded in personal economic need. But the Brown character seldom seems terribly guilt ridden, at least in any debilitating way. In this country's inverted class politics (with the left blocked from overt class claims, to the advantage of the right, which turns such claims on a resentful axis), it has long been good *conservative* strategy to play the class card.

It is also interesting that Quayle's initiative seems to have failed, at least in the short run, except in its narrowest goal of ensuring Quayle's renomination. The immediate response by the show's producer focused on abortion rights, linking women's rights and independence in a way familiar to feminists but unacknowledged by their opponents. The disarray of the Republican spin efforts, the next day, showed that they had little idea how to work this part of the political landscape. No doubt, the link to women's issues helped doom the Quayle initiative. The ghost of Anita Hill hovered over this entire election season. Even backlash could not drive it away.

The fact that Quayle's charges immediately engaged left-oriented elements of the media is also part of the reason it did not work. Although much of the American left has studiously avoided learning how to use the media, a small contingent at work in the various culture industries (several of whom were prominent in the Clinton campaign) are much more savvy about the play of codes and shifting symbols.

The 1992 election can be understood as a laboratory experiment in defeating resentments. Bush and Quayle understood the potential for backlash politics. Perot's challenge rode a more generalized resentment than any established party could mount. (And the large percentage of votes he finally amassed shows how narrow the victory over cynicism was.) But in general, Republicans found it temporarily difficult to victimize their usual, familiar black suspects, in the wake of the Los Angeles riots and the media's angry memories of the 1988 Willie Horton ads. There were still women to resent, but the lingering ill will generated by the Thomas-Hill hearings turned out to be far more important than the Gulf War that Republicans hoped would drive the 1992 election. George Bush's loss in 1992 by no means revealed ebbing cynicism or backlash. But his awkwardness at implementing the backlash strategy helps us see his strategy as a distinctive political event, whose emergence keynotes our cynical age.

Susan Faludi exhaustively tracked one set of backlash strategies, those directed against women, in her widely read 1991 book.[5] As she details with an abundance of examples and cases, when resentful or opportunistic appeals are directed against the victims of social arrangements and institutions, the name for the strategy is backlash. Every threatened cynic-in-power knows how to "turn the tables" on a challenge: Say it is going too fast, injuring too many weak egos, inviting backlash.

In one narrow sense, backlash strategies build on a kernel of truth. A new form of activist has emerged, a category that was almost invisible before the late 1960s. There is a strong, utterly attractive, articulate, and revolutionary new person around — the independent woman. Many men and women both fear and desire her. Some women who want to be this person fear her, too — that is the character of freedom. This desire is a key. Our social theories, liberal in general, do not easily incorporate a strong conceptualization of desire. Desire breaks out of liberal categories, displacing liberal calculation and reserve with desire's own needful calculus, which is an entirely different thing. Desire gone awry produces its dark variants, backlash and resentment.

As an effect of cynical politics, backlash shares all the problems that apply to cynicism. Although Faludi stayed well away from theorizing, much of her book confirmed this combination of desire and backlash. She uncovers the hidden, complex motives behind the vehement statements directed against the new woman by people who are made stronger by their attacks on someone with no more (and often much less) institutional authority than themselves. Consider Conservative Caucus founder Howard Phillips: "We must prove our ability to get revenge on people who go against us."[6] Or Jerry Falwell of the Moral Majority, accusing feminists of launching a "satanic attack on the home.... With all my heart, I want to bury the Equal Rights Amendment once and for all in a deep, dark grave."[7]

Falwell received great attention throughout the 1980s. From the level of that attention, we might expect that he was the sort of centrist, "responsible" voice that we so often hear is the only type of voice allowed on the national scene. But as Faludi shows, Falwell was a wild, wiggy analyst of conspiracy, resentment, and backlash. Faludi characterizes Falwell's *Listen, America!* as an outline of a "global feminist conspiracy — a sinister female web of front organizations spreading its tentacles across the free world."[8]

Even women were enlisted to this backlash project. Some of Faludi's best material covered Connie Marshner, a high-profile figure throughout the 1980s, in part due to her resentful op-ed pieces on National Public Radio. As Faludi showed, consistency is not required of our backlash masters. Marshner lived the busy, political, often independent life of a feminist, if in service to the antifeminists. Continuing to work while pregnant (and then through the youngest years of her first three children's lives), Marshner sometimes lived apart from her husband in order to continue her career. She gratefully received day-care help from her boss, the well-known conservative Paul Wyrich.

Marshner remained personally disinterested in the housewife role she had so vividly advocated. "I'm no good with little kids and I'm a terrible housekeeper," she told Faludi in an interview. "To me, it's very unrewarding, unfulfilling work. By contrast, what I'm doing in Washington has real tangible rewards, accomplishments." Faludi notes that "neither she nor her husband believes this makes her a 'macho feminist,'" the phrase she had used so acidly against other women who dared to pursue careers (246). Marshner knew that family commitments carry with them a set of choices and self-examinations. But she did not say that publicly at the time when she was saying so much, so publicly.

Marshner finally disappeared from the scene, returning home to the housewife role she thought so confining when she gave birth to her fourth baby. She then began a publishing enterprise whose first book was her screed against day care. Faludi thought her notably quick, in an interview, to criticize mothers (like herself, until just months earlier) who continued to work after a child was born. This is opportunistic ideology, the kind of talk that doesn't even persist through the rest of the speaker's own day. It may have seemed like standard political talk, batting values and policies back and forth. Marshner got plenty of airtime from NPR to criticize people who lived much more consistent lives. This was not politics as usual. It was a cynical and strategic application of backlash, and it worked.

As Faludi explained, the backlashers developed their tactics throughout the 1980s, taking their dark practice out to the public and honing their execution. Reagan-era conservatives had converted backlash into a set of tactics within a strategic context. Find female intermediaries (like Marshner, Phyllis Schlafly, whom Faludi also cited, and Mona Charen, who has assumed their duties on talk shows and in a widely syndicated column). Have them launch their diversionary attacks, cynically fending off charges that the backlash strategy is what it obviously is — antiwoman.

The backlash tactic then is grafted onto an economic policy. Most of us remember George Gilder as a markets analyst or a new-technology guru, but Faludi reminded us how much backlash venom filled the big-selling *Wealth and Poverty,* which brought him to public attention. In that book Gilder wrote that "the man has the gradually sinking feeling that his role as provider, the definitive male activity from the primal days of the hunt through the industrial revolution and on into modern life, has been largely seized from him."[9] Never mind that the connection is pure wig complaint. Obvious cantankerousness only confirms a wig's conspiracy—and promotes his backlash.

The next tactical graft is a classical basis, a root system set in an honored antiquity. Enter the Professor Emeritus of Resentment, Allan Bloom: "The latest enemy of the vitality of the classic texts is feminism."[10] This language, the "enemy of vitality" complaint, is obviously bruised male ego stuff, hardly the sort of erudition supposedly required of a successful public intellectual like Bloom. The bashing of new intellectual movements (including multiculturalism and postmodernism) by such authors as Bloom, Dinesh D'Souza, and Camille Paglia is also an outbreak of backlash. Each presents some trappings of serious scholarship, but their intended audience, drummed up by supportive media conservatives, is more interested in partisan attack on the scholarly project. Better targeted, funded, and promoted than the old familiar American anti-intellectualism, this new genre is a tactical wing of the backlash.

Then, the backlash tactical workbook seeks to neutralize some familiar opposition voices, frightening them into joining the backlash diagnosis. Aware of this tactic, Faludi criticized some important feminists rather sharply, especially Betty Friedan: "By accepting the New Right language, Friedan has walked right into the New Right's 'pro-family' semantics trap. She is reacting to the backlash rather than setting her own agenda, even referring to the women's movement now as 'the feminist reaction'" (325). This is a tricky path. Solidarity is one possible response to backlash. But, as Faludi's analysis of Friedan shows, a sense of politics, the field in which backlash traps are encountered and must be answered, is even more important.

This ensemble of backlash tactics forced feminists into hard political choices. In particular, feminists had to reconsider gender solidarity, or the idea that there is something essential about women as women that could be the basis for political action. As appealing as such a stance is politically, it was too susceptible to backlash tactics. Although *essentialism* is too technical a term for Faludi, she knows the danger of the pop psychology elevation of "essential" female characteristics. Carol Gilligan, a star with liberals and communitarians, was far too unprotected from appropriation by the backlash. Gilligan corrected herself on this point, but her protests appeared in a small-circulation journal, while her much more widely read book made all sorts of lazy "natural woman" arguments possible.

Faludi's analysis of backlash tactics helps illuminate several recent political events. Michael Dukakis's 1988 campaign collapsed in the face of the backlash. Dukakis ran away from then-unknown Texas state official Ann Richards, whose playful assault on "poor George" Bush had genuinely scared Republican campaign operatives, as was finally reported long after the campaign. Dukakis was tricked into accepting the Republican spin, that Richards's speech was divisive, when in fact she was responding to divisive, resentful wig assaults by Reagan-Bush Republicans. Presented with opportunities to expose "Bush's family-values façade," Dukakis squandered a big gender gap, a gap that Bush's crew knew they had to close. In one case, a Dukakis aide who "dared to comment in public about the possible hypocrisy lurking behind Bush's family-man show, was fired for her frankness — and a nervous Dukakis hastily apologized to Bush for his aide's indiscretion" (275). The conservative commentator Kevin Phillips published a widely read book arguing that a similar failure to respond to backlash strategies had also typified Dukakis's handling of economic issues.[11]

By contrast, Bill Clinton's 1992 campaign responded to backlash tactics with overt appeals to gays and lesbians, and with Hillary Clinton's visibility. The president's "in your face" approach worked where Dukakis's accommodation had failed. There was one moment when the real dynamics of this campaign — and the real way to confront backlash — came through clearly. In the second televised debate, Bush was asked when the country would have a woman or a black on a winning ticket. Bush went on about his wife Barbara's popularity, admitting that it was too late to put her on the ticket. While walking back to his seat, he mumbled a wish that women would lose in their bids for the Senate. That made sense. Most of the women candidates that year were Democrats. But Bush's offhand remark defeated his statement's sense. He'd been floored again.

Bush was unnerved. After the debate, he asked, "Who got me into that?" The answer might well have been Jesse Helms, Jerry Falwell, media adviser Roger Ailes, and the rest. Bush had made backlash his strategy, as had Reagan and hundreds of lesser candidates. They became so bold with this strategy that the Democrats could (finally, with great trepidation) just push them over. Clinton's win wasn't just good marketing; it was more specific than that. He did just enough "in your face" to win...barely. That is at least one element of a successful response to backlash, as Faludi argued briefly in her book's conclusion. Democrats did not lose for twelve years because they were too bold, and they did not win in 1992 because they tamed their message. Clinton's courting of the conservative Democratic Leadership Council (DLC) had been a good way to run until the election started. Once on, the election was won with sometimes daring attention to potential constituencies, even if those constituents had been subjects of Republican backlash.

Obviously, the victory did not last long. From the very first days of Clinton's administration, conservatives flung the backlash device (always more comfortable in opposition mode) against the new crowd. The success of the 1992 campaign—a shock to Republicans, who thought they deserved to own the White House—set up a withering round of backlash. In particular, Hillary Rodham Clinton quickly became the lightning rod. This does not indicate that the Clinton campaign tactics were wrong, however. It does show how adroit backlash has become, how uninhibited it is, how quick it is to locate new targets and tactics, and how resistant it is to repudiation. The success of the anti-Clinton campaign suggests we have much to learn about how to oppose and contain backlash.

Subsequent events in the Clinton presidency confirm this analysis. Backlash attacks persisted. Whereas a campaign provides a finite arena for backlash, a presidency offers a continuous opportunity. Clinton's opponents deployed backlash to set up surprisingly massive Republican wins in the 1994 election. But after that, Clinton's partisans became somewhat more adroit at countering the backlash with a double-sided strategy. Clinton used Republican political adviser Dick Morris to move to the right, but he also used opportunities presented by Gingrich, then Speaker of the House and leader of the revolution, to shore up a Democratic base. In the absence of a Republican president or an active presidential campaign, backlash became somewhat harder to sustain.

Or so it seemed, before Special Prosecutor Kenneth Starr and his many allies on the right, including those who had sponsored

Paula Jones's complaint, went into high gear. When Clinton's poll results started to diverge from the daily news trajectory on the Jones lawsuit and then on the Monica Lewinsky story, this was widely reported as evidence of a resigned cynicism among the populace. Poorly attuned to backlash, if also delighted for the great stories issuing forth from the scandal, media commentators missed the obvious. If the only issue is Clinton's alleged personal behavior, the diagnosis of voter cynicism makes sense. But there is a missing or at least unnamed third element—backlash and citizen reaction to it. If the backlash strategy becomes an issue, the debate is back onto political grounds, rather than merely on the perilous grounds of assessing character via televised hearing, grand-jury leaks, and speculation by the commentariat.

Conservative editorialists bemoaned the loss of civility. George Will, in particular, seemed particularly frustrated. The problem with "having vulgarians like the Clintons" in power is that they "further coarsen American life."[12] Evidently, it is not so coarsening to have vulgarians on the editorial page of the *Washington Post*. Will compared Clinton "and his hirelings (who must really need the money)" to the queen in *Through the Looking-Glass*, who exclaimed, "Why, sometimes I've believed as many as six impossible things before breakfast." He then compared Clinton's remarks on the case to "Alger Hiss's denial about espionage, Nixon's about Watergate, O. J. Simpson's about murder." One could either take this as partisan frustration or as evidence that Will knows, at some level, that the number has been called on the backlash strategy and that a new round of right-wing triumphs will first require that the fire of resentment be rekindled.

On the continued public support for Clinton, Will said, "Watergate divided Americans between those who believed Nixon guilty of abuses and of lying about them, and those who did not. However, no significant group said he was guilty but that they did not care because they approved of, say, his China policy." The other possibility—that the public had, with some prompting, discovered the partisan potential in the prosecutor's job description (at the same time that prosecutors had become much more partisan in their service to backlash)—did not seem to occur to the astonished Will. And given the relatively apolitical play the Clinton scandals often received, nobody was forcing Will to ruminate over

whether this was a case of his vulgarians against theirs. To equate
Clinton with Nixon seems quite a leap, but Will's column didn't
even stir the dust. Cynical about Clinton, and about everyone else
in this sordid scene, Will's readership may have just assumed that
such bomb lobbing was in his job description.

The effect of James Carville's campaign against Kenneth Starr
was to raise the backlash issue. The public was cynical, all right,
but there was some question what the targets of its cynicism were.
At this writing, the story of the so-called Clinton scandal is still itself being written. Further revelations could change its trajectory
completely. But some implications of the matter are emerging, even
if these implications have not yet been widely understood. Surely,
the scandal story shows how weak a solution civility is, given the
enormity of stakes and the availability of the backlash strategy. But
there are other responses. Carville's contentious attack on Starr is
a start. A better response might be formulated if we knew what
backlash was and treated it as the significant element it has become.

For her part, Faludi proposed forthright and political challenges
against backlash. The overt "Me Decade" individualism of the 1980s
and its attendant nervousness about politics only set up new opportunities for backlash. Faludi suggested a more explicitly political response: "Under the '80s backlash, in the very few instances
where women have tried . . . a vocal and unapologetic strategy, they
have managed to transform the public climate, set the agenda on
their own terms, and change the minds of many individual men."[13]
She might well have added that backlash is durable. It revives itself and recovers from setbacks. There is no silver bullet. The survival of feminist politics at all may properly be seen as an accomplishment from the angle of backlash analysis: class politics did
not fare as well.

Faludi's accomplishment was to identify backlash as a genre of
public speech, a category of strategic interaction between powerful cynics and their wig sidekicks. Backlash is not response and
argument but fear and hate, often disguised as response and argument. It does not announce what it is. Backlash reveals itself in its
dark desire to punish, to get revenge. But neither is backlash entirely
a function of personality and authoritarianism. It acts in league
with a media that thrives on contentious sound bites and provides

more opportunities to hone and repeat coded backlash appeals. And like the cynicism at its core, backlash brings with it extraordinary defenses against successful response.

Backlash cuts through the resistance to politics built into American politics, or more precisely, backlash puts that resistance to use, cynically. As broad and simple as it seems, however, backlash provides a sophisticated solution. It neutralizes calls to unity and solidarity, substituting partisanship instead. But backlash partisanship is a ruse, since it appeals to a tradition of fair competition but allows only one partisan side into the arena. Although backlash must be struggled against, it carries with it a defense against that struggle, since it provides a way to diminish potential opponents. There is more to understand, however, about the persistence of backlash in our cynical era. There is the more specific basis of backlash, namely, resentment.

Chapter 11

The Age of Resentment

Advanced Applied Cynicism

> Nietzsche does not repudiate reason, but he does deploy a rhetorical style designed to bring the self up against the limits of reason. Reason is necessary to life, but it is also insufficient to it.
>
> William E. Connolly, *Political Theory and Modernity*

The one area where the social psychology of cynicism turns out to be central to this analysis is, in turn, the one area that many of the more public laments over cynicism tend to avoid. Political life in a democratic state is plenty complicated, even if we stay with the arid conceptual vision of that political condition that has long been popular in the mainstream. Groups, ideals, programs, and opportunism are enough factors to make for a very open system, as well as a system that can be dominated by cultural norms, making it seem remarkably closed. Mix in the elements of Faludi's backlash, and you have a very difficult grid that gets more complex.

But there is also a depth to the backlash strategy discussed in chapter 10. When politics turn toward resentment, the other elements can be inverted or skewed. Instead of functioning as a corrective to deal making, appeals to values can twist out of shape, providing an opportunity for resistance or even hatred. Resentment closely relates to cynicism; in some ways, resentment functions as a cynical strategy.

In his 1968 campaign and then in the presidency, Richard Nixon honed his appeal to the resentful impulses of the "silent majority" he identified and then deployed as both defense mechanism and justification for a range of policies and actions. Reading words written by White House speechwriter Pat Buchanan, Vice President Spiro Agnew opened another front against elites who could be both ally in power and resented force that justified the emerging Republican conservatism.

During the 1968 campaign, Kevin Phillips focused the attention of the New Right he was helping to create. Sure, the military was still important to them, as was a smaller government. But the New Right was really about "domestic social issues." The meaning of that bland phrase was clear to everyone, even if the "law and order" code that carried the message was still indirect. E. J. Dionne explained what these codes meant: "What [Phillips] really had in mind were domestic social resentments. He listed these as 'public anger over busing, welfare spending, environmental extremism, soft criminology, media bias and power, warped education, twisted textbooks, racial quotas, various guidelines and an ever-expanding bureaucracy.' "[1]

When contemporary conservatism hit its stride in the 1980s and 1990s, it did so by adopting a populist, even playful tone and rhythm. Reagan's "aw shucks" demeanor, arrayed against his critics' high seriousness, was the first break. The movement that Nixon started found a way to carry on without Nixon's disabling paranoia. With Reagan, the impulse to resentment gained a new and effective tone. For a while, the newly empowered ruling cynics' social spending continued unabated (and they even increased it, if the domestic elements of the massive military budget are included) while they simultaneously honed the tools of social resentment. As Dionne explained, support for some kinds of government persisted throughout the 1980s, notably for education, the environment, medical insurance, the elderly, and day care.

Reagan could deliver liberal social benefits (especially "entitlements," like Social Security) while simultaneously giving resentment its seemingly kind, small-town, "father knows best" tone. The double movement to build the coalition with well-funded programs and to deny any public good became the home turf for conservative politics. Soon the right began to promote the "political correctness" critique, a sustained taunt at the self-absorbed seriousness of the liberals and the ideological left. George Bush partook of the opportunity, deploying Willie Horton to get elected, if only once. Rush Limbaugh emerged as this song's lead singer, adopting all sorts of showbiz gambits to poke fun at a presumably powerful left. Whether the left was as powerful as Limbaugh thought they were, there is no doubt that Reagan had confounded his adversaries, who criticized him vehemently and were perplexed by his continued popularity.

When the Reagan-Bush era ended, a new game emerged with stunning speed. The first sign of this new game was the bitter and sustained bashing that Bill Clinton encountered as president. Having suffered the sustained and often sarcastic assaults on Reagan, conservatives came to the role of opposition with undeniable vigor. Hate radio emerged as a social phenomenon and quickly went far beyond the partisanship of Limbaugh. But Rush expanded, too; he finally got on the air in the D.C. market, then gained a nationally syndicated television show with the help of the Republican insider turned TV producer Roger Ailes. Jerry Falwell came back to life, marketing *The Clinton Chronicles*, a bizarre videotape of snide charges and conspiracy theory.

On the more distant fringe, militias formed and began a stunning rise to popularity and visibility, especially in the rural West. It soon became evident that the potential constituency of the militias was remarkable. Kenneth S. Stern dates the emergence of the militias from the February 1994 founding of the Militia of Montana by John Trochmann, who was explicitly reacting to the deadly raid on Randy Weaver's cabin in Ruby Ridge, Idaho. Carolyn Trochmann, John's wife, had delivered supplies to that cabin — and had assisted when Vicki Weaver gave birth during the period when the Weavers were holed up to avoid federal prosecution of Randy for breaking gun laws.[2]

In 1994, intense militia organizing meetings sometimes drew hundreds, even in sparsely populated rural towns.[3] Observers said that the militia movement was growing more quickly than any previous radical-right movement had ever grown.[4] Eventually, the militia movement could count well over two hundred militias and support groups in thirty-six states.[5] Shortly after the 1995 Oklahoma City bombing of a federal building, an ABC/*Washington Post* poll found that 13 percent of Americans supported private armed militias, 12 percent said they were afraid of the government, and 9 percent said violence against the government could be justified. Six percent called the government their "enemy." Nearly apologizing for these stunning numbers, the pollsters took care to explain in their summary of the results that "six percent, while a small share, is 11 million adults."[6]

The antigovernment, anti-Brady (gun control) Law, and generally antileft (feminist, environmentalist, or multicultural) message of the militia had obviously found a sizable audience. Poll numbers such as these were unimaginable, even years into the mass movement organizing of the left in the 1960s and 1970s. The numbers are even more remarkable given that the poll was taken after the possible connection between the militias and the Oklahoma City bombing had been established. It is difficult to imagine that any radicals in American history, having been linked to domestic terror so vividly, could have enjoyed such massive support. Congress felt compelled to hold hearings on two of the militia's favorite topics, federal law enforcement's excesses at Waco and Ruby Ridge. Mainstream conservatives struggled to decide what to do about this new political form.

Militia organizing focused on Waco and Ruby Ridge but also developed a larger analysis. The Militia of Montana routinely warned of international conspiracies featuring the United Nations' presumed effort to enforce a new world order. Militia videos warned of black surveillance helicopters and storage of old Soviet army equipment in Louisiana. The antigovernment litany opposed environmental laws, affirmative action, and above all, gun control. Most of the groups proposed greater states' rights, thus forging connections with a rightist antienvironmentalist movement that was flourishing in the West under the umbrella rhetoric of "wise use."

It is not too much to say that in the rural Northwest, the mid-1990s became a Me Decade for disillusioned working-class white guys. Given the impossibility of consumption as a reaction to their dread, their self-fulfillment took a different tack. The popularity of Rush Limbaugh on AM radio displaced that of the increasingly vapid FM music stations or even the omnipresent country-western stations. Camouflage replaced plain flannel as the fabric of choice for men's apparel. More gun racks on old pickup trucks carried guns instead of fishing poles or carpenter's levels. Guns had always been popular in the rural West, but the gun shows now featured more exotic models, some of them clearly not intended for the traditional deer hunt. Resentful and racist propaganda took its place on the tables at those gun shows, too. The cultural movement of resentment found a form. And its unifying theme was a broad, often well-articulated rage.

Eventually, the shock over the Oklahoma City bombing registered with the public and left the militia movement diminished. By the time the McVeigh trial concluded in 1997, the militias had been ignored more than they had been refuted or dismantled. Limited by Judge Stephen Matsch, McVeigh's defense lawyers were unable to defend their client by casting aspersions on the larger militia movement, the tactic Morris Dees had earlier predicted would be used. Indeed, the media's silence on the militias has been odd, especially in comparison to the continued bashing of the left over its various excesses. The sixties era University of Wisconsin math building explosion and the Boston Brinks robbery linger forever as instances of left transgression. The Oklahoma City Murrah Building explosion, hugely more deadly and just as political an act, has been transformed into a story about its victims' suffering. This in itself says something about the uneven effects of resentment.

Of course, resentment did not suddenly emerge for the first time in the early 1990s. The resentful turn has a long history in American politics. In the same moment that the sons and daughters of the Enlightenment sense distress and begin the search for solutions, plans, and policies, some of their neighbors turn to another path, beginning a resentful hunt for enemies, villains, and scapegoats. The same cues and signals can trigger either response.

Resentment is a control device, but it is also a condition and a response. Like cynicism, resentment sits at a special turning point of political life. Critique, as understood by Marx and every other theorist of the Enlightenment, was supposed to transform its audience into critics, problem solvers, and solution seekers. Those *lumpen* elements more susceptible to resentment, the poor and uneducated, for example, were simply a sideshow for Marx. No world-changing analysis would bubble up from the most forlorn of political groups. The mainstream vaguely hoped for education, higher voting percentages, and better public behavior, but it, too, largely wrote off those elements that did not share the basic temperament of public life. These modernists — left, right, or center — understood that a resentful mass had to be relegated to the margins.

The philosopher Friedrich Nietzsche had long ago anticipated these attempts. He explained that resentment had other dimensions. Facing suffering and transient life, people learn to resent their fate. And they learn that this works even better if they can identify some agent who has caused their suffering, and who can be bitterly targeted. Resentment is at least potentially a political event, since its parameters — agency, decision, and action — match those of public life. A discernible political effect begins to emerge. The rationality that believer communitarians stress as a solution to public problems can discover more than one kind of resistance. Rational discourse can try to defeat self-interest and unreason. But it can also, perhaps at the same time, serve as resentment's code — its Trojan horse. Routine elements of political dialogue seem to change sides, turning against their own stability. The target of this reversal is the role that reason plays, as political theorist William E. Connolly notes in the epigraph to this chapter.

Resentment persists because people continue to attribute some of their suffering to public events in ways incompletely covered by reason or rationality. In Nietzsche's terms, "Every sufferer instinctively seeks a cause for his suffering, more exactly an agent; still more specifically a guilty agent who is susceptible to suffering."[7] Both the human condition in general and specific sufferers resist rational solution. For resenters, the pursuit of remedies comes to look like a self-destructive sucker's game. Recalcitrant sufferers avoid extending respect to fellow victims or obedience to those perceived as unjustly powerful. Any public project, any political movement or reform attempt, can encounter a segment of the public already equipped to fend off its supposedly benign efforts.

Resenters deploy their defenses in a savvy way. They resent the injustices that arise from the messy activity of governing. This double movement against death and against injustice generates stability for resentment, which might otherwise be volatile and hence subject to restraint. Each component of contemporary resentment blocks attempts to deal with its other components.[8] This is what intellectuals sometimes call an overdetermined relationship. The double bind is functioning, or an effect is twice-produced, over-loaded with causal energies.

Resentment is more stable and durable than fear. Resentment is the form fear takes when it's in the game for the long run, translating an impulse into a strategy sophisticated enough to respond to many of the countermoves its targets attempt. Resentment is a matter of life prospects, as abstract as ideology. Well applied, resentful attack can be phrased so as to escape any reality test. The habit of conspiracy theorists to think in terms that cannot be refuted is a quirk neither of psychology nor of logical ability. It reflects a pattern or culture, and resentment captures that pattern in conceptual terms: "That's just what they want you to think!"

Once unleashed, resentment burrows into the resenter's self, taking over other possible reactions to the world. Connolly reminds us how easily Nietzsche can be expanded on this point: "The priests (including later judges, therapists, teachers, confidants, spouses) deflect resentment against suffering in life back into the self, manufacturing it into energy 'for the purpose of self-discipline, self-surveillance, and self-overcoming.'"[9] Resentment turns sincerity inside out, taking advantage of our presumption that leaders are sincere but also using doubts about an adversary's sincerity as a signal to the resentful ones. Every modern political argument relies on a causal link: despair leads to diagnosis leads to progress. Nietzsche insists we remember that every such link can be misappropriated.

Powerful cynics love the resentful possibility. Employing resentment, the cynic can manipulate resentful constituents, cutting through the resistance to politics to generate an advantage. The powerful cynic thus reaches out, creating accomplices. This is a more efficient way to proceed than the lies or violent acts that comprise "dirty politics" as we usually know it; the cynic's opponents are well prepared to detect those gambits. Perhaps having once believed in this arrangement, cynics are well situated to manipulate those who still believe.

The cynic-in-power can be a very attractive character, retaining some of the vitality picked up during those youthful experiments with idealistic belief. They are recruiters, and resentment is what they can offer. These cynics thus have legions of collaborators—

powerless, resentful haters who will clear the space for the powerful cynics' work. Receiving none of the recognition and glory that their leaders achieve, there are millions of them. They are the apologists for power, equipped to provide a steady, Main Street drumbeat that explains how tough it is to rule amid all those special interests. They resist with unbelievable energy when gender, race, or class appears as a political issue. No longer believing their own voice, they have thrown their lot in with those who rule.

In contemporary America, the varieties of cynicism continually cross paths, refusing to stay neatly sorted. Sometimes powerful cynics try to mobilize wig cynics for temporary benefit. But the wigs, too, have been watching television, studying it for their own purposes. They learn some of the routines of the powerful. And even if the wigs are seldom capable of the polish accomplished by powerful cynics, what they have is sometimes enough — to confuse, to reveal.

Barely two months after the Oklahoma City bombing, Senator Arlen Specter (R-Penn.) convened an extraordinary congressional hearing.[10] The Senate Judiciary Subcommittee on Terrorism, Technology, and Government Information entertained testimony by five leaders of the militia movement. Included in the group were officers of state organizations that news reports had tied to Timothy McVeigh, the man then charged with (and two years later, convicted of) what observers called the worst single terrorist action in American history.

John Trochmann began his statement to the committee by calling the militia movement "a giant neighborhood watch" and entering a copy of the U.S. Constitution into the committee's record. (Another panelist, James Johnson, an Ohio militia leader and one of few militia leaders who are African American, called the militia "the civil rights movement of the nineties.") Trochmann's statement began with mainstream (if overstated) claims: "The high office of the Presidency has been turned into a position of dictatorial oppression through the abusive use of executive orders and directives, thus leaving Congress stripped of its authority. When the President overrules Congress by executive order, representative government fails." But moments later, Trochmann took a different approach:

When the government defines human beings as a biological resource under the United Nations ecosystem management program, maintaining that state and local laws are barriers to the goals of federal government,... while billions of our tax dollars are forcibly sent to bail out the banking elite,... Congress wonders why the constituents get upset. When government allows our military to be ordered by foreigners under Congressional authority, then turns its tanks on citizens to murder or destroy, or directs a sniper to shoot a mother in the face while holding her infant in her arms, you bet your constituents get upset.... A nation can survive its fools, but it cannot survive treason from within.

Trochmann's statement displays the militia's resentful approach clearly enough. He asserts the identity of his position with that of the nation, a theme the professorial Ken Adams of the Michigan Militia later repeated. Although Trochmann seems to be trying to stay in the mainstream, the habit of wild charge (suggesting that the government directed "a sniper to shoot a mother in the face while she was holding her infant," as if that precise effect was intended by the FBI bureaucracy) breaks through. But the psychology of the militia leaders is less interesting than the interaction this testimony generates — an ebb and flow of discomfort as genres of public speech collide. Trochmann should have been easy prey for Specter and his colleagues. But that is not exactly how the session turned out.

In one of the hearing's more noteworthy exchanges, Senator Specter involves himself in an extended (if not entirely comprehensible) conversation with Norman Olsen, the fatigue-suited Michigan Militia spokesman:

> Specter: "Mr. Olsen, I heard you say on national television that you could understand why someone would bomb the Oklahoma City federal building. How could you say that?"

Olsen first tries to deploy the usual public dodge, claiming his remark had been taken out of context. "You, Mr. Senator, soundbited Leslie Stahl and were wrong to do so." Specter fends off that dodge and asks again, "Do you now understand why someone bombed the Oklahoma City federal building?" Olsen tries to turn the question into an occasion to criticize the FBI, also mentioning the historic force of such motives as vengeance and retribution. Ignoring Olsen's turn toward muckraking or sociology, Specter stays with it, repeating the question once again. This time, Olsen uses another dodge, suggesting that the alleged bomber was "innocent until proven guilty." Strangely enough, Specter will not let the point go:

> Specter: "The Oklahoma City federal building was bombed.... What I'm looking for is your statement about understanding why the building was bombed. You talk about vengeance and retribution.... Is there any justification whatever for the bombing?"

In response, Olsen falls back on familiar anti-Semitic code, calling Specter a "clever attorney" and raising the possibility of more than one bomber and a "conspiracy at a higher level." But Olsen then catches himself and turns the conversation to Lee Harvey Oswald, reminding Specter that he was "the single bullet theorist.... You believe that he alone did it. We don't necessarily hold to that opinion." The swirling character of contemporary conspiracy begins to assert itself, but Specter defers — "Well, if we can leave the single bullet theory for another day..." — and draws a laugh from the audience. Then he veers back to the "understanding" issue.

Olsen mentions other enduring conflicts, including that in Northern Ireland and elsewhere in the world. Although Olsen is inarticulate, he actually has managed to answer Specter's question in several ways. But the tension is too much, and he issues a charge, telling Specter, "you represent corruption and tyranny." Strangely, Specter does not even answer that charge but goes "back to your statement about retribution and violence." But Specter does not have much to say about that, lamely continuing: "I want your ideas fully exposed.... I want your ideas compared to mine and I want to let the American public judge whether you're right or I'm right." All of which begs the question of what Specter's "ideas" are. Does he deny the force of revenge in politics? Finally, the spell broken, Specter responds to Olsen's earlier charge: "I don't take lightly your comment that I represent corruption.... I want you to prove it when you say that."

Olsen then brings up the CIA, which he calls "probably the grandest conspirator behind all of this government," suggesting that "puppeteer strings of the CIA may reach even to the Senators before us." Senator Herbert Kohl then tries unsuccessfully to pin Olsen down on his charge that the government of Japan blew up the Murrah Building. Kohl then asks Militia of Montana leader Robert Fletcher about his statements on the corrupt character of high government officials, including a charge that the FBI director is a "sex pervert, child molester advocate, or Christian-hater." Fletcher denies making such a statement, suggesting it came from a book sold by the Militia. ("It's a book we carry, same as the library.") Fletcher then segues to conspiratorial charges, including claims about "hundreds of flat cars of Russian equipment all over the U.S. . . . and the Army creating civilian prisoner camps," both mainstays of the militia's New World Order diagnosis.

So far, so good. Kohl at least knows what he wants out of this hearing. He wants to let Fletcher make himself look foolish. But then Kohl, too, runs into the conspiracy spiral, when he asks Fletcher about claims that the government is using "weather tampering techniques so the New World Order can starve Americans." Fletcher turns the question around, citing Senator Claiborne Pell's statement on the matter, adding helpfully, "You might want to touch base with Senator Pell," whom Fletcher quotes as calling such technology "the greatest weapon ever created in the world."

Senator Fred Thompson then makes the issue more or less explicit. Leading James Johnson through a set of questions, Thompson concludes, "Bad laws are one thing . . . but you don't organize a militia to lower taxes. You organize a militia [to have] some military ability." Clearly, the Republican members of the committee wanted to protect their relationship with the militia constituency, which at that point they suspected was significant, while also taking the mainstream view that the militia posed a danger. This is the same impetus that likely drove Specter into his strange line of questioning with Olsen. Are militia members demons or constituents? Or is there a way to make them both?

After Adams scores a minor point by noting that militia allies in Congress had sent letters of inquiry regarding a March 1995 rumor that Attorney General Janet Reno planned to "attack militia leaders," it was Senator Diane Feinstein's turn. She asked Trochmann the standard question, whether "there are situations when you can take the law into your own hands?" Trochmann gave her a familiar self-defense answer, then changed the subject: "I am told you have a concealed weapon permit, so you I guess you probably feel the same way we do."

   Feinstein: "Well, let me put that aside. I do not have a concealed weapon permit."

   Trochmann: "Well, then you recently had one."

   Feinstein: "No I had one in the 1970s. I have not had one since then. [It was] after a terrorist incident that took place involving myself. . . . I have not had one since."

Trochmann answers that he will have to get back to his California informants, to which Feinstein gratefully patronizes, "Yes, I think you should." But the damage is already done. The line between mainstream and wig can be hard to police.

Powerful cynics have learned to love the resentful possibility. That tactic cuts through resistance to politics, changing resistance into resentment, an impulse that can be manipulated. The cynic-in-power tries to use resentment, setting citizens against each other in circles of resentful charge and countercharge. In this important sense, some of what we call cynical politics is the energetic pursuit of resentment politics, set off by the generation of conservative cynics who learned their craft from Richard Nixon.

   The politics of resentment poses a special challenge for American politics. Given the complexity of democratic systems, we invent ways of talking about politics that unify an otherwise bewildering array of possibilities. We invent, learn, and pass along to new generations stories of American heroism or tales of the pure ideals that somehow govern this obviously messy scene. We sing democracy's song. The resentful possibility turns this process inside out. Appeals to democracy's values are twisted into occasions for resentment and anger. Appeals to a common heritage split that commonality. The best of our impulses turn into the worst.

Part III

Alternatives

Chapter 12

Marge the Stoic

The Coens' *Fargo* and Civic Solutions

Ill-fated folk! For would they but obey
With understanding heart, from day to day
    Their life were full of blessing, but they turn
Each to his sin, by folly led astray.

Glory would some thro' bitter strife attain
And some are eager after lawless gain;
    Some lust for sensual delights, but each
Finds that too soon his pleasure turns to pain.
    Cleanthes the Stoic, "Hymn to Zeus"

Cynicism causes trouble. In its more sinister forms, cynicism can be corrosive and even disruptive. It interrupts patterns that most citizens would rather not have to think too much about. Cynicism sows doubt among believers and undermines solutions that would otherwise make perfect sense. Our culture has honed its ability, in ways sometimes sophisticated, sometimes crude, to articulate values or virtues and to imply that these stated virtues then solve problems of conflict and governance. Perhaps the most devious interruption cynicism promotes is to undermine the claim that ideals can simply and directly inform political possibilities. The cynic knows better and teaches others that knowledge.

    This last part of the book turns to alternatives. Once the cynical strain has been set loose, where might we search for the antidote? This chapter considers the possibility that despite the tensions placed on belief in a cynical age, there still might be a cultural way to foster belief. This possibility has been widely circulated, from ancient times to the present. In contemporary America, the communitarian argument has been particularly popular with intellectuals and commentators. At the level of community, so the argument goes, the habits of belief can still do their work, overcoming the corrosion cynicism sets loose. Communitarians look to the civic realm — a mix of cultural habits, institutions, and prohibitions that might still revitalize life in a democratic society.

Communitarian arguments are often compelling. The costs and tensions of community are more visible in actual communities. Accordingly, it makes sense to examine the communitarian remedy as it is realized, in community. This is risky business. Discussion of community quickly devolves into anecdote or ideology. In drawing attention to the fabric of community, the sense of balance or imbalance experienced in social life, it is useful to study stories that seem to capture a culture's patterns. Carefully studying a novel or opera or, in the instance I have chosen here, a movie, can reveal connections without promising to reveal more than is possible in the study of culture.

It helps that a cultural study is inevitably partial and evocative rather than complete and certain. The built-in precaution is as useful as a safety switch on a power tool. But like all safety switches, cultural interpretation carries its own frustrations. The example I have chosen to study will no doubt seem inappropriate to some readers, who will not recognize their own clan in this story and would choose another example of community values. Without question, there are many kinds of community not reflected in the discussion that follows. An analysis of that range would be useful, but is, for better or worse, not the book I chose to write. What this chapter tries to do, instead, is to suggest that communitarian remedies, when implemented in their full, cultural forms, have costs and tensions not necessarily represented in the values or virtues that justify those cultural forms. These perils may be better understood if one lets oneself be immersed in the culture, the better to feel its rhythms, commitments, doubts, and even its catastrophes.

Fargo,[1] the Coen brothers' 1996 movie, tells the story of a lurid series of crimes set in motion by the desperate attempt of a Minnesota car dealer to extort money from his wealthy father-in-law. The film also reveals a crucial point about the ongoing theoretical discussion of community and values. Calls to "community" resolutely insist that social business be discussed in the sober and somber dialect of conscious, rational decision and commitment. Whether in sophisticated intellectual argument or the popularized canon of Bill Bennett, community business is done in the voice of the preacher, the legislator, and the teacher, in their most civil and civic modes. *Fargo* reminds us of the actual social implementations stoic communitarianism requires of its subscribers. Social practices — the daily habits, behavioral ticks, and adaptive strategies brought to theoretical prominence as an analytical field by feminists, postmodernists, and others — form the actual terrain on which communities build themselves upon stoic precepts.

The central character of *Fargo*, Brainerd police chief Marge Gunderson (Frances McDormand), has barely been introduced before we see her at one of a cop's worst moments, surveying a bloody crime scene. Prominently pregnant with her first child, Marge picks her way over the snow and ice, locating bodies and reporting to her deputy in a tone one might use when locating early tomatoes in the backyard garden. "It's in the head and the hand there. Guess that's a defensive wound." Of all the post-Tarantino violence films, *Fargo* may be the most defensible. The legitimacy of the stoic's claim is established at extremes, when it is most vividly tested.

Throughout *Fargo*, everyday banter becomes anthemic. Everybody except one of the hired kidnappers speaks with a prominent Minnesotan accent. Sentences end with a grammatically unnecessary "then," "here," "now," "yah," or "there," with words clipped and inflection rising as members of the clan seek reassurance that the public codes are still in order: "That's the best we can do here." "I'm doing really super there." The lilt becomes slower and more precise when each speaker most needs a reminder of the community values that will, they hope or believe, carry them through whatever dark moment impends. At such times, the clichés become almost infantile: "there in a jif," "okey dokey," "thanks a bunch."

Nietzsche explained the debilitating quality of professional discourses deployed by preachers, teachers, and social workers. But while Nietzsche resorted to aphorism and outrage in an attempt to avoid replicating the discourses he criticized, the Coens use cinema to provide a glimpse of the daily life generated in a society that takes its stoic communitarianism very seriously. If we were to ask a historian or sociologist about the sources of Minnesotanism, she would likely talk about ethnicity, religion, and ethos. Ask a film director and he responds with manners, habits, and modes of speech. *Fargo* is loaded with actor "business," the small pieces of behavior that compose a culture.

Fargo portrays a stoicism that requires extraordinarily strong social norms, constantly reinforced by habitual public and private performance. When Marge meets former classmate Mike Yanagita (Steve Park) in a hotel bar, there are conventions to be kept up, to ensure that loyalty and remembrance persist as value commitments. Cynics in the audience may immediately assume that Mike is manipulating Marge, but when she later finds out that his deception has been profound, Marge is put off her perfect tone — that persistent chin-up outlook that carried her through murder, frustration, and even pregnancy. The next morning, her anxiety shows in an interview at perpetrator Jerry Lundegaard's (William H. Macy) car-lot office ("Oh, for Pete's sake, for Pete's sake. He's fleeing the interview! He's fleeing the interview!"). The repetition shows that doubt has been planted — how could one of us stray?

There is reason for her distress. Marge's community imposes strong social norms. Stoicism suspects that madness would be a willful and selfish response, an indulgence that might spread if not kept rigorously under control. In any social setting, borders are constantly being imposed and policed; some things are just not spoken. In an ideal communitarian setting, the borders are extensive, and breeches are very serious business. One person's outburst might undermine important social commitments. In the film, Marge maintains her composure, in one scene even tolerating the juxtaposition of live worms (bait) with her roast-beef sandwich (lunch). Stoicism is not for the squeamish.

While communitarians advocate discussion as antidote to potential or present catastrophe, this commitment is continually at tension with the countercommand that much remain unspoken. The most important community themes — among them race, the crucial but unspoken element of Marge's meeting with Mike Yanagita — are best treated if we can pretend they don't exist. The "color-blind" proscription currently so popular among conservatives is but one example. The racial erasure of the Yanagita scene could also be used to condemn the Minnesota insularity replicated by the movie, but this erasure seems more strategic than that. When Mike first telephones Marge, her pronunciation of the name (applying a slight Minnesota lilt to the first syllable — itself already a joke on spoken Minnesotan — and lowering the second syllable, then slightly increasing inflection on each successive syllable) already signals that the old classmate is calling-under-erasure. We wonder what nationality the name could represent and try to re-translate the name back from Marge's high-Minnesotan, with its unconventional vowel sounds.

Reviewers hostile to *Fargo* found the Yanagita subplot unfathomable. John Simon could find no better explanation for the scene than the Coens' "predilection for the bizarre," then blasted it summarily: "This episode takes up considerable time, but to what purpose? . . . The brothers do show guts in making a Japanese-American and, in another case, an Indian unsympathetic; but it would be even more daring for them to tell a story straightforwardly and economically."[2] To see Mike and Shep Proudfoot, the Native American mechanic, as carriers of a noble anti-PC project is to miss the Coens' project profoundly.

Mike Yanagita is one of several victims who populate *Fargo,* but he is a victim of a different sort, injured by his accidental placement into a society into which he doesn't fit but which also suppresses consideration of difference. We might hope that such victims would heroically resist the perils of their situation, but that outcome is not guaranteed and might even be rare in a culture that polices itself effectively. We also, and rightly, remain skeptical of artists who portray victims in their abject suffering without making their own perspective emphatically clear. *Fargo* tests these social boundaries when it treats the Yanagita subplot with such casual aplomb. Whether their risk pays off is for the viewer to decide. It is not an easy decision, but it is the kind of decision actual politics, in a social setting, constantly requires.

It should not surprise that stoics think that race can be sublimated to community, or perhaps that it must be sublimated, else the social enterprise collapses. Seeming to deny the importance of such threats as social pathology or race, stoics may actually make them more important, giving them a force and establishing a space in which they can fester. This is always the stoic's potential tragedy. Carefully policing borders to keep threats out, a stoic culture might actually have been covertly generating desire and anxiety.

Some viewers of *Fargo* disliked the film because they thought the Coens were simply making fun of Minnesotans. The Coens have clearly given their Minnesota a fabulous quality, and viewers might well object, as many real Minnesotans did, that such a place does not exist.[3] As I will discuss below, the Coens have treated their story as a fable. As such their film, like any artistic project, calls for interpretive judgments. Irony, sarcasm, and other genre-shifts invite judgments that are inevitably interpretive. Politics, too. Whether or not the Coens intended to take revenge on their childhood home, *Fargo* can be interpreted as a fable of stoic community.

There could be reasons for the critics to be sensitive to sarcasm. Stoics have long made fine comedic fare, as Garrison Keillor (the film's obvious cultural mentor) understands.[4] The reluctance to emote that so often gives humor its edge is, it turns out, a vestige of classical stoicism. The classical scholar E. Vernon Arnold described the stoic style as "a severe intellectual and moral discipline" in which "the speaker was called upon under all circumstances to speak the truth, the whole truth." But instead of producing naughty, critical, or showy arrogance, this commitment encouraged plainness. The stoic "could add no word which would touch [his audience's] sympathies or kindle their indignation."[5]

To be a stoic is to exhibit a plain, virtuous truthfulness, avoiding emotion. In a community governed by such a norm, mutual commitments become hugely important, since rhetorical appeal is largely avoided. Criticism is conducted in understated, even ironic terms. Marge corrects her deputy's reading of a "DLR" license-plate report by a dead trooper. Rather than pull rank on the hapless deputy (who had missed the obvious possibility that the patrolman had seen dealer plates) or risk an overt joke, Marge's response is perfectly understated: "I'm not sure that I agree with you one hundred percent on your police work there."

Stoic community is built on a commitment to a shared realism and rational negotiation. Writing about classical stoicism, Arnold summarized this commitment neatly — the "starting-point, 'the universe is.'" The commitment implies a cultural outlook, setting the basis for contemporary stoic culture: "Wisdom is considered by Zeno not only as the first of the virtues, but as the foundation of all; so that Courage is wisdom in suffering, Justice is wisdom in distribution, and Soberness is wisdom in enjoyment." Even though the programmatic aspect of classical stoicism does not translate into contemporary cultural stoicism, the precepts still resonate: "The standard of daily duty is that which when done can reasonably be defended." Classical stoicism did not insist on a stern and simple adherence to the demands of reason. Instead, Stoics rely on "shrewd good sense and worldly wisdom; in short, the doctrine of 'making the best of both worlds.' "[6]

Still, even if this stoic accommodation to the real world persists, so also do the threats to realism of fables, myths, and stories. After all, *Fargo* reminds us, Brainerd fashions itself the very home of Paul Bunyan. Although few of *Fargo*'s reviewers made the connection, the Coens have concocted another rather elaborate joke on the relationship of fable to reality. Extensive references in the film's opening credits, production notes, and interviews with the brothers assure viewers that *Fargo* is based on real events. As the film opens, this message sets the scene: "This is a true story. The events depicted in this film took place in Minnesota in 1987. At the request of the survivors, the names have been changed. Out of respect for the dead, the rest has been told exactly as it occurred." Some reviewers noted the reference to "respect," and rightly so; viewers' reaction to the film surely turns on their reaction to the social caricature of Minnesotans. But there is a larger joke here. There is considerable doubt whether such a crime ever actually happened.

The *Minneapolis Star-Tribune* tried to track the story down and failed, concluding that the "incidents it details never occurred, according to the state Bureau of Criminal Apprehension, which maintains crime records."[7] No murders remotely resembling those depicted in the film occurred in Brainerd, Minneapolis, or, for that matter, in the state of Minnesota. One reviewer, writing in *Cineaste*, cited Ed Gein as a precedent.[8] Although Gein's crime is well known in the upper Midwest, its details completely diverge from *Fargo*'s plot, and it occurred in 1957, not 1987. In short, the realism that attends *Fargo* is a hoax. Or a fable. The Coen brothers carried this hoax to considerable extremes. Asked by one national publication how close the script was to the actual event, Ethan Coen replied, "Pretty close," but offered no details. A representative of Gramercy Pictures acknowledged that the Coens presented the film to the studio as a true-crime story: "We didn't investigate it. The studio doesn't do research. . . . We love the project, we believe in the project, and if they say it's based on a true story, then we believe it."[9]

Only in the film's published screenplay does Ethan Coen hint at the hoax. His introduction concludes that the story "aims to be both homey and exotic, and pretends to be true."[10] He then tells the story of his grandmother, who told the boys crime stories long accepted as true within the family but which, on later reflection, did not stand up. But, however dubious, the stories had become part of the family's experience. No matter how committed a culture is to a flattening, rationalistic community ethos, the Coens imply, experience remains irreducibly personal. If the stoic begins with "the universe is," the Coens counter with "experience is," and is personal. And experience continually bends toward the fabulous, testing the realism stoics insist must be maintained.

No matter how persistently we might try to suppress disruptive emotions, experience asserts itself, sometimes turning into fable. As Ethan Coen explained, "Paradoxically, what is closest to home can seem exotic. We can't read about the South Seas without comparing it to Minneapolis, and can't describe Minneapolis, even to ourselves, without it seeming like the South Seas."[11] As flat as a culture seems, it still contains and is constructed on its members' experiences, some of which may strain at the flatness. Examine a culture closely, perhaps as the Coens eventually examined their grandmother's stories, and the parts may not fit the grand theme. The ideological commitments that seem to hold a community together may not function as straightforwardly as they promise.

But even after it has been revealed as fable, the cultural story can still function. The claustrophobia endemic to stoic communities suppresses emotive appeal. Apathy, supposedly the postmodern culture of artists and intellectuals, is more fully realized by the stoics. The resolute stoicism of the Coens' characters (at, say, the buffet) beats anything happening at the university coffeehouse. Stoic culture — again, dating back to the classical stoics — does not identify pleasure with virtue, as, say, a reward.[12] The stoic substitutes a kind of aesthetics of sense making for the more straight-forward appreciation of pleasure. Everything is thought out, talked out, and a sensible conclusion clicks into place with plea-surable precision. When Jerry's businessman father-in-law (Harve Presnell) and his accountant (Larry Brandenburg) talk about Jerry's parking-lot acquisition "making sense," they speak in tones of confidence and pleasure hardly found elsewhere in the film.

Although the Coens reserved the topic of bowling leagues for their subsequent film, *The Big Lebowski,* we can fairly assume that there are bowling alleys in Brainerd. And we know that the lanes are filled with bowling leagues and that much pleasure attends the precise clipping of pins. In short, the demise of community that Harvard professor of government Robert Putnam hopes to mea-sure by the decline of such civic associations as the neighborhood bowling league has more complex undertones. The good citizens of Brainerd would not go "bowling alone," to quote Putnam's won-derful title, but their sociability and civic commitment have un-usual dimensions. The pleasures associated with those commit-ments are carefully flattened.

Likewise, the unmistakable visual theme of the film is the flat, frozen landscape. The Coens grew up in Minnesota and as teenagers longed to escape. Ethan told an interviewer, "We were misfits grow-ing up in a bland, nothing place. Everyone there just accepts their lives at face value, no questions asked. We were ice dwellers."[13] In introducing the published screenplay, Ethan writes that the film pursued a specific effect, "the abstract landscape of our child-hood—a bleak, windswept tundra, resembling Siberia except for its Ford dealerships and Hardee's restaurants."[14] Of course, stoic cultures thrive, sometimes even where the terrain is not flat. It is the expressive and rhetorical features of culture that stoicism flat-tens. The paradoxical elements that remain (the car dealerships and fast-food restaurants) are not indicators of depth so much as they are flatteners of a different sort, referencing nothing but themselves.

Fargo contains several references to the management of flatness. One of the villains, Carl (Steve Buscemi), is the only character who does not speak Minnesotan, and is thus immediately marked as an outsider. By several standards Carl is a flat personality, too. Although talkative, he is pathetically unimaginative, dull witted, and inflexible. But even he can pose terrible disruptions in a community that preserves its own flatness so seriously. In two separate scenes, witnesses are unable to offer much of a description of Carl. A bartender, taking a break from shoveling snow, describes him as a "little guy, kinda funny looking [pause] in a general sort of way." Two prostitutes come up with no further description than "funny looking." Carl is so obviously "not from around here" that he is almost invisible.

When Carl returns to Brainerd, injured but in possession of more money than he had expected, his effort to hide the cash turns into hilarious misfire. There is not even a good place to hide a satchel of cash on this frozen, featureless landscape. There is no access to depth in this place; life is on the surface. As an outsider, Carl simply assumes the possibility of hiding places and markers, but he has miscalculated this, along with so much else. Everything is visible. The space extends indefinitely along the boundary fence next to which Carl has planted the cash. This flatness does not simply exist. It persists as a consequence of considerable communal effort. And with such effort comes the suspicion that the careful, self-negating routines have marshaled much energy for little reason. It is, after all, a culture with an enormous regard for reason. And with reason comes the skeptical turn that undermines the project. Scholars of classical stoicism refer to this as one of stoicism's paradoxes. At the core of stoic life is the resolve to leave matters where they are, instead of examining them with all of one's faculties.

This reluctance is reenacted in *Fargo,* at the crucial point of the heroine's reflection on the drama's climax. After Marge has found the surviving villain, Gaear Grimsrud (Peter Stormare, an accomplished Swedish actor), she expertly delivers a leg wound and, in a scene left to our imagination, bosses him across the frozen lake and snow-covered ground into her cruiser before help arrives. Driving the villain to jail, Marge allows herself a few moments of contemplation — a vanity seldom allowed in this stoic culture, no matter how much time for contemplation seems offered by Minnesota's wretched weather. Marge's rumination is not about evil, human nature, or fear. Indeed, this stoically chipper law enforcement officer starts off with a straight-faced pun: "So that was Mrs. Lundegaard on the floor in there. And I guess that was your accomplice in the wood chipper. Those three people in Brainerd." After a long, thoughtful pause, she continues, "And for what? For a little bit of money. There's more to life than a little money, y'know? Don't you know that? And here you are and it's a beautiful day. Well. (sniffs) I just don't understand it."

This speech stands out, and not only because of its role in the story's narrative. The film's Minnesotans are not much given to out-loud reflection. Several reviewers noted its simple character. John Simon pointed out that "when Marge . . . adds, 'Don't you know that?' folksiness and absurdity enjoy their preposterously entwined apogee."[15] A more favorable reviewer, Michael Wood, also criticized the speech: "It's right that Marge shouldn't understand it, of course, and that we shouldn't understand it either. But there is something too easy about this orchestration of our failure."[16]

There is something "too easy" about the speech precisely because "I don't understand" is a deliberately empty gesture, fully consistent with the ritualized, empty, yet vaguely sociable verbal gestures the film uses throughout to signify stoic culture. Marge knows there are some things one shouldn't try to understand, to really confront. She's a good stoic, an able representative of her tribe. To examine this ugly sequence of events too closely is to put the entire enterprise at risk. Stoic community is premised on the notion that this is perhaps the worst chance you can take — to risk an emotional reflection on one's experience. Marge long ago decided not to go down that (white and icy) road. In the currently popular stoic adage, you don't want to go there. It wouldn't be prudent.

Marge's speech is about the breakdown of social commitments. Everyone knows they are supposed to act according to a broader set of values than the simple pursuit of money that otherwise dominates American life. To keep at that sometimes-unpleasant path, one needs to suppress the obvious. It was not a beautiful day in that bleak, frozen place, by any measure. In some other interpretive context, it might well be the stoicism, even more than the criminal transgression, which is incomprehensible. This, in a nutshell, is the stoic commitment: no emoting to win social solidarity, no rhetorical appeals to establish an authoritative position, and above all, no cynicism. Stoic community establishes boundaries and polices those boundaries. Many of the social devices we learned at the movies are out of stoic bounds.

Still, *Fargo* only takes us part of the way along the path it sets. The film is mostly apolitical. We can only imagine the admirably stoic commitment to affirmative action that informed Marge's selection as police chief. Similarly, we have only brief glimpses of the culture's implications for *Fargo*'s racial others (Yanagita and Shep Proudfoot, who, one reviewer noted, "would be very out of place in a Kevin Costner film").[17] It is thus necessary to look elsewhere in order to fit stoicism in a more fully political context.

The political scientist Thomas Dumm helps in this regard by taking stock of a culture in which a conscious stoicism inevitably implies a set of commitments involving cruelty, complacency, realism, and depth. Dumm asks how we should approach the facts of daily life — in his example, the supermarket, that flat space of pure consumer manipulation and commercial uniformity. A communitarian would, no doubt, see the supermarket as flat and miserable. But that judgment, Dumm counters, would foster "the complacency of despair. This stoical move, associated with a particular shrug of the shoulders, looks, but only looks, knowing and wise.... In fact, it participates in a different ignorance, one that associates the perpetuation of cruelty with ubiquitous qualities of life."[18]

Dumm identifies this "ignorance" (a literal ignoring impulse) with several prominent modes of social thought — postmodernism, contemporary liberalism, and communitarianism. Each school of thought contains a "constant struggle ... to resist this religious impulse," an impulse that advises acquiescence in the face of ongoing cruelty, citing a recognition of the ubiquity of life's woes. "The struggle involves not only trying to maintain perspective as perspective becomes flattened, but trying to deepen one's sense of something (flatness) that is not deep to begin with."[19] This is a difficult paradox for theory. Every modernist impulse pulls theory toward depth answers in which culture (e.g., a persistent commitment to accept ongoing cruelty as inevitable) immediately evokes structures, whether psychological, economic, or moral. Every intellectual learns to confront flatness by raising the ghosts of class or group interest, social pathology, or a crisis in values.

Stoic communitarianism insists that this quandary be settled in favor of sober, rationalist analysis supported by broad values rhetoric and the continual move toward common ground. The stoic assumption has proved enormously popular among opinion leaders in the American media. Every talk show or opinion column models the grave, serious discourse of confident rationalism, the pragmatic ignoring of some public problems, and the insistence on the efficacy of common values to solve public contentions. *Fargo* presents no alternative to the community's stoicism. That is stoicism's trap: alternatives are always perceived as threats and thus must be guarded against, suppressed, or otherwise relegated to the margins.

The stoic position can be attractive (as the Coens strain to show us), but it revels in its boundary-policing commitments; this is flatness in response to flatness, a road map to cruel obliviousness. As Peter Sloterdijk explained, "Seen on the whole, Stoicism was a philosophy of the comfortable. Diogenes, however, really was without possessions and he could convincingly shake his contemporaries' consciousness, as later, on Christian soil, the Franciscans first were able to do again."[20] A cynic has discarded some comforts, including the comforts of belief, casting it aside in the day-to-day routine of job and family. Belief can still be appealed to, but each such appeal is suspect, since it could be cynical.

Under pressure, stoicism risks a collapse into cynicism, the danger modeled by *Fargo*'s bad guys and capitalists alike. Call that the collapse of rulers into the cynicism of the powerful. This cynicism manipulates the governed in the name of necessity, weaving fabrics of official pronouncements, excuses for coercion or worse. And this happens amid television commercials that deliver a sophisticated and manipulative cynical drone on behalf of powerful corporations. The cynic stoically goes to work, suppresses concerns about what the work requires, and then prospers. Still, the cynic can save the moralist from potential debilitations inherent in morality itself. Cynicism emerges as a cultural role when stoics rely too much on suppressing conflict, thereby damaging the balance they try so hard to maintain. For stoics, the appealing drive of cynicism is incomprehensible, or it is a forbidden pleasure to which the stoic can be drawn, as if by a compulsion. Finally unable to police this boundary, the stoic can experience unpredictable out-comes, as in the case of the car dealer turned criminal in *Fargo.*

Every stoic communitarian urgently works to redefine the cyn-ical breakout as an irresponsible choice, as evidence of a weak sub-mission to an impulse that would have passed. *Fargo* asks us to understand a culture by attending to the ways it makes itself gov-ernable. What cultural practices or images are deployed to police the boundaries? Which boundaries are important and why? At least for believers, stoicism presents a stable alternative. *Fargo,* in its res-olute effort to portray Marge as an attractive character, poses the issues sharply. There can be a charm about the stoic. One must imagine Marge happy.

But Marge's stoical happiness has its costs. A society that bends too resolutely toward the stoic misses other possibilities. What is more, the fables that inevitably attend social life bend and contort the stoic's commitments into shapes not entirely prefigured in the values used to justify those commitments. The violence this inflicts on those who differ from the community's imagined ideal can be terrible. But consequences adhere to the well-policed community, too. The perils of stoic community lie not only in external disrup-tion, but also in its own, internal paradoxes and corruption, includ-ing the collapse into cynicism. Settling for what might otherwise be a disappointment, settling for, say, the ambivalent honor of il-lustrating the intermittently useful three-cent stamp, as Marge urges her artist husband to do at the very end of *Fargo,* may in-deed turn out to be settling short.

Chapter 13

"So What?"

Another Side of Cynicism

> The fully developed ability to say No is also the only
> valid background for Yes, and only through both does
> real freedom [begin] to take form.
>
> Peter Sloterdijk, *Critique of Cynical Reason*

Having met the cynic, do not make the mistake of assuming that
the inverse of a cynic is necessarily a believer. This is one of Peter
Sloterdijk's boldest insights. It could be that the phenomenon of
cynicism is diverse. And even though the cynic is defined largely
by an antagonism to belief, it could still be that the question of
power plays just as important a role in understanding how cynicism works. I have already noted how slippery our everyday use of
the word "cynical" can be. We call things cynical that have many
different, more useful names. But now, having focused more narrowly on cynicism as crisis of belief and cultural pattern, we discover that cynicism splits again.

Specifically, Sloterdijk proposes "kynicism" (a cheeky, subversive
practice, "the motif of self-preservation in crisis-ridden times...
a critical, ironical philosophy of so-called needs") as the antidote
to modern cynicism ("a kind of shameless, 'dirty' realism that,
without regard for conventional moral inhibitions, declares itself
to be for how 'things really are' ").[1] The spelling of kynicism is in-

tended to evoke the Greek spelling and, in turn, the tradition of Diogenes.

But Diogenes is by no means the only kynic we know. Quite the contrary: it is remarkable how often the characters and entertainers who draw our gaze are impudent nonbelievers, acting out challenges to power. Our literature and, more important, our cinema, television, and pop culture are full of cheeky, exasperated, yet attractive kynics. Humphrey Bogart was perhaps the most famous. Dave Barry and Hunter Thompson are revered curmudgeons, precisely because of their charismatic cynicism, displayed in edgy diatribes against oppressive or just plain stupid power. I'm not making this up! Many of the best figures from recent and current pop music, including Randy Newman, Bette Midler, and Elvis Costello, often play the kynic. The list of profound jokers seems almost endless: Nicole Hollander, Richard Pryor, Lily Tomlin, Robin Williams, Paula Poundstone, Al Franken, and many others — every one a kynic.

If Americans could see their political process close up, they would find more kinds of cynics than they knew existed. The cynic's naughtiness and edgy energy could be written into the job description of the successful campaign manager. Sometimes high humor issues from the cynical glee of having manipulated voters, as in Robert Redford's *The Candidate*. But some campaigners look more like Diogenes. James Carville and his famous "the economy, stupid" sign were kynical in a way that Clinton voters loved. Bush supporters liked the cynical bumper sticker the candidate himself promoted: "Annoy the Media: Vote for Bush." One suspects that Mary Matalin, or one of her comrades-in-attitude, must have given it to him.

Even if his career otherwise could serve as a model for the powerful cynic, Lloyd Bentsen's famous 1988 line to Quayle ("John Kennedy was a friend of mine") was purely kynical: rhetorically excessive, done in high mock paternalism, undermining the future Veep's authority and confidence. This is not only a game of the left. Reagan's "there you go again" retort to Carter in the 1980 presidential debate had the same force for the same reasons. Most of our most memorable political punchlines are kynical refrains, even though in the context of power and office, some of the jokers turn out to be cynics-in-power. Often, activist kynics are almost indistinguishable from their outsider-cynic counterparts.

Some left-kynics have made good use of conspiracy, including Dick Gregory, Russell Means, and in his more self-conscious moments, Oliver Stone. They portray conspiracy theories gone giddy: causation flaps in TV-driven winds. There were kynics in Perot's crowd, too. Whoever gave Ross the Boss the Patsy Cline tape playing "Crazy" was a troublemaker. The candidate himself could affect the kynical swagger: "I'm all ears."

Deciding who is the kynic and who is the outsider-cynic, or simply a servant to powerful cynics, is a crucial political act in a cynical age. Some kynics lose their edge over time. Yippie-turned-New-Ager Jerry Rubin suffered this fate in his last years. Others turn dogmatic — say, Oliver Stone on a bad-idea day. It is always possible that the kynic is really a believer under a veneer of disbelief. Bogart usually ended up a redeemed believer in his movies. Could it be that all his movies were fables of the kynic's recapture? Perhaps. But it is also possible that we come for the early reels — to watch the kynic. We put up with the obligatory conversion at the end because we know, cynical fans that we are, what outcomes Hollywood allows.

Kynics form a long tradition in Western society. The trouble-makers, balloon puncturers, and hot-air detectors play an important role whenever pomposity reaches its fullest bloom. Some of us recalcitrants react with a reflexive distrust, sensing cynic-in-power manipulation or outsider hatred and destruction. We start looking around, out at the margins, at the back of the room where the jokers hang out, for the spirit of Diogenes, the original kynic.

There are plenty of models. The problem is not that we have generated too few kynics. It is that we discount them too quickly. We enjoy the kynics as a sideshow, a source for funny stories. But our disrespect feels a little uneasy. We know that power can be pompous. How could citizens of a society governed by innumerable Dilbert-staffed bureaucracies not know that? In a thoroughly cynical setting, the liberal, preachy, carefully self-constrained citizen's role is no threat at all. Powerful cynics learn early on to allow much complaining. Have another hearing on this environmental impact statement. These are challenges that governments easily absorb.

There are limits to the success the kynic can attain. It is not even always clear what the kynic's success would look like. Kynics do not just advocate the things (the credulity of representation, responsibility, and the like) that powerful cynics abuse. The kynical project aims at destabilizing the powerful cynic's system, not only his institutional system but also his systematic and self-interested arrangement of attitudes, opinions, and categories of thought. The kynic does not aim at institutional success, at least in any direct way. Most of the time, the kynic probably would not make a very good senator. Institutional triumph, especially in institutions underwritten by the same coherent, sober belief that sets the kynic off in the first place, does not much interest the kynic.

But there are other rewards. The kynic wants to undermine the philosopher, from a point outside of but also just adjacent to the philosopher's hardened position. Playing that role, performing it so well that it is remembered and its liveliness noted, kynicism scores an important win on its own terms. As it turns out, the philosopher has long needed the company of the kynic, even if neither of them seems all that thrilled about the other. Sloterdijk calls the kynic's cheekiness "a source of enlightenment in which the secret of its vitality is hidden." Coherent, somber belief could hardly form a successful system on its own. The long-standing inability or unwillingness of people — even philosophers — to live coherent, somber lives would surely doom such a system. This unacknowledged, cheeky attitude toward truth provokes and makes problematic the (seemingly functional) self-control philosophy requires. The philosopher's measured and naturalistic pronouncements on values and possibilities meet a foe from outside its frame, one that uses "apparently irrelevantly provocative gestures" (99–102).

Still, the kynic probably knows that any successes will be temporary. It would not necessarily occur to kynics that the philosopher needs their participation to complete some larger system of truth. Kynics do not usually treat "larger systems of truth" very well. Although uncertain of success, kynics do have a sense of what their success would mean: "Those who rule lose their real self-confidence to the fools, clowns, and kynics" (102). A particular kind of confidence in belief — the commitment to belief's efficacy — would be more visible, more problematic, easier to question, less able to rule.

A whole set of impudent practices follows from Sloterdijk's recognition of the kynic's role: "Certain small phrases irrefutably ad-

vance cheeky realism from below against the 'law.' " The phrases
he has in mind deflate false pretensions by asking insistently and
kynically, "So What? and Why Not?" These are not unfamiliar questions: "With a persistent So What? many young people have driv-
en their incorrigible parents... to frustration." Revising the cheekiness of youth, Sloterdijk praises the activity of children at play.
Such play is schooling for freedom, training the participants in
"the saying of So What? incidentally in a natural way." More fully
socialized folk have a problem with their timing and resolve. They
find it difficult "to say No always at the right moment." "So What?"
is training for that important political act.

Sloterdijk's list of cynicisms also reconfigures practices whose
power we have not taken seriously enough. On the map of his political practices, the joke emerges as a key. The most common topics of humor, "the elementary satirical themes and most important
genres of jokes," are also "the cardinal cynicisms." For Sloterdijk,
moreover, jokes are important not primarily as a key to uncon-
scious activity (as they were for Freud). Instead, jokes "represent
the main battlefields of elevations and humiliations, idealizations
and realistic disillusionments. Here, vices and insults, ironies and
mockeries have their largest playing fields." In these jokes, these
"frivolous sideswipes" at the pompous, liberal presumptions of
society, jokers everywhere keep alive a "morally regulative sense"
of response (304). The usual domains of the joker correspond to
a map of pompous power, unacknowledged personal influence, and
political anxiety. When we have been composing and appreciating
jokes, we have already been developing an impudent regimen, a
discourse that not only provides comfort and release but also responds to power and the anxiety it produces in us.

Consider the fields we joke about: "The military with its tensions between hero ethics and cowards' realism, between officers
and subordinates, front and rear echelons, war and peace, command and obedience, is ... an inexhaustible generator of ... jokes."
Charlie Chaplin meets Kilroy and Ernie Pyle. "It is no different
with sexuality, which, with the juxtaposition of the covered and
the naked, the forbidden and the permitted, constitutes a vast field
for jokes, obscenities, and comedies." Most of what Hollywood has
ever called comedy fits here. "Likewise the medical domain, with
all its possibilities for sarcasm about health and sickness, madness

and normality, the living and the dead" (304). M*A*S*H meets Dr. Kildare at ER, all viewed through a dark humor familiar to many a "real" doctor, too.

"And all the more so with the entire domain of religion," Sloterdijk continues, "which is more serviceable for swearing and joke telling than almost any other theme. For, wherever there is so much sacredness, a large profane shadow arises, and the more saints are honored, the more comical saints can be found among them." Whoopi Goldberg meets the Flying Nun and a legion of drunken, good-hearted Irish priests. "There is also the area of knowledge, which is crisscrossed by tensions between intelligence and stupidity, joke and citizens' duty, reason and madness, science and absurdity." Even Ronald Reagan once played a slapstick professor, in the movies. And, of course, there is "politics, with its ideologies, state actions, its great words and small deeds, which provides an infinite source of pranks and parodies" (304–5). For which Johnny Carson, Jay Leno, David Letterman, and stand-up comics everywhere are eternally grateful.

The joke is instructive, but one cannot dwell solely in its realm. The tired tension between intelligence and stupidity impends, and besides, we all know what happens to a joke too much explained. To understand how kynics are positioned, we must also look at some of their serious targets.

To take the kynic this seriously is to make an important point about how we judge political roles. Simply put, the kynic makes it obvious, in a practical, understandable way, that there is no absolute, unproblematic reason why a citizen should have to recreate the world with his or her own statements and actions. It may seem a small point, but the kynic knows how strategically it is placed. Too often, political acts are judged on the basis of their coherence as representations of a preferred future, an institutionalized alternative. It is as if there were a rule: only political statements as careful, rational, concerned, and boring as those made by political figures will be allowed political significance.

The coherence from action to proposal to preferred world is indeed one possible way truth can be applied in politics; call it one possible "truth rule." It is a very popular rule with liberals and environmentalists, but also with police, public officials, and even journalists. But it is not the only possible truth rule. And it has its own problems, as Sloterdijk employs Diogenes to explain. What if it turns out that the powerful, the arbiters of acceptable responses, are not actually living the way they say everyone must live? Does your sloppy departmental recycling operation disprove your eco-philosophy? Does the need to run a deceptive foreign policy operation or two render your commitments to democracy hypocritical? Isn't it just a little too convenient that those in power define the rules of political engagement in a way that preserves their justification for precisely what they do best — making abstract statements about the public good and values and what is or is not possible?

Sloterdijk explains that kynics test such questions by pressing another claim. Perhaps the way we act politically should reflect the lively, disruptive, impudent, and cantankerous way we live — a different coherence than the one promised by the believers who would control these impulses. This is a question of political style, of the aesthetics of political judgment. Those in power hope to show by the style of their communiqués that their moderate proposals make sense, that it would be reasonable to extrapolate their respectful, individualistic, juridical proposals onto the entire populace. The model for the mainstream proposal is the judge, even-handedly deciding among competing claims, demonstrating the validity of the regime's rule by showing that even matters of great emotion and even violence can be treated with this sonorous, almost boring vehicle. Express your concerns moderately. Compose rational and reasoned arguments. Above all, bring politics to this higher road of discourse.

This mainstream style has long ago been brought into doubt. In the most famous case, Marx and his followers explained that a challenging, confrontational, struggling style might be appropriate in order to counter exploitation and produce justice. Marxism's characteristic political style, that of the class warrior, would reflect the dimensions of the battle, not the utopian hopes for a solution. The marxist warrior's style would reflect a certainty of purpose and an appropriately urgent sense of the need for abrupt change. In short, the marxist style reflected a political project, just as the contemporary mainstream style does. And this model informed several generations of working-class populists. It had the further virtue of containing its own model of motivation, explaining how one moves masses to political action.

Most of us now see the marxist model as excessively optimistic, willing to do violence on behalf of an unworthy goal—the tricky, undependable hope for justice in a workers' state. Most modern citizens are more concerned that bureaucrats could capture that workers' state, mismanaging it for their own, cynical purposes. Some citizens have delved deeper into the question, coming to understand that the inevitable collapse of capitalism (which helped justify the struggling style of a politicized working class) was no longer such a sure thing. Capitalists responded to various crises by becoming managers, finding new ways to generate satisfaction, fear, individualism, security, and other useful feelings among their employees. The managers even took to public relations, using the mass media that began to emerge during the maturing stage of industrial culture. Although culture continues to be a scene of conflict, the managers at least used some media capacity to spread the word that it was flexible, powerful, and thus able to respond to changing circumstance. The marxist optimism withered away.

But even after we put marxism aside, the question persists: Does it make sense to emphasize the quiet, careful, highly rationalistic style of the individual-as-judge? For a while, the cautious, individualistic style championed by American liberalism was good cover for critics who wished to avoid the violent surges of red baiting that swept through American society. But now, even that excuse has become passé. The Cold War, as we say, is over. Still, the liberal style is so familiar, so reassuring. Surely it has value as a common, recognizable role, available to all without being too terribly dangerous. And what harm could it do? Coherence and universality must surely still be the primary criteria of political action.

This is the point at which Sloterdijk intervenes in the argument. As it turns out, the cynicism widely attributed to socialist bureaucrats had long since become an organizing principle for capitalist managers, too. And every cynical manager understood how useful the modest liberal style could be. The individualists could even be recruited. Not all cynics have power. Some are satisfied to apologize for the powerful, identifying with them and organizing other, powerless citizens to likewise draw their identities from the master's needs. And in a setting where the entire context might be cynical, the liberal, preachy, carefully self-constrained citizen's role might not be very threatening at all.

The kynic has an answer ready for the liberal. There is no reason to assume that our public expressions should model the order we would like to see imposed. The problem is no longer how to impose order in a disordered context, perhaps wracked by religious wars or corrupt monarchies. Now the problem is how to disrupt a very secure order that might be much more cynical in its operations than in its rhetoric. What needs to be modeled is no longer the coherence and stability (the *responsibility*) of a preferred order. Instead, the critic should model the liveliness, the humor, the embodied messiness of a citizenry on whom "responsibility" has been imposed, often cynically.

There is even a sort of perverse justice in the shift from liberal to kynic. At least the kynic reminds the communitarian that solemn testimony to the public good is not the same thing as public good itself. What would a public good look like if it actually knew how to laugh at itself? If it were self-confident enough to embrace the various Others in society, rather than to keep them carefully excluded at the margins? Or put it negatively—can we imagine an order that did not have the kynic's correction built into it? The kynic intervenes with considerable precision into the realm of power. Sloterdijk explains the kynic's disdain for sober civility: an "essential aspect of power is that it only likes to laugh at its own jokes." The unwillingness to share a giggle—to laugh at its own expense, as the saying goes—is central to the workings of power. We are left to chuckle only at the opponent or the dispossessed. In this sense, the now-popular claim for civility is a partisan initiative, an attempt to discredit an embarrassing adversary.

Posed this way, some potential objections to the kynic's intervention can be more easily answered. The assumption that responses should model preferred institutional outcomes is one choice, but it might not be the most appropriate one, strategically speaking. If institutional outcomes are excessively stable (so much so that they might operate cynically), it might be better to search for different ways to express opposition. It might be better to tease the cynic, reminding onlookers that the pompous, wealthy, and powerful cynics have not exhausted us yet.

There are other objections the kynic will have to face. Isn't your performance just a substitute belief? Attempting to unnerve the powerful cynic, haven't you just put yourself in the superior role of exemplar? The kynic answers that cynical power has no grounds on which to issue such constraints, no good reason to insist that our responses should be positive or even consistent. The kynic keeps reminding the authorities of what their beloved order excludes and suppresses, of the truth it cynically prevents from emerging. To be sure, this will be a tricky shift. Contemporary society is well trained in its expectations of politics. To undermine that consensus, the kynic will be a constantly self-marginalizing character, acting intermittently and frequently failing. Even the kynic's successes will be poorly understood. Some kynics will lose focus, drifting into sour resentment. But as a cultural response, kynicism persists.

Kynics pose problems, not the least for the political analyst. At their best, kynics are so attractive that any attempt to describe them ends up sounding like a recruiting pitch. But what is important about the kynic is their role as a key to understanding society. This confusion stunted the development of American politics after the sixties, when remarkable kynical interventions could not be sustained and then became the target for a counterrevolution that has been massively successful. Sixties culture survived, but mostly as a private culture.

Most of our political crises now stem from the moral inconsistency of individual politicians. We hear endlessly about Clinton's affairs, just as the Bush nominee for secretary of defense, John Tower, was disqualified by similar complaints. Journalists love the Clinton sex stories, because they form a coherent drama. Did he lie and cheat? Such stories are much easier to tell than policy failures, which are usually ambiguous stories, unless they involve the failure to implement a new policy, as in the case of Clinton's failure to reform health care. Policy inconsistency never quite forms into as good a story, as Iran-Contra and the savings and loan stories show. This is not only a fault of the media, with its preference for some stories over others. After all, the media's audience is much better prepared for the stories of moral inconsistency of politicians' private lives. We know cynicism, but we have focused on only one of its modes.

Our political system was designed to be hard to move. Our institutional arrangements offer an almost endless obstacle course of veto points, opportunities to block almost any given reform proposal, for reasons honorable or not. Those institutional arrangements have fostered an apolitical culture. As proud as we are of the political system, we have nonetheless learned not to expect too much of it when we have a problem. Given this hard-to-move system, politics will necessarily involve both policy and strategy. What makes a proposal sound and what makes it possible are inextricably linked. This is a cynical connection — strategic thinking will often be at odds with policy thinking. This kind of cynicism has been much discussed. Kathleen Hall Jamieson cites it as a central cynical moment. But her critique of the strategic is antipolitical. It is not wrongheaded to pay attention to both policy and strategy.

This is a lesson E. J. Dionne learned, between *Why Americans Hate Politics* and *They Only Look Dead.* In the first book, Dionne sang the praises of solutions, diagnosing our problems in terms of our willingness to speak of strategies applied to campaigning or governing. In his more recent book, Dionne explains that reform is so difficult that for it to succeed, reformers will have to attend to both policy and politics. Ignoring that balance may maintain the purity of solutions talk that Jamieson promotes, but it will also defeat reform, which needs to account for the political strategies as well as the policy implications.

This makes for a complex mix. And those who love politics revel in this complexity. Simultaneously walking and chewing gum has nothing on politics as a model for complexity. This is not the complexity of "too much information," the standard criterion ever since Walter Lippmann praised expert solutions. The crucial political complexity of our time is the mix of policy and politics. At its best, the cynicism complaint is a way of policing that tension so that politics does not overwhelm policy. Again, it becomes important to understand the various modes of cynicism. A politician who sacrifices policy for political considerations is displaying (or more likely trying to hide) cynicism. That is the complaint the left made against Clinton's willing acceptance of the 1996 welfare proposals, for example. But the cynicism that citizens or critics develop, after seeing such a display, is not the same thing. It has different characteristics and different effects. In short, it works differently.

In a system that preserves existing arrangements as well as ours, those who rule have tremendous advantage, and that advantage is growing rapidly. The communitarian or civility analysis describes an insider rhetoric but does little to destabilize the advantage of those who rule, who can cynically use the rhetoric of civility or community. This problem becomes especially acute in a society that neither understands politics nor appreciates it much. We end up in a bind — bored into passivity but injured by the policies that result. It makes sense to apply a stern civility test to Dick Morris, whose behavior displayed so much cynicism. But it does not make the same sense to apply the same test to community activists who criticized the effects of the advice Morris gave Clinton. This lack of symmetry is a problem. Journalists like rules that apply to both sides, the better to uphold their self-promoted image of objectivity. The solution to this symmetry problem is politics — a better understanding of the process by which we make public solutions.

We can begin to better understand the political process by better understanding cynicism. The different varieties of cynicism make a difference. The cynicism of those who rule is not the same as wig cynicism or kynicism. Cynical rule may not be best controlled by application of believer talk, since the sincere talk of community and values has itself been cynically appropriated so often. And the wig cynicism that loves conspiracy theories and sometimes lapses into hatred does not prove that our only recourse is believer talk. Nor must we ignore the danger of wig cynicism in order to keep open the kynical possibility. Kynical responses can pose dangers, too, but have another potential effect. The kynic can destabilize power in a way that values talk cannot accomplish.

The rules are not the same for all political actors. Wig cynics endanger the political enterprise by driving people away from the game altogether, in extreme cases, toward disruptions that are violent or harmful to the political game itself, a game the kynic wants to revitalize, not to destroy. Kynics, who are not defending wealth, power, and privilege, have wider latitude for action. The standards by which a powerful cynic is judged should be much tighter than the standards applied to the outsider. The civility movement needs to understand this, and fast.

Politics requires multiple roles, and this requirement is not refuted by the fact that it genuinely complicates the political game.

Activating a cynical citizenry means finding ways to reengage them in politics, even if they don't much understand or like the game just now. In this apolitical society, there is no great surplus of examples that model political engagement. But there are a few prominent examples, readily available for analysis and interpretation. There are a few visible kynics whose act we know very well.

Chapter 14

Teachings of the Demonstration

Representation in the Streets

Rebellion is, by nature, limited in scope. It is no more
than an incoherent pronouncement.
Albert Camus, *The Rebel*

The events of 1989 and 1990 in China, Eastern Europe, and South
Africa reached us as a sequence of images, mostly televised
glimpses — the mise-en-scène of postmodern revolution. Mandela
walked from prison and later the same day addressed a crowd of
supporters. The Berlin Wall went under the wrecking ball of what
can only be described as a band of reveling partygoers. A simulated lady liberty rose in China.

For me, one image stands out, in some way enclosing each of
those events. It is familiar, available to each of us as a text we could
reinterpret. A lone Chinese student steps in front of a column of
tanks in Tiananmen Square. As the lumbering, awkward tanks try
to turn, first one way and then the other, the student easily blocks
them. He is more agile than the tanks. For the moment at least,
his visibility is a ghost shirt. Finally, the tanks stop trying to turn
and briefly become symbolic of doubly frustrated authority. As if
wanting to escalate the play just a bit more, the student climbs the
lead tank and appears to be trying to speak to it. Words against
metal. A few of his friends appear in the frame now, pulling him

back into the crowd. Perhaps he could yet be safe. The next few days in the square would hold his fate.

Or, what is more to the point, the protester's gesture went into orbit. One of its reentry points was, of course, American politics. At the first opportunity, President George Bush, a sophisticated China hand from way back, he would tell you, praised the student's courageous action as an expression of the students' thirst for freedom. Bush saw the student as confirming the most basic elements of democratic social thought. The president's reading of this gesture was a commonplace one in those months between Beijing and Bucharest. In each instance, in Asia, or Europe, or Africa, following stunning disruptions, every political development was described in terms of the values that supposedly drove movement.

In one story after another, we heard of an almost uncontrollable yearning for freedom breaking out, pushing every network anchor to frenzied travel schedules. Commentators spoke of communism's demise or capitalism's triumph, readings that held only as long as one suspended notice of South Africa or the Palestinian *intifada,* for example, or the notable lack of interest in capitalist ideology among the Chinese students. Others, perhaps sensitive to those exceptions, spoke more generally of the collapse of outmoded governmental, political, and social systems. That abstraction had other problems. A net wide enough to capture both communism and apartheid would be wide enough to capture other outdated political modes as well. The explanations offered for these remarkable events lacked specificity, leaving enough anomalies unexplained to let us reopen the issue. What was happening in those scattered yet somehow connected events?

My reading of the episode with the tanks — and of this entire sequence of events — diverges from the most commonplace explanations. By gesture and posture, the student had appropriated more than one genre. The resulting ambiguity gave his protest its intensity. This was a story of "bodies and tanks"; his body improbably stopped the machines of oppression. But the student's action made other references as well. The dance of student and tank column was more Charlie Chaplin than John Locke, more cinema than physics, more play — dangerous, self-obliterating play, to be sure — than ideology. Bush's reading of the image was opportunistic, a rushed effort to reinscribe a perilous moment with an explanation that fit into the plot he preferred. Bush saw no signal that order itself was at stake, no sign that irreverence had reached new levels. He didn't notice the genie leaving the bottle, entering the (television) tube, and starting to move around the globe.

My response emphasizes something he excluded: a subtly different kind of freedom carried by the actual political mechanism that accomplished each transformation — the televised street demonstration. The floating, propelled network news anchors narrated these events as if they had no vehicle at all other than an abstract ideology of freedom and a simplistic functionalism of collapsing systems. I do not disagree that protesters expressed values of liberation or that systems could reasonably be called outdated. The rhetoric of freedom flowed abundantly before turning sour and unmistakably opportunistic with the onset of the Persian Gulf crisis in August 1990. But to emphasize only the liberal ideology of these events would be to miss their media — the practices, vehicles, and genres that carried what was in each case a light ideological load.

The mode of change received little direct attention during this period. In prevailing mainstream political thought, it is the content of messages that matters, not the vehicle that carries them. This exclusion carries an ideology, as do all such important exclusions. The mainstream prefers to accumulate developments incrementally, in the manner of engineered change. Radicals often agree with this preference for content. When the poet Gil Scott-Heron announced in the 1960s that "the revolution will not be televised," his message was subversive precisely because it mirrored a liberal judgment. Television was not "real" and could not provide the arena for something as dramatic as revolution. As appealing as he was, Scott-Heron was also wrong.

Insisting on content, we misunderstand televised demonstrations. Protesters invite such error with their populist claims that demonstrators represent a constituency. "The people" are represented in the demonstration, the populist asserts; "the people, united, will never be defeated." In this story, an economy of representation underwrites each demo. The difference between turnout and majority, discounted for danger or inconvenience, equals an event's political weight. The demo, as even a political scientist might grudgingly admit, is one representative form among many, a political tactic enabled by free-speech provisions of a constitution as mediated by a judicial mechanism. But the mainstream reading habitually misses how protest works. Political science texts can explain that demonstrations have effects, but they can't quite explain how this works or how the effect might be calculated, given the tiny proportion of any population that demonstrates.[1]

This mainstream rhetorical link of demo and representation has other problems. As *constitutional representation,* the demonstration is inevitably defective — simplistic, too ill behaved for a congressional hearing, more evidence of injury or impulse than citizenship. (If this sort of demonstration presented a food processor at a department store, representing it for sale, we'd be entertained, but we wouldn't learn what the gadget did.) Rather than merely grading the demo down for its "bad citizenship," I would study politics at the point of disjunction between the citizen role and the protester role. These two styles are tellingly different, as are their goals and their standards of efficacy. Liberal democracy strives to produce one kind of citizen, an actor in a well-established context of legalistic, constitutional authority.

Protesters, by contrast, constitute themselves along different lines. They appropriate a subtle, second meaning of *demonstrate.* In most uses, the word *demonstration* suggests objectivity: to demonstrate is to point out, to make known, to describe and explain, to prove through deduction. Protesters' usage moves toward the contingent realm of strategies and emotions. Their demonstration doesn't establish objectivity and logic, demonstrating the relationship of gravity and eggs, say, so much as it "shows up" the objective order, assertively getting in its way. Protesters undermine the citizen's connection to authority, threatening to expose illegitimacy. Their demonstration is "a show." Publicly but irreverently, they show that the way we live is necessarily at odds with prevailing knowledge. Their action thus may be minimally programmatic by intent, not defect.

By contrast, citizens demonstrate that they have interests, complaints, and proposals — they are the ones who petition government. When citizens stray from this carefully circumscribed role, their stands are soon discredited. Citizens emphasize the severity of their concern. Protesters demonstrate themselves, their lives, against a framework, not merely its consequences. A demo shows irrepressible bodies, engaging through humor, outrage, and a distinctively expressive urge, not by protesters' compliance with rules but by resistance that says, *in your face, deal with me*. Demonstrations show a life not encompassed by civic philosophy nor represented by institutions. Every "official story" takes on a suspicious tone after the demonstrator has reinterpreted them. Such stories are at odds with the rowdy, transgressive urge that actually makes life lively.

The televised street demonstration reveals something about social and political change. The demo shows how kynics produce change by creating new kinds of political persons. Here my reading produces a better understanding than Bush's of what that Chinese student was doing with those tanks. The student's protest made sense within this alternate rhetorical framework, announcing his own freedom in ways not entirely contained by ideology, plan, or program. He campaigned for the vitality of intersecting genres of public speech, for an irreverent disassembly of institutional order that had controlled him simply by determining the conditions under which he could be seen. Turning into Chaplin for a moment, the student *demonstrated*.

The history of protest is intertwined with the history of revolution, crossed with the sociology of crowds. The sociologist Joseph Gusfield began his review of social movements with a reminder of "France in 1789, Russia in 1917, and China in 1949," but quickly moved on to "Civil Rights movements,...ghetto riots, and... utopian settlements, to list some from among many."[2] He thus traced the origins of social protest through such diverse precedents as the abolitionist movement of the mid-1800s, nationalist movements in India, German Nazism, eighteenth-century food riots in Europe, Marcus Garvey's Universal Negro Improvement Association, various labor movements, and millenarianism.

The notion of leftist social protest, so commonplace today, may be a relatively recent development. The *Oxford English Dictionary* dates this usage of the word *demonstration* only back to 1861, when an issue of *Saturday Review* reported, "We read how the students of [a] University 'made a demonstration'. This we believe means, in plain English, that the students kicked up a row." In *Political Man,* Seymour Martin Lipset notes that "before 1917 extremist political movements were usually thought of as a rightist phenomenon. . . . After 1917 politicians and scholars alike began to refer to both left and right extremism, i.e., Communism and fascism."[3]

This newness should not be too surprising. The demonstration is an element of our age, with its images, communications, and public appeals. On its face, the demonstration is always rhetorical. It *demonstrates* (shows, exposes, replays, and tests) in distinctive ways. The demonstration *shows* (positions or criticism or commitment) without seeking to *institutionalize* that representation. The leap from representation to law remains problematic, ready to be overturned by the next demonstration. For Americans, this aspect of the demonstration may be best encapsulated by the career of Martin Luther King, Jr., who reacted to legislative successes on civil rights issues by moving to other moral challenges — poverty and the Vietnam War — rather than by consolidating institutional advantage. That move was controversial, both within the civil rights movement and in the Johnson administration.[4]

Other political forms presume success. After all, they are grounded in nature and truth. Institutionalized, the values of liberal democracy attain the status they expected to attain. If that institutionalization fails, nature and truth collapse. The demonstration, in contrast, expects to fail, as any system based on escalating risk and instability must. In that sense, the flagged viability of the demonstration during the 1970s and 1980s, and then the spectacular failure of the Tiananmen Square demonstration, did not signal the ultimate demise of the form. Institutions such as Soviet communism are subject to collapse. Such an institutionalized truth regime can be disproved or discarded. But the demonstration is not disproved by its failures. Many protesters do not understand this aspect of the demo. Asked to participate, some will always ask, "How do I know this will do any good?" Their confusion between demonstrating and, say, expending effort to study for exams misses the point. But their misunderstanding does not always undermine the demo, which thrives on such ambiguities, vaulting from them to yet more subversion.

The wit and verve of the demonstration necessarily diminish, sooner or later, or are susceptible to cancellation, sometimes by assassination or other armed interference. American demonstrations became more predictable after the 1970s. Mass Washington gatherings became formulaic and safe. Environmentalists and human rights advocates mastered the demonstration-as-rock-concert genre. The women's movement, at least partly founded in demonstration, moved on, leaving the streets to their antiabortion opponents. Still, none of this "disproved" the demonstration. When Randall Robinson's Trans-Africa movement revitalized the form with small but highly visible demonstrations at the South African embassy in Washington, the demonstration reappeared, presenting itself (for arrest) as if nothing had happened. The demonstration hadn't died, as a failed institutionalization of truth sometimes expires. It waited, as it were, in videotape vaults around the world.

Early on in the contemporary American development of the televised demonstration, the participants had already announced the terms of success for the form they were inventing. In the antiwar protests at the 1968 Democratic Convention in Chicago, protesters chanted, "The whole world is watching." The crucial majority was formed in the audience's gaze, not by an action, presence, or even opinion. The credulity of their chant upset the liberal processes of "popular will"; social force could now emanate from bodies-in-view. The institutions of electoral "representation" began to face a new test, a challenge that soon proved as vital a radical form as anything had since the demise of class warfare.

The demonstration seeks to alter the balance of what the sober and serious realm of civic discourse includes and excludes. The demo tries to "break into" public conversation. The sociologist and New Left veteran Todd Gitlin reminds us that early SDS gatherings went so far as to debate and then orchestrate their picket-sign slogans, the better to focus their message.[5] The chant, a less organized form (implying a spontaneous vox populi), worked better on television and thus became the privileged instance of the slogan. Derogatory press reports of demonstrations always note that organizers contrived unimaginative and excessively organized chants. More supportive press reports select particularly outrageous or humorous slogans as evidence of a demonstration's mood. Nobody confuses protesters with potential candidates or appointees.

It is hard to portray the demo as opportunistic, since it causes so much trouble. By staying on the street, the demo protects its integrity.

Liberal society contains assumptions about the role of the citizenry, which is supposed to be a knowing, controlling "audience." There are strong expectations regarding potential responses that link the powerful back to that audience. The citizen-as-audience watches government-as-mirror of the citizenry. This circuit is strongly self-referential and circular, which may help explain its remarkable stability. Liberal responsibility summarizes that circular relationship. Government responsibility implies a willingness to *respond* to citizens who in turn deserve to be heard in proportion to the "responsibility" of their claims. It is the citizen's responsibility to frame demands in terms the circuit can handle: appreciative of power's problems, careful, partial (not absolute), and patient rather than impulsive.

Questioning these sociopolitical "manners," demonstrators present a different model of the citizen, even as they also articulate demands and insist that attention be paid. The demonstrator is, in other words, an alternate citizen, a different kind of public person. The demonstrator, in his or her most effective moments, is nothing less than a rival expression of the popular will. This version emphasizes everyday life and presumes to contrast the common practices and attitudes of that life with the restricted, self-controlled version required by Western representative democracy.

The demonstration implies an entirely different sort of participant, as Peter Sloterdijk explains. The demonstrator distances himself or herself from the citizen, even though they can claim citizenship when necessary, reversing course to their own advantage. Demonstrators position themselves as *cheeky* citizens. The measured, naturalistic pronouncement on values and possibilities meets a foe from outside its frame, one that uses the "apparently irrelevantly provocative gestures," a tactic Sloterdijk traces back to Diogenes' attack on a prematurely enshrined harmony between life and doctrine. Kynics confront power in ways outside the frame allowed by liberal responsibility. Kynics deploy "bodies as arguments, bodies as weapons."[6] This concern for the body, for how one lives rather than how one idealizes, is characteristic of the kynic.

One of the defining triumphs of American protest, reported long after the fact, was Richard Nixon's obsession with the demonstrations taking place within view of the White House during the Vietnam War. Most of those demonstrators likely expected that the White House would ignore their message, but they repeatedly spoke to the void, intervening with their ill-clothed and unwashed bodies. They reenacted Diogenes more precisely than most of them could have known. Nixon denounced them as irresponsible. But the kynics bothered Nixon so much that he worried endlessly about them and eventually positioned buses to block his view. Nixon specifically enacted Sloterdijk's description of the powerful cynic's demise: "Those who rule lose their real self-confidence to the fools, clowns and kynics."

The kynic repositions criticism to the margins of discourse and beyond the bounds of seriousness, and thus remaps public space. The street, the space of everyday life, is important. Also playing "an essential role in the history of cheekiness" are "the carnival, the universities and the Bohemian" neighborhoods.[7] These sites have little or no institutional authority but provide a place where the kynics can stand apart, formulating their assault on pompous power. Being located away from "legitimate" locations of power is obviously no handicap; how could the kynics function anywhere else than at a margin, a cusp, a thoroughfare?

One obvious objection to Sloterdijk's schema is that demonstrators have often sought to cloak themselves in the legitimacy and moral force of a Plato, rather than his public tormentor, Diogenes. Sloterdijk's kynic functions at the margins of the marginal, camped out at the fringe of the demonstration while the serious spokespersons intone severe moral critique, nearer its core, at the microphones. But in another sense, the kynic is where the actual force of the demonstration resides, no matter what happens at the microphone. The oral histories of demonstrations (the next day, over coffee) linger at the jokes and funny signs and slogans, the outrages and improprieties, more than at the speeches and carefully coherent position papers.

Even the most solemn demo speeches sometimes revert to a cheeky, joyous impudence. The performances of Malcolm X and Martin Luther King, Jr., set the genre of the contemporary demonstration, and their performances were continually ambivalent in form. A bit too loud, a touch too joyous, occasionally naughty in their choice of metaphors, these performers know they are misbehaving, even while they accomplish their announced aim to speak truth to power. We recall King's "I Have a Dream" speech as pure moral force, but some of its power flows from its songlike qualities, a feature King drew reference to when he made explicit reference to "the old Negro spiritual." Even this most serious, legitimacy-pursuing speech, perhaps King's most carefully prepared text, had its playful, kynical moments. One of its most sustained metaphors transposed the social contract into a moral checking account, reversing the familiar role of poor blacks writing checks that bounced, and playing with the implicit connection between the liberal social contract and capitalism.

Knowing that he could not directly address capitalism, King still knew he could raise some dust. He recast the Declaration of Independence as a "promissory note," issued to blacks as a "bad check, a check which has come back marked 'insufficient funds.'" But the innocent recipients of that fake payment (e.g., his audience that day, who by this point in the speech are laughing loudly at the playful reference to expressly forbidden topics) "refuse to believe that the bank of justice is bankrupt." Even the form of their complaint, the huge public demonstration, enters the play when King reminds them that there are many "demands" that are legitimate in society: "So we have come to cash this check, a check that will give us *upon demand* the riches of freedom and the security of justice." Five years later, it would be big news when King targeted economic justice for his next campaign. But his constituents had heard the message long before then.

There are many other examples. The shows staged by Abbie Hoffman offer the most outrageous examples, but the irreverence also can be found throughout Woody Guthrie's work, passed down to his son Arlo, whose recording of "Alice's Restaurant" is surely a kynical masterpiece. Anyone who has ever attended a large American demonstration, by whatever left group, on whatever issue, cannot have missed the cheeky core of the action, on placards, in costume, in the joy of kynics gathered in the street.

As populism moves to the right, there have even been instances of right-wing kynics. Randall Terry's Operation Rescue movement, a militant antiabortion protest movement, explicitly used the kynical form. Placing themselves at the doorstep of their adversaries, Terry's group practices a confrontational style surely learned from predecessors on the left. The blood, pain, and bodies are disrespectfully flung in the face of power. To be sure, Terry's movement is weak on humor and on ideology; portraying pregnant teenagers and the people who help them as a power establishment is quite a leap. But the demo is not primarily a consistency game. The demo will likely remain a practice of the political left, given that disrespect for authority is not a typical conservative position. Still, Terry's case suggests the independence of the form, not entirely subsumed by ideology and not thoroughly attached to an interest group or institutional structure.

But if the U.S. left inadvertently instructed the right, it also sent the demo around the world. Sometimes, American journalists do a better job of reporting on foreign examples than on more familiar domestic instances. The *New York Times,* which seldom notices the cheek in domestic gatherings, carefully reported this aspect of a major Moscow demonstration. A front-page article on a significant 1991 Pushkin Square demo was subtitled "Rally Takes Kremlin Terror and Turns It into Burlesque." The reporter cited "a grinning marcher" with a sign reading, "Is Communism done yet? Or is it going to get worse?" The *Times* described the gathering as "ebullient, peaceful, . . . an impish violation." Reenacting the Chinese student (and Chaplin), "the people moved through the falling snow . . . savoring the simple act of public assembly. They took pleasure in circumventing an armada of water cannon, military trucks and combat troops and police of every description in the center of the city, a stunning gathering assembled by the Kremlin in fear of public disorder."[8]

Muscovites had already begun to import more from the United States than Pepsi, Big Macs, and MTV. They had begun to notice the unique and practiced form of the demonstration. Not only entrepreneurs, it would seem, have headed to Moscow. Via the tube, a new sort of public person — cheeky, kynical, and out in the streets — had also made the trip.

The kynical dimensions of civil rights protests, even the most "high serious," respectful gatherings at the Lincoln Memorial, do

not much survive in the subsequent two decades of legislative response. Even these protests survive as memory, however, to reemerge
as founding events of contemporary black culture and as international precedent. It is even easier to see campus protest and antiwar movements as primarily cultural, since these events never had
much of a legislative legacy. These movements survive as attitude
and gesture. It is hard to imagine anyone thinking them fulfilled
by, say, the War Powers Act or the occasional university peace studies department.

The events surrounding the Gulf War present an example of the
demonstration's strange efficacy, as well as its ambivalent legacy.
That war was often justified by the need to revise the history of
Vietnam. And the core of that revision involved a demonstration.
The Gulf War summons to "support the troops" (explicitly tied to
a massive yellow ribbon redecoration of the American cityscape)
was itself a war cry. It is explicitly more limited than calls from
previous conflicts. "Support the war," "the Great War," "the war to
end all wars" — such slogans refer to a policy or an objective. "Support the troops" almost begs for subversive completions of the
sentence "even if the project they are conducting is dubious, at
best." There was more going on than an attempt to stop Iraq's
Saddam Hussein — a newly discovered project in the summer of
1990. Perhaps as important, the image of "the vet" had to be re-
captured from kynical veterans who had staked their claim as
profound critics and demonstrators.

The kynical soldier has a long history as the dark humor of the
battlefield attests. Nonetheless, through the vehicle of the demonstration, the kynical veteran of the Vietnam War found new ways
to cause trouble, even after leaving the battlefield. Oliver Stone's
film *Born on the Fourth of July* emphasized one particular demonstration. The Vietnam Vets Against the War (VVAW) demonstration at the 1972 Miami Republican Convention made its point
with a thunderous silence. Other VVAW actions throughout the
country spread that eloquent and ironic silence, making the antiwar vet an important figure. Through protests, the real parades
honoring returning vets, kynical vets captured the political stage.
The Ron Kovic book depicted by Stone's film had emphasized the
last patrol, the convoy of cars driven cross-country by California

vets going to Miami for the protest. Hunter Thompson wrote the most dramatic account of the demonstration:

> [The Vets] were moving up Collins Avenue in dead silence; twelve hundred of them dressed in battle fatigues, helmets, combat boots...a few carried full-size plastic M-16s, many peace symbols, girlfriends walking beside vets being pushed along the street in slow-moving wheelchairs, others walking jerkily on crutches.... But nobody spoke; all the "stop, start," "fast, slow," "left, right" commands came from "platoon leaders" walking slightly off to the side of the main column and using hand signals....
>
> I left my car...and joined the march.... No, "joined" is the wrong word; that was not the kind of procession you just walked up and "joined." Not without paying some very heavy dues: an arm gone here, a leg there, paralysis, a face full of lumpy scar tissue...all staring straight ahead as the long silent column moved between rows of hotel porches full of tight-lipped Senior Citizens, through the heart of Miami Beach.
>
> The silence of the march was contagious, almost threatening. There were hundreds of spectators, but nobody said a word. I walked beside the column for ten blocks, and the only sounds I remember hearing were the soft thump of boot leather on hot asphalt and the occasional rattling of an open canteen top.[9]

Given the VVAW's importance, it was a matter of crucial importance when Kovic, a leader of that demonstration, spoke to the (ostensibly moderate, perhaps even conservative) Democratic convention that nominated Jimmy Carter only four years later. An important boundary had been transgressed. The kynic, having successfully cast a pall over one convention, had attained the rostrum at another, only four years later.

Once empowered, if only briefly, the kynical vet did some damage. A Vietnam memorial was commissioned and built in Washington: a gleaming black trench wall, it menaced the State Department's back door. As planned and originally constructed, the monument had no reassuring, unifying narrative; it had, instead, a text of individual, singular names, listed by chronology of their death (not alphabetically, which would have implied a false unity, making it a bit too easy to find a specific name). No other American monument has ever become such a site of enduring contestation, finally requiring an amendment, a heroic statue, to tame it. The fight over the Vietnam Memorial was but another sortie in an ongoing battle over the kynical vet. Rewriting the history of Vietnam-era demonstrations played large after Reagan's small simulated wars in Grenada and Panama and Bush's large simulated war in the Persian Gulf.

The promise to honor "the troops" when they returned from the Gulf was an attempt to bring that contested era to an end, at long last. The last act of this contest would be a grand rhetorical turnabout, something even flashier than the "night into day" fireworks displays that marked most Gulf War celebrations (as well as the war itself, in night-vision video form). Fanatically welcoming the troops of Desert Storm (sometimes even calling them "Storm Troopers," to exuberantly deploy yet another revision), the yellow-ribbon folk hoped to finally close the contest by pinning the antiwar demonstrators with the blame for dishonoring returning Vietnam-era troops.

Never mind that this reversal was dubiously founded. As Thompson explained, the antiwar movement had almost unlimited respect for the VVAW, with good cause: "There is no anti-war or even anti-establishment group in America today with the psychic leverage of the VVAW."[10] At any rate, only the vet who returned with a keen kynicism intact would have wanted a parade conducted by demonstrators, whose parades are typically unpredictable and disrespectful. Indeed, it probably helped that the yellow ribbon tied together a false case. To exhaust the memory of the kynical vet, the memory of the VVAW, nothing less would really do. This was the powerful cynic's run on the kynic's stage, but even the wild success of the Gulf War reinforced the kynic's role, if indirectly.

There are many ways for a kynic to fail. And not all demonstrators are kynics. Some insist too much on literal and consistent condemnation. They find it hard to understand why their approach works so poorly. The tendency to remain linked to the message, to an ideological vision that would fit within modernism, is too comfortable for some demonstrators to abandon. The best demonstrators, however, have always understood that the message — the ideology of the demonstration — composed only one of its dimensions. The status of this intervention includes an edge toward performance and action, remaining subtly uncomfortable with the stability and reliability of ideology. The demonstration knows that it cannot go on forever. The demonstration, this oddly efficacious but ambivalently realized rhetorical reenactment of modernity's demise, does not survive. It recurs.

Chapter 15

Politics after Cynicism

> My wife and I and the vice president all called him
> [Dick Morris, the campaign aide who resigned in dis-
> grace] and just had a purely personal conversation.
> Bill Clinton

The demonstration is useful as a way of isolating the kynical impulse so it can be more clearly seen. But kynicism is by no means
only a protest role. It becomes important in understanding the
broader phenomenon of cynicism precisely because the cheeky, disbelieving form extends throughout political culture, often vying
for a place where we might not expect to find it. It is in these more
ambivalent locales that kynics mix with cynics of various stripes,
setting off a struggle over the political system.

Democracy has long contained tensions that are not entirely reflected in its seemingly obvious and natural doctrine. Someone has
to rule, to assemble the legislative coalition, and to make genuinely
tough decisions. And the people must add their stamp of legitimacy. But the voting public may not be sufficiently attentive or
politically attuned or expert to make rational or even sensible decisions. One solution to this problem would involve considerable
deference to elites. That is the solution founder James Madison
preferred, and there is much of his legacy in the civility strategy. The
basis for contemporary cynicism was set there, when the founders

affixed the label "representative," with its powerful rhetoric, to institutional arrangements that could not live up to the words. Madison's accomplishment, documented in the *Federalist Papers*, was to redefine civic attitudes about representative democracy, turning that hallowed political value into a danger to be avoided at great cost. To insulate ourselves from actual politics, we substituted a civic faith, which flourished.

Eventually, this belief, so well argued that it couldn't be convincingly contradicted, simply exhausted itself, running down from overload and rust. Every cynic knows that civic faith no longer credibly organizes political life. Over and over, the American arrangement makes promises it cannot keep. But this exhausted, battered system retains great utility. Cynics-in-power find the rhetoric of consent and civic values terrifically useful. It can be deployed to convince people that they are free because they have an abstract power of rebellion. Rendered merely symbolic, consent can help a cynic-in-power rule. This is the grandest sting of our greatest con men and women.

This arrangement puts elections at a crucial intersection in our cultural life. The rituals of democracy might seem innocuous enough between elections, even if renting out the Lincoln Bedroom probably strikes most of us as a bit much. But in a campaign, the chips are in the center of the table. Power is at stake, so the struggle becomes more immediate and less constrained. Winners need to retain some legitimacy, since they' will later govern. But winners must first win. With so much at stake, the incentive grows to use the manipulative tricks and deceptions. At this point in the democratic saga, the campaign manager performs the core civic role.

We are nervous about our campaigners, and there is reason to be nervous. Their project, to present a candidate or issue in a way that will connect with a broad electorate, is rife with opportunity for abuse. There are lies to tell, fears to exploit, and influence to purchase. We express our anxiety about the political system's worst moments when we use the word *politics* as a synonym for nearly every foible of social life, for manipulation, unfairness, influence, and untold smaller sins. Whatever else Americans are cynical about, we are hugely cynical about politics. Still, Americans avoid politics, and it took a long time for the political operative to emerge as a public figure. Histories say little about specific operatives before this century. Interest in big-city machines brought a few of these characters to the public eye, but their real heyday came later. Everybody of a certain age knows minute details of Richard Nixon's career, but how many could identify Murray Chotiner, the hard-driving campaign pro who helped chart Nixon's rise to power?

Television's need for talking heads now makes the campaigner a public figure. Lee Atwater, Ed Rollins, Roger Ailes, George Stephanopoulos, Dick Morris, and Susan Estridge are well-known names. The insider journalist Joe Klein generated a huge fuss with *Primary Colors*, a book that focused as much on the process of campaigning as on its thinly veiled satirical take on Bill Clinton. But no campaign pros have ever captured public attention like our oddest political couple, James Carville and Mary Matalin.

Each of them is an effective campaigner at the highest level. Carville so personified Bill Clinton's 1992 campaign that a documentary largely focused on him, *The War Room*, enjoyed a successful theatrical release. Matalin played an important and visible role in Republican presidential campaigns before graduating to flashy media visibility on the CNBC cable channel. The book they coauthored raised dust and sold units. They posed for an American Express advertisement that ran in the slick magazines. The ad pictured them surrounded by the spoils their success — and their credit card — had purchased. How could they be sincere, effective — and married? And what explains their continued visibility and popularity? Doesn't this amount to a pair of thumbed noses in the face of society? Surely, they must be the First Couple of American cynicism.

Here's Matalin on Lee Atwater, the bad boy of Republican politics who ran the 1988 Bush campaign: "Atwater always had a three-cushion shot. There was always something in it for the candidate, something in it for Atwater, something in it for somebody else so they would be loyal to Atwater. It was quite a technique."[1] Atwater was Matalin's mentor in national Republican politics. She isn't criticizing him here. This is high praise.

Carville is every molecule the Democrat's bad boy. He made his mark in national politics with Bob Casey's 1986 campaign against William Scranton III for governor of Pennsylvania, honing his signature ability to convince a reluctant candidate to "go negative."

Casey, an antiabortion candidate and a cultural conservative, needed to run to Scranton's right. Negative ads had become an issue in the campaign, but at the end, Casey was still behind. Carville helped assemble the famous "guru" spot showing a college photo of Scranton with long hair. "Sitar music twanged in the background. If we could've filmed it in Smell-o-rama there would have been at least incense in the air."[2] The voice-over quoted Scranton praising possible uses of transcendental meditation in government. The ad tried to brand Scranton a hippie. A subsequent Carville accomplishment was to boost Texas governor Ann Richard's negative ratings in a nasty Democratic primary. She won reelection but subsequently lost the job to George Bush's son.

Anyone can think up a nasty ad. The campaign manager's prized talent is the ability to talk the candidate into "going negative" and putting the ad on the air. Describing his conversation with Casey, Carville is much less descriptive than when he describes the ad itself: "Casey wasn't wild about it, but we had very specifically not mentioned drugs, which was his promise, and ultimately he gave us the okay." One imagines the actual conversation was more entertaining than the description. The campaign manager does the dirty work, convincing a candidate who sees himself as honorable to abandon the high road, to discard civility. The pro is the carrier of the news: the stakes are enormous and you will lose if we don't do this. This is the very cusp of the cynical turn.

The best campaign managers give us a clue. The public realm is a location of wonderful if sometimes guilty fun. In the struggle, in politics, there is a sophisticated response to the demons of cynical society. But the game mocks simplistic explanations. The political world, with its long-abandoned faith in simple civility and values, nonetheless keeps on going — a perfectly cynical environment. At times, the cynical moves seem innocuous or even justifiable, given the stakes in play. At other times, the manipulations seem corrosive of the democratic possibility. No principle can convincingly settle debates over which moves are good and which are bad. The cynical problem and its various antidotes do not array themselves neatly on different sides, as on a football field.

To make sense of this mess, it helps to broaden our understanding of what democracy requires in the contemporary age. Contention is not a dysfunction or mistake in a system in which powerful cynics work hard to create marginal identities for their political opponents, sometimes using a resentful politics to complete the deal. The rampant wig politics of our age only make the cycle of cynicism harder to eradicate. Wigs are immune from centrist calls back to the middle, and their excesses make the powerful cynics' job easier. When the cynicism turns as thick as it recently has, the appropriate response is democratic politics, not generalized center-mongering. That politics will be contentious, but it will also be lively. It is in that liveliness that powerful cynics and wigs might finally meet their match.

The political science article of faith, that politics is inevitably Tweedledee and Tweedledum, described our centrist parties in the 1950s and early 1960s fairly well, but it is not a necessary condition. After the mid-1960s, it stopped being a good description of the political system. But it lived on as a code for American distrust of politics. In our era of heightened contention, when someone says they can't tell the difference between parties, candidates, or interest groups, they're telling you about their cynicism, not about the level of difference and contention in our politics.

The contingency of events — the propensity for politics to change directions, based on an always impromptu mix of manipulative skill, lucky timing, and accident of situation — confounds an apolitical citizenry that hopes, above all, not to have to worry about politics. But that same contingency energizes the tiny minority of the general population that has been politicized. It keeps political folk reading the newspaper. In a lively democratic culture, more citizens would understand the constant unfolding of events. More of those citizens would be involved in interpreting those events and playing out the possibilities that arise.

The democratic activist understands that the contingency of political events is a fact of democratic life, rather than an injustice to be railed against. As the political theorist Wendy Brown explains, "The late twentieth century could be said to be 'a time of events.' Not the time of The Event — as in the French Revolution or Munich, the Tonkin Gulf Resolution or even the Dreyfus affair — but of relatively banal events, of events that acquire their status not by being part of a larger historical force or movement but precisely by erupting out of the everyday."[3] Such names as Anita Hill, Clarence

Thomas, Gennifer Flowers, Tawana Brawley, Rodney King, and O.J. signal these events.

Nonetheless, in itself, democratic activism may not be much of a solution. Powerful cynics also take advantage from the way events unfold. They are the manipulators, and contingency invites manipulation. Cynics-in-power assume the impossibility of belief, which contingency reaffirms, over and over. They can manipulate every effort to resolve the tensions of cynicism at a general level. There can be no general "solution" to the various ills cynicism produces. We are left with tactical and strategic moves, rather than a solution.

In a lively democratic setting, with its continual reference to unfolding events, judgments are seldom as clear as they may seem. The civic belief position emphasizes the utility of political values, but in actual political action, those values may not be very useful or may only be useful under extreme and unusual conditions. In democratic practice, political events test our reliance on values. Sometimes kynics stage protests against pompous and hypocritical adversaries. Sometimes powerful cynics use values to manipulate their constituents. Sometimes citizens and manipulators alike use values talk to underscore positions that are more partisan than they wish to openly admit. And sometimes those values offer very real reassurance that we are, after all, "doing the right thing," often when that thing is partisan, lively, and not all that clearly connected to those reassuring values.

Another way of putting this is that politics is often composed of reversible positions. There remains no enduring, certain way to decide which competing interpretation is correct. President Clinton's moderation might be evidence of his conservatism or it might be the necessary, if unfortunate, context for his more agreeable accomplishments. Newt Gingrich's radicalism before and during his term as Speaker of the House might have been seen as moving the Republican coalition away from some of its internal paradoxes or setting his party up for a fall. From a distance, such questions are easier to answer. The historian, building a consistent narrative out of an era that didn't know it was living that story at the time, resolves such puzzles with ease. Likewise, the moralist, standing away from the fray, has an easy time describing what each event means. But in politics, these judgments are seldom so obvious. At the same time, it is never the case that "anything goes" — that we have somehow endorsed nihilistic relativism when we take serious note of the political world's contingency.

Trying to simplify this inevitable difficulty, we continually refer back to historical situations in which values played a clearer role. Hence the enduring usefulness of Hitler as object lesson, as proof that extraordinary evil sometimes shows up in the political arena. But in daily practice, politics is seldom that obvious. Unless one takes some pleasure in tracking the political to-and-fro, there is much incentive to opt out — to deny the relevance of politics, to adopt the cynical distance characteristic of our age. The values position, seemingly a call for reengagement, can end up encouraging this flight from politics. The political world is at least as hard to reconstruct as an egg fallen from a wall.

The believer always wants to impose order on this scene, urging us to believe that good values produce good outcomes. But this is not at all assured. Sometimes good values lose, since their bearers are unable to navigate the difficult political maze to implement policies informed by those values. Sometimes good values win but for reasons unacceptable to the believers, as when congressional Republicans, wary of their poll ratings, helped pass a minimum-wage increase in early 1996. Success is therefore a difficult matter for the moralist. Could it be better to lose and retain the moral voice? A victory is a perilous — maybe even a terrible — thing.

The contingency of events, the propensity for politics to change directions, based on the luck of timing and situation, is what keeps that unlikely smile on the face of kynical activists everywhere. The political world does not exist to confirm or refute our values. Instead, it provides an arena in which we can negotiate our differences, assess possibilities, and create movement. To evoke the image of the kynic is not to offer irreverent protest as the only solution to our ills. It is only to suggest that the real culture of democratic politics itself, an often dangerous, funny, and challenging practice, will have to be rebuilt if any solution can emerge.

The kynic is prepared for things to turn out well, in a way that the believer seldom is. But the kynic, scoffing at utopian dreams, knows better than to hope for permanent correction. The best outcomes, pertaining as they do to events, are transitory, so a kynic may not even imagine the utopian possibility. The ideal is the kynic's target, not the goal. The wig fatalist reconfigures hope into despair, prospects into pessimism. For fatalists, these things are already settled. The playing out doesn't matter; it cannot interest them, since their defenses are already up. The kynic doesn't worry about that too much — or at least, not too long, or in too debilitating a way. Kynics will take a momentary win, retreat, attend to other business, or begin planning the next action. They know that is the way to disengage from authority, to trick the powerful into losing their self-confidence.

The tendency in American politics, always, is to split the difference, make conflict go away, retreating to the signs of consensus even if a refolding of prior events is necessary to support the lost consensus. So I've saved a discussion of how to do that until very late in this book, hoping it will be harder to fall back on the split difference and refolded event. But any practiced American cynic is way ahead of me, thinking how the activist kynic and believer could be mixed together. Inevitably, the solution is to reinterpret the kynic as a secret believer, a partisan with bad manners.

Without doubt, kynics have a moral streak. Their complaint about the hypocrisy of those who govern or those who preach can even be a corrective that helps repair broken commitments to morality. But kynics have other complaints that are not so easily encompassed by morality. They complain that nobody, no matter how well repaired, can or should live solely by the universal nostrums our moral traditions invoke. Kynics remind the stuffed shirts of the function that vitality, humor, and healthy disbelief can play, especially in a society that requires a political activism that it simultaneously inhibits. The kynic is not Nietzsche's overman, forcing a heroic transformation of all values and habits by refusing the public morality. The kynic's irreverent cheekiness serves as a self-imposed limit on the dangerous slide into self-righteousness. The role itself contains a sort of balance, if you will, a studied imbalance.

Kynicism is a culture. It informs roles and ways of being in the world. There are examples of kynical culture, as these last chapters have endeavored to show. But kynicism is no more encompassed by its examples than cynicism is contained by its instances. I have exaggerated the coherence of the kynical role in order to make it visible as an alternative to the cynics we know better. Kynics come and go. They fade in and out of view. Some of them turn bitter or private. This is the point; the kynic differs from the believer, the wig, or the cynic-in-power in dramatic ways. The kynic has to be identified as a role or a possibility if we are to understand cynicism in general. But the kynic is no more a "solution" than are the various targets of kynical criticism. Kynics issue a reminder, not a program. They compose a gesture, not a project.

Kynicism differs from civic belief in that it offers no foundation from which to build subsequent arguments and proposals. Denying such a foundation, kynics show that there are other ways to live — other bases for moral claims, other ways to frame expectations, other ways to imagine politics. Foundations are much debated these days. The kynical example engages that debate in a different way, showing recognizable precedents and evoking the rhythms of life-as-lived. Not content to battle it out with the believers on their chosen ground of foundational abstracts, the kynical heirs to Diogenes change the character, locale, and temperament of the debate.

If the kynic has a foundation, it is an odd one. Democratic practice is not really as foundational as we have been led to believe by the stultified symbols, unsatisfactory institutions, and even deceitful manipulations that have been loaded onto the word *democracy*. Behind all those abuses, however, democratic tradition offers some hope. In its radically open, contested, and variable possibility — really, a lack of structure rather than a foundation — democratic practice is worth taking seriously. This is a basis (if, strictly speaking, a base without foundation) that we recognize, still. Sometimes democracy is contentious; sometimes it pacifies. Sometimes it is stable, but at other times it forms an arena for events, for the creation of identities, and for all sorts of cultural adjustments. It is even possible that democracy positively needs the kynic. Prone to capture, democracy requires a rogue element that pries it loose from its moorings, restarts its meandering, and reminds those who follow its play that the democratic game retains the potential to surprise.

Cynicism is the condition of living after belief has been abused. The political world — its various institutions, whether official or not — has well earned a cynical response. But this is not entirely a matter of sordid individual motives, of high crimes and misdemeanors. This system has long been set up for its citizens to disbelieve. Too many paradoxes thread their way through the system's arteries. Arranged to maximize internal conflict and minimize efficiency, the system was always ready to be disbelieved.

Nowhere is this clearer than in the tension between campaigning and governing. In a campaign, a candidate and the organization promoting the candidate must develop a message, refining a simple version of their message that combines policy, politics, and a media strategy. Even though citizens complain that campaigns go on too long, from the inside perspective, a campaign's life span is terribly short. Campaigns move with ferocious speed. One serious mistake, and the campaign could effectively be over. From the inside, every campaign is about one day long. With that sense of urgency, every decision, every action, every judgment is amplified. Tricks get dirtier, money gets more valuable, and the stakes get more and more intimidating.

The rhythm of the political campaign is a clue. A campaign pro thinks about the horizon of events, the ways things will happen down the line, the gambles ahead, the events that will happen even if others don't yet see it. We can imagine that when James Carville came to the first Clinton campaign (as it was riding an early crest), then heard about some of the Arkansas dirt Clinton's opponents would surely sling, he began thinking about how you help a candidate develop to handle such nastiness. He started to explain how hard they were going to have to be on Bush and Quayle, in anticipation of these events that had not yet happened. He knew that this boldness (now, in preparation, and later, as events unfolded) would doom any hope he had of some normal job in the administration. He probably never dreamed of a White House job, knowing that he was headed for another campaign.

Although these are only examples in which we can isolate the kynical impulse, the political campaign or protest march provides the kynic with the best possible platform. The kynic cannot be institutionalized. The tensions carried within the kynical role would be fatal if the kynic came too close to the seat of government. Again, there is a precarious imbalance. The kynic is fascinated by the public world but remains an outsider. Like the gambler, the kynic decides when to hold and when to fold.

Then at the end of a kynic-run campaign, somebody's candidate wins. And the world turns. Governing requires a different set of skills. If the pace of action does not exactly crawl to a stop, the horizon is further away; most elected officials fill out their terms. Now the audience is not entirely encompassed by the polls and the audiences at fund-raising dinners. There are branches of government that impinge on any policy proposal. Internal negotiations can make or break prospects for success. The game is much better contained in Washington. Governing cannot be an extension of campaigning, no matter how much we talk about "the permanent campaign."

During a campaign, citizens sift through proposals, slogans, and commentary. The most sophisticated among them understand that many of the charges and countercharges are codes that contain much more than their surfaces suggest. But, by definition, these activist citizens already have a preference; they have a horse in the race. So knowledgeable citizens discount the codes, measuring the possibilities that their side will succeed. Once governing begins, the sides are different. A liberal Democrat might have supported Clinton in the election but would begin pushing against his moderate or conservative tendencies. The corresponding urge drives conservative Republicans. For sophisticated voters, this is not too disconcerting. They understand how all this works.

The "unsophisticated citizen," a category that covers almost the entire population when the issue is politics, will not handle this shift so gracefully. For them, campaign promises are promises, not codes designed to win a contest. With a little encouragement from a perpetually antagonistic press, these citizens quickly turn cynical. Governing never looks much like campaigning, and when it does, that's just more reason to be cynical. The pronouncements and speeches government leaders give are no help at all. Carefully evasive, so as not to disrupt the real, private negotiations, these speeches sound as false as they are. But for citizens who have little confidence that their interests are represented in those negotiations, or who would not even know how to tell whether they were represented or not, the evasions are hard to take. Smells like dishonesty.

If the public somehow had confidence that officials had their best interest at heart, or if they really respected those leaders as "larger than life," that might help resolve some of these tensions. But the cynical era has been remarkably durable. For whatever reason, and I have suggested several in the course of this book, civic faith is terribly hard to reconstruct. Political parties, journalists, and institutions have all earned our cynicism. By now, we might well start to understand that this is something like a permanent condition. The most basic institutional arrangements are not subject to radical alteration. While the rules and practices of journalism are always changing, the basic structures of that world are well set in place, too. And campaigns have always looked like a cynical mess.

Rather than focusing on reconstructing belief, it may make sense to try to escape this game of belief, disbelief, and cynicism. Sermons on civility and community may not be all that helpful. The solutions might be found elsewhere.

Chapter 16

Solutions and Conclusions

This is another fine mess you've gotten us into.
Oliver Hardy to Stan Laurel

Oliver Hardy's retort was always a good joke, because Stan Laurel was never solely responsible. But the mess was predictably extraordinary, if not exactly "fine" in any of that word's several meanings. And, of course, Oliver's bluster hid his share of the responsibility for the mess. In our case, it is truly a fine mess we've gotten ourselves into. And getting out will not be as simple as we might hope. The solution to cynicism does not much resemble the usual run of political solutions. Any number of policies and reforms would respond to America's cynicism. But programmatic suggestions are much easier to propose than to achieve. The hard part is developing the political and cultural moves that would make such reforms possible.

In June 1998, as Monicagate raged, the National Commission on Civic Renewal issued a major report on the civil realm. The commission, despite its official-sounding name, is a private foundation. Its report was funded by a major private donor, the Pew Charitable Trusts. The results received high-profile treatment in the major newspapers. The commission had clout; its cochairs were William Bennett and former Democratic senator Sam Nunn. The commission's report represented a bid for big-time visibility.

It even featured a graph of civic health, the Index of National Civic Health (INCH). Not surprisingly, the trend pointed perilously downward.

The report leaned heavily on the attitudes and behaviors of citizens: "As James Madison rightly suggested more than two hundred years ago, republican government presupposes more trustworthy human qualities — more virtues — than does any other form of government. Our nation could not have survived and prospered if this confidence in the capacity for virtue of democratic citizens had been misplaced."[1] This is a remarkable reading of Madison, who worried about the citizenry's virtue more than he relied on it to stabilize the republic. The report was persistently blind to effects that produce incivility and cynicism. In the press conference, reporters picked this up immediately. One asked why corporations and other massive institutions didn't come in for more criticism. The executive director pointed out a passage on page 39 of the report, a weak response that was subsequently ridiculed by other reporters. The director then pointed out passages on pages 18 and 46.[2] It was not a happy answer.

The commission's list of reasons why it was troubled about the country's civic and moral condition was revealing:

> During the past generation, our families have come under intense pressure, and many have crumbled. Neighborhood and community ties have frayed. Many of our streets and public spaces have become unsafe. Our public schools are mediocre for most students, and catastrophic failures for many. Our character-forming institutions are enfeebled. Much of our popular culture is vulgar, violent, and mindless. Much of our public square is coarse and uncivil. Political participation is at depressed levels.... Public trust in our leaders and institutions has plunged.[3]

The commission searched long and hard. It found the problem. It is "us," if by us, of course, you mean the public rather than the elites who composed the commission or the institutions that gave it credibility and funding. A sort of "royal us": "Much of what has gone wrong in America we have done — and are still doing — to ourselves." The problem is us, that "too many of us have become passive and disengaged. Too many of us lack confidence in our capacity to make basic moral and civic judgments, to join with our neighbors to do the work of community.... In a time that cries out for civic action, we are in danger of becoming a nation of spectators."[4]

As if anyone was still uncertain, the commission then hammered home the point: "To be sure, there are many obstacles to effective involvement.... Yes, leadership matters. It matters a great deal. But today in our democracy the core issue is not leadership; it is citizenship."[5] But as explicit as the report was about the problem it perceived, it was none too explicit about how it reached this remarkably self-serving conclusion. It referred to "countless millions of decisions, by individual citizens as well as large corporations" as a cause, but that was about it.

Buried in a section of the report that trumpets "A New Movement" among citizens in neighborhood associations and voluntary groups, a mild critique of the commissioners' peers finally slips in. Public officials need to "place the restoration of public trust at the forefront of their concerns."

> This means doing the public's business efficiently and effectively; it means speaking honestly to the people, not diminishing confidence by making promises that cannot be kept; it means keeping our democracy open and responsive to the voices of all the people, not just those with money and connections; and it means respecting and nurturing the democratic capacities of citizens and communities.[6]

But everything that surrounds this timid passage says it isn't so. The report leaves little for that honest, open, and respectful government to actually do, once it has rid itself of corruption and inefficiency. No policies or institutions are particularly at fault. The "royal us" is the problem.

This becomes yet clearer when we read the report's solutions section. The categories of solutions are individuals, families, neighborhoods, schools, faith-based institutions, and the media. Political parties, Congress, corporations, elite professional groups, candidates, and other centers of power show up only insofar as they can help the individuals, usually with trivial reforms. ("The federal government should spur the development of a voluntary national [educational] testing system with high standards.") The crushing problem of economic inequality receives a passing mention as a subcategory of neighborhood solutions.

Poverty policy is treated as a subcategory of faith-based institutions: "The federal government should revise the tax code to increase incentives for charitable contributions." Traditional conservative concerns — divorce rates, out-of-wedlock births, and the like — are featured in the report, but liberal concerns such as day care are buried. Day care for children shows up in a proposal that "faith-based institutions should take full advantage of new opportunities under federal law to receive public support." The report's schools section is longest, and contains the clearest traces of dispute:

> Some members of the National Commission advocate public support for parental choice broadened to include private and religious schools, especially for low-income students now trapped in failing systems. These members believe that wider choice will enhance educational opportunity and accountability, improve quality, help get parents more involved . . . , and catalyze civic engagement. They consider school choice to be a crucial and necessary step toward civic renewal and self-government.
>
> Other Commission members believe that public schools have been, and continue to be, vital meeting grounds in which future citizens learn to respect and work with one another across their differences. These members fear that choice widened beyond the bounds of public schools could diminish support for public education, further fragment our society, and weaken our democracy. We were not able to resolve these differences.[7]

Remarkably, the evidence suggests that the group had its biggest fight over whether to advocate the destruction of one of the only great civic institutions this country has managed to erect and maintain — public education.

The commission's pattern of selective perception is yet more obvious when one considers the flashiest element of its report — an index of civic health. With its snappy acronym, the commission's Index of National Civic Health is obviously meant for prime time.

The index tracks "political participation, political and social trust, associational membership, family integrity and stability, and crime." In the commission's main exhibit, a graph of INCH from 1972 to 1996, several crucial periods jump out. After a steep decline (from 110 to 98) between 1972 and 1975, the index levels out until 1983, then spikes briefly up to 104 in 1984. Then comes the fall, down to 82 in 1989, after which the trend levels out through 1996.

In examining the components of the index, possible reasons for this pattern fairly jump out of the secondary charts. Many of the factors the commission worries most about were either stable (association membership and giving) or trended steadily toward the worse (nonmarital births). The rise in youth murder rates contributes to the late 1980s decline. The commission did not recommend either gun control or a change in the direction of the war on drugs inaugurated by cochair William Bennett. But the index's real mover is the trust component. From 1972 to 1980, trust in government collapsed from 54 to 25, with an especially sharp drop (from 54 to 35) between 1972 and 1974, paralleling the overall index's first period of decline. Then, from 1984 to 1990, trust in government collapsed again, from 44 to 28. This parallels the overall index's second period of sharp decline.

I suppose it would represent a breach of civility to note that the early-1970s decline paralleled Watergate and the 1980s decline paralleled the Republican deployment of antigovernment rhetoric as a central element of backlash politics. INCH suggests that backlash and resentment politics, as well as abuse of power, are the driving elements in our decline of civility. Yet the commission that produced INCH itself doesn't give an inch. In the press conference that announced the results, the project's executive director, William Galston, did mention Watergate and Vietnam in passing reference when a reporter asked about the graph's intriguing shape. Bennett and Nunn each joked, "I don't do charts."

The report's preface trumpeted its political diversity. It also revealed that the commission's work had been marked by some disagreements: "Our debates have been vigorous, occasionally heated, but always civil. Civility does not mean eliminating passion and conflict from public discourse.... Civility means disagreeing with others without demonizing them."[8] But the demonizers don't much show up, after this mention in the preface. The backlashers aren't blamed for the downturn in civility, nor are they pressured to change their behavior. Citizens and churchgoers are supposed to fix a problem somebody else caused. As much as the commission strove for representation from both Republicans and Democrats, it does not seem to have also felt the need to balance its proscriptions between citizens and larger institutions and interests. The civility solution urges us to imagine Little America, in which solutions can only emerge from neighborhoods and churches but never from government and politics, much beyond the local neighborhood council. The conditions that produced a laggard citizenry seem to have emerged from nowhere.

I do not wish to blame the commission for the political effects it ignored. Instead, the reason for discussing their report at such length is this: the civility argument remains blocked from dealing with the problem it identifies. If the problem is civility, the solution must be a correction in the bad attitude that has somehow infected the royal us. It would be both out of proportion and paradoxical to recommend potentially divisive political struggle as a response to lapses in civility. This is true because incivility is a symptom rather than a cause. But it is also true because civility's solutions are inherently limited. Each solution pales in comparison to the problem it is intended to solve. Solutions are recast as gestures. And as important as a gesture can be, it remains out of proportion to the promise of a solution. The spiral of cynicism merely takes another turn. Who would believe that the commission's recommendations would really change Cynical America? Not a cynic, that's for sure.

Nonetheless, as hesitant as I am to end this book with a list of solutions, a solution being a mischievous thing in a cynical world, I understand the conventions of books such as this. Several of the items on the list that follows are negatives. The grand solutions that accompany moral exhortation are blocked from the start. Building a lively democratic culture will require narrower moves — reforms that recognize the institutional and cultural underpinnings of our cynical era, since those conditions will not soon disappear. None of the items on the list is sufficient to the task. But taken together they may evoke some idea of the kind of response that would actually do something about the problems cynicism poses.

1. Simply promoting community talk and a discourse of "solutions" isn't enough.

The wonky policy-speak Dionne advocated in *Why Americans Hate Politics* is insufficient to the task at hand. Enduring structures of American politics are so stable that they will cleverly resist our reform efforts. We have, for better or worse, permanently divided and fragmented governmental authority, a system designed to be hard to move. Our politics will inevitably involve the mix of policy and politics, as Dionne acknowledged in *They Only Look Dead.*[9] To deny that mixture is to deny the necessary, a posture that only makes the dilemma of cynicism worse.

To be sure, talk of community and values still motivates some citizens. I have argued, however, that such talk incompletely represents the political world, and that some of the exclusions are important. Perhaps more crucially, the community and values positions fail to address actual cynics in a way that matters. Powerful cynics learn to manipulate such talk. Wig cynics easily spin such sermons into their antipolitics stories. And the lively American culture just sees them as irrelevant or boring. Nobody gets organized.

If it is to function, democratic practice cannot be reduced to its ostensible topic, public policy. Neither can it be converted into an object of worship — the very move that plagues its current functioning. To address our many and diverse needs, politics needs to be a culture as well as a reference to institutions, elections, and policy claims. At its best, politics can be endlessly intriguing, entertaining, frightening, and transforming. We need to learn how to perceive politics, talk about it, and teach it in ways that bring forth rather than stifle its liveliness.

2. Complaints about the media need to get it right.

Complaining about the media has become a substitute for political talk, as well as an all-purpose solution for every ill. Given television's pervasive role, this is unlikely to change. But journalism, especially, has become a more reflective practice as its role has expanded. The response to cynicism will require that the evolving criticism of the media becomes more sophisticated. This remains true, even if the task is essentially impossible to achieve. Media practice continues to evolve at a rapid pace. And "media criticism" includes a variety of actual practices, some of which have little to do with the media, as Dan Quayle's attack on Murphy Brown attests.

One of the most widely distributed of the cynicism remedies, Kathleen Hall Jamieson's insistence that journalists minimize their coverage of political strategy, is mostly counterproductive.[10] Policy and politics are inextricably connected. Insisting on submerging strategy talk simply drives that talk underground, into codes and innuendo that are easier for powerful cynics to manipulate. A better understanding of politics would require better, not less media discussion of strategies.

To be sure, it would help if we could discourage the smug dismissal of the public world that dominates the way the journalist Cokie Roberts and her colleagues talk about politics. Mainstream commentators display a terribly narrow ideological range, but they also narrow down the range of attitudes toward politics itself. As the tiny cadre of such commentators become more and more visible, and at the expense, for example, of commercial book publishing on politics, this problem becomes more serious. It would help if the commentariat were more diverse politically and if some of them actually communicated the ambivalent appreciation the political world often deserves.

3. The manipulative and hypocritical cynicism of the powerful must become an ongoing issue.

Powerful cynics hold a tremendous advantage when they can manipulate media coverage and public attitudes. Their goal, always, is to plant the seed of doubt. They cast themselves as misunderstood or persecuted victims, or worse, they hint that all political figures are the same as the worst among them. "Everyone does it" is a popular cynical formulation.

It is also a problem that journalists have come to define fairness as an evening out of errors over time. Although there is much to be said for this approach, it can block changes that would make the cynicism of the powerful an ongoing story. Journalists need to find a way to talk about powerful cynics beyond the context of partisanship. Although sexuality can certainly be an indicator of cynical manipulation, it is by no means the only indicator. Journalists need to find ways to make wealth and power a persistent and intriguing story. For guidance, they might revisit the career of I. F. Stone, a model that is often praised but seldom taken very seriously.

Journalists once understood that it was crucial for them to make cynics-in-power nervous. It is hard to imagine how the role of journalism in a democratic society might be justified if it doesn't centrally include a penchant for exposing hypocrisy among the powerful, especially when powerless citizens are hurt. But for journalists to pursue that project, they also need to move to a better understanding of partisanship, else their work will continue to be reduced to a petty, secondary version of that partisanship.

4. Some key policies have to change—notably campaign finance laws.

The blanket of cynicism has some central symbols, among which the dubious campaign contribution may be the most important. No measure of success in remedying other public issues, tweaking television news, or promoting civility will make much difference in dissipating the cynical fog unless we change the way campaigns are financed. This is one policy issue that is truly critical in addressing cynicism's corrosive effects. It is the only issue that deserves to become a litmus test. It is a fair working assumption that any proponent of civility or community values who is not also leading the charge for genuine campaign finance reform is a cynic—of the destructive variety.

There are plenty of good suggestions available to guide potential campaign reform. As many observers have noted, the problem is not a lack of ideas but the lack of political will that might make it possible to implement them. Campaigns cannot be made polite, nice, accurate, and sedate; the stakes have become far too large to expect a return to the staid, centrist campaigns of the past when Tweedledee took on Tweedledum. But campaigns can be changed so that they do not constantly remind cynics of every stripe or station that their cynicism is fully justified.

5. The wave of wig cynic antipolitics and hate movements must be rigorously resisted.

In the wake of Timothy McVeigh's trial, it would seem that the wig politics of conspiracy and bigotry are in remission. Even Special Prosecutor Kenneth Starr finally said that in his official opinion, Vincent Foster committed suicide. The black helicopter stories are now almost solely brought up as jokes, even in Montana. Here and there, a strident talk-radio station switches over to sports talk. But the early 1990s showed how large the wig constituency is and how much damage it can do.

The wig chorus changes the political dynamic, making all sorts of cynical mischief easier for ostensibly more mainstream figures to promote. The pressure that the human rights movement, especially its most public figure, Morris Dees of the Southern Poverty Law Center, has exerted on the hate movements is one of the most heroic stories of our cynical times. The wig sideshow must be resisted if a better politics is to have any hope of surviving. If one political party or the other begins to imagine that it can build its core constituency by appealing to the worst of the wig complaints, society could once again find itself quickly plunged into awful peril.

6. Religious responses to cynicism may profoundly help some citizens, but the crisis of civic belief will not be stemmed by a general religious revival.

A general reconstruction of values remains a precarious response to a culture drenched in cynicism. Too many powerful cynics will easily adopt values talk as their vehicle, sending the cynical spiral into yet another turn. The religiosity of American society is an enduring condition, and initiatives of faith like the one proposed in Michael Lerner's *The Politics of Meaning* will doubtless help ease the deep discontent of some people, allowing them to reengage the political enterprise. But this is not a general solution. Cynics are simply inured to such appeals, and the cynical culture is constructed in such a way as to specifically inoculate the cynic against renewed faith.

Civic belief is not the same thing as religious belief, despite several shared elements and patterns. The contradictions, tensions, and paradoxes that pervade government and civil society are political issues, rather than theological ones. Actual solutions to cynicism will inevitably involve politics. And the political world is sufficiently difficult for most Americans to engage that distractions cannot help in any general way. We must gain a more sophisticated understanding of democratic practice, which involves much more than belief in underlying values.

7. Diversity or multicultural perspectives help to model a strong political and cultural pluralism. But their partisans must exhibit political savvy.

Among our society's best accomplishments has been the explicit and systematic welcoming of diverse and multicultural perspectives. "Respect" has become a central element of political discourse. Many Americans now understand how society has helped shape core identities. In the process, we have rehearsed ways of talking about a society that is genuinely pluralist, a society that neither needs nor insists on a high degree of uniformity and understands deep advantage, not a problem.

These advances have not occurred without cost. The backlash against diversity has been vigorous and consistent. The effect of this reaction has sometimes been to drive diversity advocates into a narrowly ideological trap feminists refer to as "essentialism." This is valuable not only because it helps people to engage with diversity claims but also because it models pluralism. If that pluralism is lost in dogmatism and political certainty based on gender, race, sexuality, or identity, much will have been lost.

... politics — lively, contentious, ... issues that matter.

... mire, I keep remembering ... remark made in passing a long time ago. Fresh from graduate school and clinging to my first teaching job, I made friends with the neighbors. When talk turned to politics (Reagan was challenging Carter that fall), I lobbed criticism at both sides, wrapped in my version of a funny, wise-guy superiority—the way graduate students talk. My friend laughed and remarked that I was certainly a cynic. Later, puzzling this through, I decided he was not so far off the mark. Any traces of a youthful idealism had long since been shed, but my anger remained.

I had already been thinking and reading about the way paradox works in the social world. My neighbor's comment reminded me that paradox is not only a matter of deep structural conflict, inside a personality or in a social system. Paradox reveals itself in other ways, including some familiar ones. Cynicism indicates the presence of paradox at the same time that it also provides activists with a way to make their way in a world filled with paradox, the multiplicity of cause and motive, and the persistent unpredictability of ongoing events. At the intellectual level, too, cynicism has its attractions. My neighbor had started me rethinking my relation to cynicism.

There was much to be cynical about in a post-Vietnam, post-Watergate America that had responded to these provocations by turning sharply away from politics. With the American left in decline, the right mired in resentment, and the center stuck in incompetence or worse, the broader culture was deciding to go it alone. The "Me Decade" was better named than most. Still, som particular characters had found a way to stay politically active, fi ing some kind of sustaining energy whose source was not altoge obvious. Eventually, I came to understand that the charisma of cynics, some of the time—we will no doubt disagree vigo about which, and when—was more than a sideshow ent ment. Their cynicism serves as a clue to the puzzles I had to consider.

Diogenes was the first in a long line of activist cynic cynicism of his many heirs resonated with a flair tha even in America, even as various political movemen went private. That's the irony, the key to the cynicism problems visited by dangerous, corrosive, and corru require a response that is also cynical, if in a som way. We need to imagine an entirely different kind of public person — sophisticated, truthful, energized, appealing, and bold. Once we look for them, we find an abundance of models — impudent nonbelievers, acting out challenges to power. The trick is to take that model seriously and then to inject it into the many layers and locales of democratic practice. This will not be an easy trick to perform, but given the terrible condition of contemporary democracy, we had better start practicing.

In the previous chapters, I suggested several cultural models. Let me suggest one more. All the reaction against Bill Clinton and his counterculture roots may suggest that the irreverent but engaged culture the boomers made for themselves had finally been thoroughly punished and routed from public life. To be sure, powerful elements of society would like to believe that and have worked hard to make it so. The Gulf War was partly motivated by that removal project, as were the war on drugs and the antiabortion movement. This has not been an entirely ideological enterprise; many liberals got it wrong, buying into a debilitating communitarian sobriety. My discussion of kynicism suggests that Boomer culture — irreverent, disbelieving, cheeky — deserves better than what it has thus far achieved. The kynic knows how to invite people back into the public realm with both high purpose and good spirits. And no kynic could long abide a hater.

The kynic's laugh sends important signals. Consider how Denzel Washington portrayed Malcolm X in Spike Lee's film of the same name. His thoroughly political character, able to shift positions but also to attract attention and organize commitment, was conveyed by Malcolm's laugh. For those unfamiliar with Malcolm X, Denzel's laugh was the film's biggest surprise. Alex Haley's biography seldom caught it, but Lee documents the laugh's accuracy throughout the book that accompanied the film. The old *Esquire* magazine question — why is this man laughing? — could never be more appropriately asked. Here is one of the most serious political figures of this country's terrible race war, laughing. This is not surprising to most blacks or to political activists. The political world frequently is suffused with humor, in turn grim, ecstatic, or sustaining.

In the end, the search for either a saving civic belief or effective policy solutions comes up against our deep, characteristically American reluctance to engage the public world. We are supposed to hate politics, to avoid it, and to suspect those who are having too good a time at it. In the 1992 primaries, Bob Kerry was on to something when he told Paul Tsongas that he sounded like the Grinch who stole Christmas. We have been well taught to favor civil and responsible public servants like Tsongas, Dukakis, and Carter, candidates who played the moralizing, condescending, "teacher's pet" model to the hilt. There is an emotional logic to this preference. We can feel superior to them; they don't threaten to involve us. We are suspicious of candidates who communicate a sense of joy. Joe Klein's portrait of Bill Clinton in *Primary Colors* comes to mind.

But there are limits to our suspicion, or rather, there is a kynical mischief that runs counter to it. Reagan communicated a sense of joy, and that was a large part of his genius: big on values, having a great time trying to dismantle the institutions that represented those values. These discrepancies never defeated Reagan, and his success baffled the critics. Likewise Clinton, whom a majority of Americans distrust and reject as a moral model, easily bested Bob Dole in 1996 and went on to hit highs in his popularity ratings as the scandals heated up. Some characters who communicate a sense of joy in the political process are justly suspect; Hubert Humphrey's "happy warrior" act amid the Vietnam horror is a useful corrective.

We have, in short, worked ourselves into a corner. Avoiding some important problems, managing or manipulating others, we have constructed a trap for ourselves. Our age's rampant antipolitics only makes the cycle of cynicism harder to break. Immune to the correctives informed by somber policy debate, outsider-cynics make the powerful cynics' job easier. The confusions produced by our thin understanding of cynicism only make matters worse. There is no simple way out of the mess. Cynicism is a cultural mood, and cultures are not easily transformed. And kynics offer no lasting answers. Instead, they set us loose on a path. At least they make one path passable. Recognizing the perils of moralistic solutions, looking toward politics, acknowledging cultural and institutional arrangements that harm, we finally prepare ourselves to understand cynicism. The democratic politics our present difficulties require insists on no less.

Notes

Introduction

1. Leonard Pitts, "Drowning in Cynicism," *(Missoula, MT) Missoulian,* February 25, 1998, A8.

2. David S. Broder, "Don't Write Off Character," *Washington Post,* April 26, 1998, C7.

3. Quoted ibid.

4. Quoted in Martha Sherrill, "The Health Czar, At Her Other Job," *Washington Post,* January 27, 1993, D1.

5. "State of the Union Address," *Washington Post,* January 21, 1993, A26.

1. Socrates — Gone Mad

1. Diogenes anecdotes are from Peter Sloterdijk, *Critique of Cynical Reason* (Minneapolis: University of Minnesota Press, 1987), 103, 160, and Donald R. Dudley, *A History of Cynicism* (London: Methuen, 1937), 27.

2. Sloterdijk, *Critique of Cynical Reason,* 102.

3. On irony, see John Evan Seery, *Political Returns: Irony in Politics and Theory from Plato to the Antinuclear Movement* (Boulder, Colo.: Westview, 1990), and Linda Hutcheon, *Irony's Edge: The Theory and Politics of Irony* (New York: Routledge, 1994).

4. Quoted in Frank J. Murray, "The Party's on the Road," *Washington Times,* August 23, 1992, A1.

5. George F. Will, "Serious People Flinch," *Washington Post,* national weekly edition, August 31, 1992, 29. All subsequent quotations from Will in this chapter are from this article.

6. National Public Radio, *Saturday Morning Edition,* January 16, 1993.

7. "The State of the Union Address," *Washington Post,* January 21, 1993, A26.

8. Ian Frazier, *Great Plains* (New York: Penguin, 1989), 173–74. My thanks to Margaret Kingsland for introducing me to this quotation.

2. The Values Remedy

1. The Disposable Heroes of Hiphoprisy, *Hypocrisy Is the Greatest Luxury* (New York: 4th & B'way–Island Records, 1992).

2. See Michael Lerner, *The Politics of Meaning: Restoring Hope and Insecurity in an Age of Cynicism* (Reading, Mass.: Addison-Wesley, 1996).

3. The literature of communitarianism is large and growing. See Amitai Etzioni, *The New Golden Rule: Community and Morality in a Democratic Society* (New York: Basic Books, 1996).

4. Garry Wills, *Lincoln at Gettysburg: The Words That Remade America* (New York: Simon and Schuster, 1992), 174–75.

5. This characterization is drawn from William E. Connolly, *The Ethos of Pluralization* (Minneapolis: University of Minnesota Press, 1995), 26.

6. Ibid., 107.

7. Jeffrey C. Goldfarb, *The Cynical Society: The Culture of Politics and the Politics of Culture in American Life* (Chicago: University of Chicago Press, 1991), 51.

8. Ibid., 51, 54.

9. Allan Bloom, *The Closing of the American Mind: How Higher Education Has Failed Democracy and Impoverished the Souls of Today's Students* (New York: Simon and Schuster, 1987).

10. Robert Bellah, Richard Madsen, William M. Sullivan, Ann Swidler, and Steven M. Tipton, *Habits of the Heart: Individualism and Commitment in American Life* (New York: Harper and Row, 1986).

11. My comments in this section owe much to the discussion in Michael J. Shapiro, *Reading the Postmodern Polity: Political Theory as Textual Practice* (Minneapolis: University of Minnesota Press, 1992), 73–81.

12. Alan Keenan, "The Twilight of the Political?: A Contribution to the Democratic Critique of Cynicism," *Theory & Event* 2, no. 1 (1998), online at http://muse.jhu.edu/journals/theory_&_event/V002/2.1keenan.html (January 23, 1999).

13. See Dan Baum, *Smoke and Mirrors: The War on Drugs and the Politics of Failure* (Boston: Little, Brown, 1996), 308–10. See also Richard Benedetto, "Bennett Walks Away from Republican Committee Job," *USA Today,* December 13, 1990, A5.

14. See William J. Bennett, *The De-Valuing of America: The Fight for Our Culture and Our Children* (New York: Simon and Schuster, 1992), 103–4. Discussed in William E. Connolly, "Drugs, the Nation and Free Lancing: Decoding the Moral Universe of William Bennett," *Theory & Event* 1, no. 1 (January 1997), online at http://muse.jhu.edu/journals/theory_&_event/v001/1.1connolly.html (February 7, 1997).

3. Cynics-in-Power

1. Peter Sloterdijk, *Critique of Cynical Reason* (Minneapolis: University of Minnesota Press, 1987), 111, his emphasis.

2. Ibid., 5.

3. Lewis Carroll, *Alice's Adventures in Wonderland and Through the Looking-Glass* (New York, Collier Books, 1962), 150.

4. Bob Woodward, *The Commanders* (New York: Simon and Schuster, 1991), 39.

5. Quoted in Martha Sherrill, "The Health Czar, At Her Other Job," *Washington Post,* January 27, 1993, D1.

4. Wig Cynics

1. Richard L. Berke, "Perot Re-enters the Limelight as a Watchdog," *New York Times,* January 12, 1993, A-1, A-17.

2. Howard Kurtz, "In Final Blitz, a Blur of Polls, Pontification and Sound-Bite Slogans," *Washington Post,* November 2, 1992, D-17.

3. Mike Davis, *City of Quartz: Excavating the Future in Los Angeles* (New York: Verso, 1990), 58–62, quoting journalist Morrow Mayo.

4. Quoted in Taylor Branch, *Parting the Waters: America in the King Years, 1954–63* (New York: Simon and Schuster, 1988), 380–81.

5. Limbaugh appeared on *Nightline* on April 19, 1994. It is described in Jim Naureckas and Janine Jackson, eds., *The FAIR Reader: An Extra! Review of Press and Politics in the 90's* (Boulder, Colo.: Westview Press, 1996), 139–41.

5. A Brief History of American Cynicism

1. Fred Hobson, *Mencken: A Life* (New York: Random House, 1994), 95.

2. Hobson, *Mencken*, 250; Richard Wright, *Black Boy* (New York: Harper and Row, 1945), 270–72.

3. Don Whitehead, *The FBI Story: A Report to the People* (New York: Random House, 1956), 41, 43, quoted in Curt Gentry, *J. Edgar Hoover: The Man and the Secrets* (New York: W. W. Norton, 1991), 81; see also Gentry (73) on the beginnings of Hoover's use of conspiracy at the FBI.

4. Gentry, *J. Edgar Hoover*, 87–88. For a discussion of presidential assassination conspiracy theories and a novel and entertaining review of several other historical conspiracy theories, see Robert Wernick, "Don't Look Now — But All Those Plotters Might Be Hiding under Your Bed," *Smithsonian* 24, no. 12 (March 1994): 108–24.

5. Gentry, *J. Edgar Hoover*, 354, 420 ff.

6. See McCarthy's speech in the *Congressional Record*, 82nd Cong., 1st sess. (June 14, 1951), 6602. The conversation with Hoover is reported by Gentry, *J. Edgar Hoover*, 377–78.

7. Richard Hofstadter, *The Paranoid Style in American Politics and Other Essays* (New York: Knopf, 1965), 7. This version is revised and expanded from a speech delivered at Oxford in November 1963, and was published in abridged form in *Harper's* (November 1964).

8. Hofstadter, *The Paranoid Style*, 5.

9. Tom Engelhardt, *The End of Victory Culture: Cold War America and the Disillusioning of a Generation* (New York: Basic Books, 1995).

10. Robert B. Reich, *The Work of Nations* (New York: Vintage, 1991).

11. Peter Drucker, "Caught in the Middle," *Business Week*, September 12, 1988, 80.

12. Benjamin DeMott, "Seduced by Civility," *The Nation*, December 9, 1996, 9.

6. Federalists and Liberals

1. Alexander Hamilton, James Madison, and John Jay, *The Federalist Papers* (New York: New American Library, 1961). Madison was the author of *Federalist Paper No. Ten*.

2. Robert A. Dahl, *A Preface to Democratic Theory* (Chicago: University of Chicago Press, 1956).

3. Louis Hartz, *The Liberal Tradition in America* (New York: Harcourt Brace Jovanovich, 1955), 5.

7. Why Americans Hate Politics

1. E. J. Dionne, *Why Americans Hate Politics* (New York: Simon and Schuster, 1991).

2. Ibid., 17.

3. See Murray Edelman, *Constructing the Political Spectacle* (Chicago: University of Chicago Press, 1988), 12–17.

4. Dionne, *Why Americans Hate Politics,* 17.

5. John Dewey, *The Public and Its Problems* (Chicago: Swallow Press, 1927), 138–39.

8. Medium, Media, Mediate

1. Fred Hobson, *Mencken: A Life* (New York: Random House, 1994), 218, 251.

2. Quoted in ibid., 255–56.

3. Quoted in Marguerite Michaels, "Walter Wants the News to Say a Lot More," *Parade,* March 23, 1980, 4.

4. David Antin, "Video: The Distinctive Features of the Medium," in John G. Hanhardt, ed., *Video Culture: A Critical Investigation* (Layton, Utah: Peregrine Smith Books, 1987), 147–66.

5. David Ross, "Truth or Consequences: American Television and Video Art," in Hanhardt, ed., *Video Culture,* 167–68.

6. Mark Crispin Miller, *Boxed In: The Culture of TV* (Evanston, Ill.: Northwestern University Press, 1988), 97, 106.

7. Ibid., 14–15, quoting "Insider," *TV Guide,* January 10, 1987, 18.

8. Miller, *Boxed In,* 326.

9. Robert C. Allen, *Channels of Discourse: Television and Contemporary Criticism* (Chapel Hill: University of North Carolina Press, 1987), 2.

10. John Ellis, "Cinema and Broadcast TV Together," in Hanhardt, ed., *Video Culture,* 258–59.

9. Bush, Burned

1. A thorough review of the several Willie Horton ads can be found in Kathleen Hall Jamieson, *Dirty Politics: Deception, Distraction and Democracy* (New York: Oxford University Press, 1992), 43–63.

2. Carl Bernstein, "It's Press vs. Bush: A Bruising Fight," *Los Angeles Times,* October 25, 1992, M1, M6.

3. Ibid.

4. Tom Brokaw's response to objectivity questions, quoted in Mark Crispin Miller, *Boxed In: The Culture of TV* (Evanston, Ill.: Northwestern University Press, 1988), 101–2.

10. The Uses of Backlash

1. Andrew Rosenthal, "Quayle Says Riots Sprang from Lack of Family Values," *New York Times,* May 20, 1992, A1, A11.

2. Quoted in ibid.

3. Michael Wines, "Views on Single Motherhood Are Multiple at White House," *New York Times,* May 21, 1992, A1, A12.

4. "Ease Up, Dan," (*Missoula, MT) Missoulian,* May 21, 1992, A1, A9.

5. Susan Faludi, *Backlash: The Undeclared War Against American Women* (New York: Doubleday, 1991).

6. Quoted in Thomas J. McIntyre with John C. Obert, *The Fear Brokers* (Philadelphia: Pilgrim Press, 1979), 156.

7. Faludi, *Backlash,* 232, quoting Jerry Falwell, *Listen, America!* (Garden City, N.Y.: Doubleday-Galilee, 1980), 151.

8. Faludi, *Backlash,* 234.

9. Ibid., 290, quoting George Gilder, *Wealth and Poverty* (New York: Basic Books, 1981), 115.

10. Faludi, *Backlash,* 290, quoting Allan Bloom, *The Closing of the American Mind: How Higher Education Has Failed Democracy and Impoverished the Souls of Today's Students* (New York: Simon and Schuster, 1987), 65.

11. Kevin Phillips, *The Politics of Rich and Poor* (New York: Random House, 1990).

12. George F. Will, "Vulgarity at Home," *Washington Post,* February 3, 1998, A17.

13. Faludi, *Backlash,* 457, her emphasis.

11. The Age of Resentment

1. E. J. Dionne, *Why Americans Hate Politics* (New York: Simon and Schuster, 1991), 230.

2. Kenneth S. Stern, *A Force upon the Plain: The American Militia Movement and the Politics of Hate* (New York: Simon and Schuster, 1996), 12, 26.

3. Attendance figures for meetings in Montana—150 in Billings, 200 in Great Falls, 250 in Hamilton, more than 300 in Big Timber, and 800 in Kalispell—are cited in Stern, *A Force upon the Plain*, 72.

4. Ibid., 13.

5. "Special Militia Task Force Edition," *Klanwatch Intelligence Report* 78 (June 1995): 7–11, and Stern, *A Force upon the Plain*, 96.

6. "Distrust of Government," ABC News/*Washington Post* Poll (May 17, 1995). Posted to America Online (keyword ABC/NEWS/POLLS, May 17, 1995), transcript ab5np036–7.

7. Friedrich Nietzsche, *On the Genealogy of Morals,* trans. Walter Kaufmann and R. J. Hollingdale (New York: Random House, 1967), 127.

8. William E. Connolly, *Political Theory and Modernity* (Oxford: Basil Blackwell, 1988), 171.

9. Ibid., 158, quoting Nietzsche, *On the Genealogy of Morals,* 128.

10. "Militia Hearing in Congress," televised on C-SPAN, June 15, 1995.

12. Marge the Stoic

1. *Fargo,* director Joel Coen, written by Ethan Coen and Joel Coen, Gramercy Pictures, 1996.

2. John Simon, review of "Fargo," *National Review,* April 22, 1996, 60–62.

3. Film critics in Minnesota warned "readers to gird themselves for caricature, exaggeration and heavy-handed dramatic license in the guise of local color" (Adam Platt, "The Case of 'Fargo' vs. Minnesota," *Chicago Tribune,* May 9, 1996, 1).

4. Keillor "is considered to be one of those who thought the film mean-spirited." On his radio program, he referred to *Fargo* as "slow... you had a lot of time to see where you were going and wish you didn't have to" (ibid., 1).

5. E. Vernon Arnold, *Roman Stoicism* (London: Routledge and Kegan Paul, 1911), 150.

6. Ibid., 200, 306, 303.

7. Colin Covert, "'Fargo' Events Never Happened," *Minneapolis Star Tribune,* March 3, 1996, 10F.

8. Thomas Doherty, review of "Fargo," *Cineaste* 22, no. 2 (Spring 1996): 47–48.

9. Covert, " 'Fargo' Events Never Happened," 10F.

10. Ethan Coen and Joel Coen, *Fargo* (London: Faber and Faber, 1996), x.

11. Ibid., ix.

12. E. Zeller, *The Stoics, Epicureans and Sceptics*, trans. Oswald J. Reichel (London: Longmans, 1892), 235–39.

13. Mal Vincent, "Interview: Ethan and Joel Coen on 'Fargo,'" *(Norfolk) Virginian-Pilot*, March 20, 1996, C-1.

14. Coen and Coen, *Fargo*, 19.

15. Simon, review of "Fargo," 63.

16. Michael Wood, "The Life of the Mind," *London Review of Books*, June 20, 1996, 18–19.

17. Doherty, review of "Fargo," 48.

18. Thomas L. Dumm, *united states* (Ithaca: Cornell University Press, 1994), 148.

19. Ibid.

20. Peter Sloterdijk, *Critique of Cynical Reason* (Minneapolis: University of Minnesota Press, 1987), 165.

13. "So What?"

1. Peter Sloterdijk, *Critique of Cynical Reason* (Minneapolis: University of Minnesota Press, 1987), 193.

14. Teachings of the Demonstration

1. Thomas E. Patterson's introductory political science text is probably a representative example. He covers the demo in four paragraphs of a large book, conceding that early civil rights legislation "can be explained only as a response by Congress to the pressure created by the civil rights movement." After a nod to diversity ("American history would be very different had not the abolitionist, labor, suffragist, and other major movements pressed their claims"), Patterson effectively dismisses protest due to the small proportion of the public that participates in or supports protests (Thomas E. Patterson, *The American Democracy* [Hightstown, N.J.: McGraw-Hill, 1990], 215–16).

2. Joseph R. Gusfield, ed., *Protest, Reform, and Revolt* (New York: Wiley, 1970), 1.

3. Seymour Martin Lipset, *Political Man* (New York: Doubleday, 1959), 128.

4. David L. Lewis, *King: A Biography* (Urbana: University of Illinois Press, 1978), 297–312, and David Halberstam, "When 'Civil Rights' and 'Peace' Join Forces," in C. Eric Lincoln, ed., *Martin Luther King, Jr.: A Profile* (New York: Hill and Wang, 1970), 187–211.

5. Todd Gitlin, *The Whole World Is Watching: Mass Media in the Making and Unmaking of the New Left* (Berkeley: University of California Press, 1980), 32–54.

6. Peter Sloterdijk, *Critique of Cynical Reason* (Minneapolis: University of Minnesota Press, 1987), 101, 109, 99.

7. Ibid., 117.

8. Francis X. Clines, "100,000 Join Moscow Rally, Defying Ban by Gorbachev to Show Support for Rival," *New York Times*, March 29, 1991, A-1.

9. Hunter S. Thompson, *Fear and Loathing on the Campaign Trail '72* (San Francisco: Straight Arrow, 1973), 387.

10. Ibid., 392.

15. Politics after Cynicism

1. Mary Matalin and James Carville, *All's Fair: Love, War, and Running for President* (New York: Random House, 1994), 49.

2. Ibid., 40.

3. Wendy Brown, "The Time of the Political," *Theory & Event* 1, no. 1 (January 1997), paragraph 2, online at http://muse.jhu.edu/journals/theory_&_event/V001/1.1brown.html (January 23, 1999).

16. Solutions and Conclusions

1. National Commission on Civic Renewal, preface to *A Nation of Spectators* (Washington, D.C.: National Commission on Civic Renewal, 1998), available online at http://www.puaf.umd.edu/civicrenewal/finalreport/(June 25, 1998).

2. The transcript of the press conference can be found online. See "NCCR Delivers a Briefing at the National Press Club Regarding the Erosion of Civic Life," *Nation of Spectators*.

3. "Defining the Challenge of Civic Renewal," *Nation of Spectators*.

4. Ibid.

5. Ibid.

6. "A New Movement," *Nation of Spectators*.

7. "Meeting the Challenge," *Nation of Spectators*.

8. Preface to *A Nation of Spectators*.

9. E. J. Dionne, Jr., *They Only Look Dead: Why Progressives Will Dominate the Next Political Era* (New York: Simon and Schuster, 1996).

10. See Joseph N. Cappella and Kathleen Hall Jamieson, *Spiral of Cynicism: The Press and the Public Good* (New York: Oxford, 1997).

Index

William Chaloupka is professor of environmental studies at the University of Montana, where he also teaches courses in political science. He has also taught at the University of New Mexico and Ball State University. His books include *Knowing Nukes: The Politics and Culture of the Atom* and, coedited with Jane Bennett, *In the Nature of Things: Language, Politics, and the Environment*, both published by the University of Minnesota Press.